Colford/Lipsett

IMMIGRANTS, ELLIS ISLAND

The Story of a Family

Joseph E. Colford III

"Colford/Lipsett: The Story of a Family," by Joseph E. Colford III. ISBN 978-1-62137-870-9 (softcover).

Published 2016 by Virtualbookworm.com Publishing Inc., P.O. Box 9949, College Station, TX 77842, US. ©2016 Joseph E. Colford III.

Table of Contents

The Story of Our Family

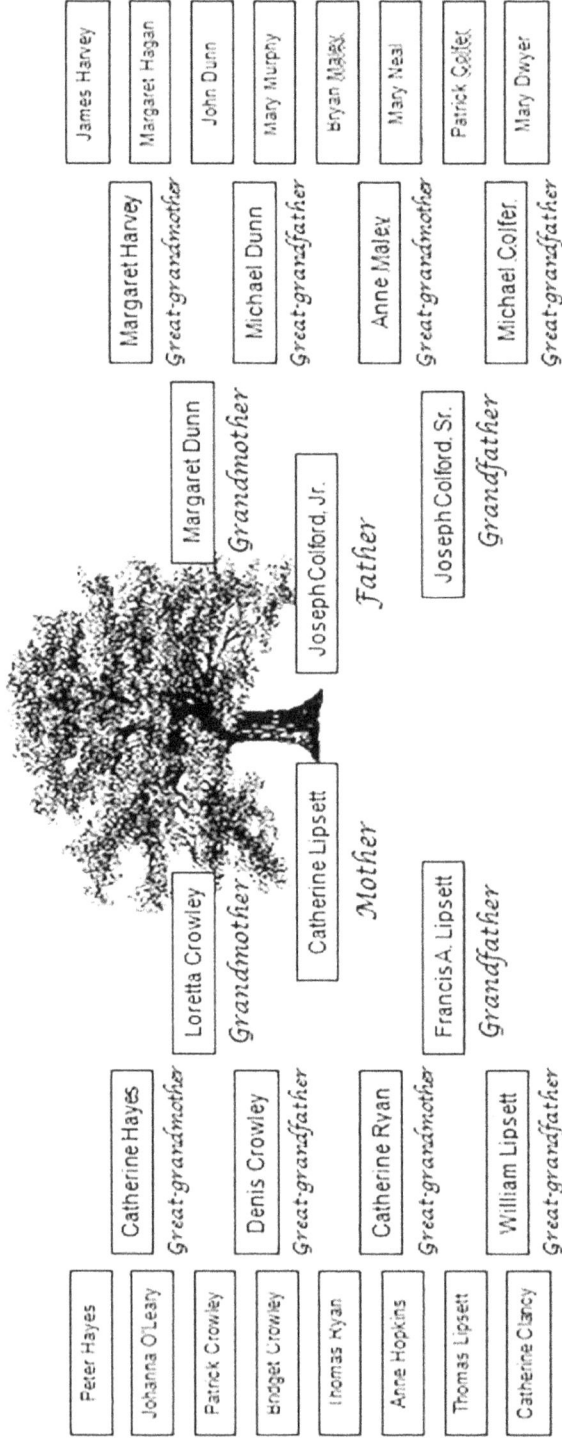

		James Harvey
	Margaret Harvey	Margaret Hagan
	Great-grandmother	
Margaret Dunn		John Dunn
Grandmother	Michael Dunn	Mary Murphy
	Great-grandfather	
Joseph Colford, Jr.		Bryan Maley
Father	Anne Maley	Mary Neal
	Great-grandmother	
Joseph Colford, Sr.		Patrick Colfer
Grandfather	Michael Colfer	Mary Dwyer
	Great-grandfather	

	Catherine Hayes	Peter Hayes
	Great-grandmother	Johanna O'Leary
Loretta Crowley		Patrick Crowley
Grandmother	Denis Crowley	Bridget Crowley
	Great-grandfather	
Catherine Lipsett		Thomas Ryan
Mother	Catherine Ryan	Anne Hopkins
	Great-grandmother	
Francis A. Lipsett		Thomas Lipsett
Grandfather	William Lipsett	Catherine Clancy
	Great-grandfather	

The Eight of Us:

Mary, Joseph III,
Francis, Paul,
Christopher, Peter,
Loretta, Brian

Prologue

Perhaps it's just folks in middle age, those *"Baby Boomers"* among us, including myself, who have become interested in family history. Since I have become involved in it, there is not a day goes by that I don't rue the missed opportunities of being able to question at great length our grandparents about their recollections of family and family lore: of Grandpa Lipsett's 16 years in Ireland before he left for good; of his thoughts and emotions regarding the departure itself and of his first marriage to Winnie; of Grandpa Colford's stories told to him by his immigrant parents, Michael and Anne, and his uncle James; and of Grandma Colford's sad story of a childhood marked by the early death of a father and a young, overwhelmed widowed mother. Of course, I suppose that it's less about missed opportunities and more about a simple lack of interest in such things among younger folk.

As you can imagine, we have been incredibly fortunate to have had Mom as a source of information which has allowed me to verify many family history data bits with her recollections. She's been the next best thing to having our grandparents around again to tell their stories.

I have spent many, many part-time hours over the years researching our Colfer/Dunn/ Harvey/Lipsett/Crowley family histories. My first family history-related email was in August of 2000 when I emailed a Kevin Colfer from Manchester, England, about our possible Colfer family connection. Although we could not come up with any commonalities in our ancestry, the correspondence energized my family search. Jeanne, Matthew, and Michael often roll their eyes when I discuss some recent genealogical discovery. When asked what I was doing all this for, I always have said simply, *"It's history, and even family history is history."*

I have included in this narrative all the information I have found about five generations of our Lipsett/Crowley families, and of our Colford/Dunn kin. The story of our great-grandmother, Margaret (Harvey) Dunn, however, has been the most elusive of all our family lines, but I have managed to piece together a fairly accurate, yet brief, account of her life in the Greenwich Village section of New York City where she settled after she arrived on our shores. Nevertheless, there are still more gaps in her story and in that of Grandma Colford's upbringing than there are in our other family tree branches. I dare say, however, that Grandma's childhood was not a very happy time for her, thus the reason why, Mom reports, she shared none of her childhood memories.

Would Grandma have filled in Grandpa Colford about her childhood woes? Did she and Aunt Molly commiserate with each other from time-to-time about growing up in a disrupted family? Or did Grandma confide in her best friend and her Virginia Ave. neighbor, Annie Cochrane, she the mother of Bill Cochrane, St. Peter's Prep legendary football coach?

Perhaps, but maybe she thought that unpleasant recollections were best left unsaid.

Read Grandma Colford's story later in this narrative.

Some of this story borrows from Paul's earlier Colfer family history which he penned back in 1991. He picked up our history with our great-grandfather, Michael Colfer's, arrival in the States and took us all through the 20th century. My Michael Colfer/Colford story includes a prequel to his Colford history, a narrative of the Colfers in Ireland and a clarification of some of his thoughts on their early days in Newark and Jersey City.

Paul undoubtedly paged through dusty, yellowed pages of census and other records in order to piece together part of our story so many years ago. A considerable amount of my research, however, has been facilitated by the internet connections I have made with other family researchers and by the on-line resources of so many genealogical websites.

I have to admit that I developed my first interest in our family history in the summer of 1975 when I visited Ireland and England for the first time. My visit that summer to the last surviving of Grandpa Lipsett's 10 siblings, Aunt Lillie, in Leamington Spa, England, was the defining moment for me. She mentioned at one point during my three-day visit that Grandpa had been married before he married our grandmother, Loretta (Crowley) Lipsett. Considering all that I knew of Grandpa, this news came as quite a surprise. Her recollection resonated with me for many years, and I was determined to investigate that bit of family history one day. His story is the first one which I completed some time ago before I began my search for the Colfords.

The multiple spellings of the same names which you will find in this story are neither misprints nor misspellings on my part; I have presented them all exactly as they have appeared in the many records I have come across in my genealogical search for our family.

I had hoped to be able to place, beyond a reasonable doubt, all of our Colfers, Dunns, Harveys, Lipsetts, and Crowleys in a very specific townland in Ireland, despite the vastness of their number. The townland is the smallest land subdivision in Ireland; approximately 62,000 of them comprise the whole of Ireland, ranging in size from less than one acre to 7,012 acres. The average townland size, however, is 350 acres.

I think that I have been able to locate the home townland for most of our forebears. I have placed the Colfers, on the other hand, within a very small area of County Wexford with a suspicion of either of two townlands where they lived. I also believe that I have come across our possible third cousins, direct links to Patrick Colfer, our great-great grandfather.

At the conclusion of our story, I have added a separate section entitled *Footnotes*, a compendium of sorts of several parts of our narrative containing information which, although somewhat tangential to the more core elements of our history, elucidates some characters and events from our past.   Read them also.

I have two regrets about completing our story with some "unfinished business," both of which involve Grandma Colford's family and which I will discuss in some detail. First, the death certificate for Grandma's mother and our great-grandmother, Margaret (Harvey) Dunn, is among the missing records I have yet to find. Neither I nor any of the other paid and volunteer genealogical resources I have tapped have been able to locate it. Her demise is known only to some higher power, I presume. Her whereabouts between the death of her husband, our great-grandfather, Michael Dunn, and her own death 23 years later also is another gaping hole yet to be filled. Second, I have not been able to locate the townland of origin of our great-grandfather, since his professed county of origin (Clare) is not verifiable. However, I have offered some speculations about where his parents, our great-great grandparents, John and Mary (Murphy) Dunn, may have lived.

I wish that I were telling a tale of the "good old days" in our story. However, those days were far from "good" for many of our forebears, particularly for Grandma Colford, a mere eight-month-old when her father died.   Please read on for her story and more.

I just ask two things of this family history:

- That you all read it and hold onto it . . . it is who we are
- That you save it for all your sons and daughters and encourage them to read it as well . . . it is part of who they all are

(Our sons and daughters will just have to add another *great* to the many layers of family *greats* included here in our story in order to understand the family connections.)

Introduction

It is as if there were two stages for conducting research into Irish family history; the year 1864 provided the line separating these stages. It wasn't until then that civil registration was required of all Roman Catholic Births, Marriages, and Deaths (BMD) in Ireland. Prior to this central public listing, only records of the Protestant Church, the official religion of Ireland, had to be registered. Catholic family researchers had to rely on the good graces, the organizational ability, and the meticulous record-keeping of local Roman Catholic priests who would have presided over the BMD in their individual parishes and recorded them for posterity. Some undoubtedly were better at doing so than others, since these records are sorely lacking in some parishes.

Joseph Buggy, a professional Irish genealogist whose lecture I attended recently, said that tracing one's Irish ancestors before the 1830s is a challenge and requires lots of luck due to the paltry amount of records available. However, if a family were middle class, known for a particular skill, living in an urban rather than a rural area, or simply Protestant, then these more intact records would provide access to a much earlier period. None of these qualifiers apply to our family, however.

I exchanged several emails with Celestine Rafferty, the librarian at the Wexford County Library, who said that some parishes were notorious for missing and/or inaccurate records of their BMD. One such parish was Rathangan, the probable home of our Colfers; our name became Colford around 1878. It had been Colfer until then, although considering the fact that our Colfer forebears could neither read nor write, it is highly likely that they were unaware of the correct spelling of their name.

Another parish, Carrig-on-Bannow, had most of its records destroyed in a fire in 1920, according to Ray Colfer, one of the Colfers I contacted during my 2008 Ireland trip. This latter parish also was another likely home parish for our family, so many of our Colfer records may be forever lost to the ages.

Ireland census records from the nineteenth century also are non-existent. Practically all such records at 10-year intervals from 1861-1891 were destroyed by the order of the British government, the latter two for use as pulp during World War I. The remaining records covering the years 1821-1851 were destroyed during the Irish Civil War in 1922 after the British left the Irish Free State; only a few fragments of these census records survive today.

These census records were among approximately 1,000 years of irreplaceable Irish archives which were obliterated when the Irish Free State's Commander-in-Chief of the Irish Army, Michael Collins, ordered the bombing of the Four Courts Building in Dublin in which the anti-treaty Irish Republican forces had garrisoned. The Irish Public Records Office which housed the records in the rear of the building disappeared in a single explosion; the occupying forces had stored their arms and munitions there, practically insuring a massive explosion when bombardment began. Almost a thousand parish registers belonging to the Church of Ireland were lost as well, since they were required to be reported to the central government.

Roman Catholic parish registers, however, were not among those destroyed, leaving them available for anyone lucky enough to be able to track them down elsewhere. Genealogists realized such luck on July 8, 2015, when the National Library of Ireland released online digitized copies of 1,091 Roman Catholic parish records, free of charge, for all to access at www.registers.nli.ie. I have spent many hours scouring these records to uncover missing information and to confirm what I suspected but never knew for sure. These registers, however, are not complete; some parishes have available for distribution only a few years' worth of birth and marriage records. Parishes rarely recorded deaths, since it was not a sacrament, thus freeing them from the obligation of including them. Other records besides these digitized ones are not readily available, if indeed they even exist.

Perusing these records has been as frustrating an experience as it has been a fascinating one. Finding the names and dates I was looking for has been the fascinating part; however, as I will discuss throughout this narrative, not knowing the exact Roman Catholic parish of one's forebears makes locating them nearly impossible. And the poor quality of some of these handwritten registers also challenges one's ability to decode what is on the page. Some of the folks who entered these events in the registers really could have used a few hours of instruction in the Palmer method of handwriting from some Sister of Charity. Yet another research killer is the faded script in many registers which makes their contents completely unreadable. A parish register of critical importance to us, Carrig-on-Bannow's, had its official baptism entries faded and useless to any researchers, ensuring that its information will be forever unavailable. In addition to these parish records, the 1901 and 1911 Irish censuses also are available to researchers today.

Another critical bit of information which is among the missing is the 1890 United States federal census. A fire and the resulting water damage in 1921 destroyed all but a few small fragments while they were warehoused in the basement of the Commerce Building in Washington, DC. This census would have been particularly helpful in tracking Grandma Colford and her family at a critical time in their story. Finally, save for a couple of photo albums Mom held onto, none of our grandparents left behind any other family records which could have illuminated parts of their stories, like letters, diaries, photos, etc.

As you can imagine, without these records, piecing together the stories of our family and of all Irish families from the early part of the nineteenth century can be a challenge. If fortunate, family researchers will have found early 19th century information for their ancestry searches from parish records, or they will have had their own family historians who would have handed down an oral and/or written history of multiple generations.

In the absence of any official 19th - century Irish census, a fairly reliable census substitute for genealogical research has been the *General Valuation of Rateable Property in Ireland* conducted by Richard Griffith (aka: *Griffith's Primary Valuation* or *Griffith's Valuation*). Griffith, the director of the Irish Valuation Office, conducted the first survey of property ownership in Ireland at the behest of the British government. The purpose of the survey was to determine the amount of taxes people should pay toward the support of the poor within their Poor Law Union (PLU), those districts or *unions* in which the local taxable inhabitants were to be held financially responsible for all *paupers* in their area.

This first Valuation of property ownership in Ireland took 16 years to complete, from 1848 to 1864. Two of the counties of interest to us, Cork and Wexford, had their valuations completed a year apart, Cork's in 1853, and Wexford's a year later. I have made good use of Griffith's Valuation which is now online, since it provides names and property values of the inhabitants of each townland. Although the best census equivalent itself, it really underestimates the number of residents in each area, since it lists the number of *"occupiers"* throughout the country rather than the actual number of people. *"Occupiers"* were those who owned, leased, or rented a property, usually, but not always, the head of the household. Even though there may have been several families living in one household, Griffith's named just one household head as *"occupier."* The Valuation recorded approximately 70 – 80% of householders throughout the country.

As many family researchers have found, the gaps in information created by these imperfect records have led to less-than-seamless story lines of their families. Connecting the dots, as it were, requires some speculation and conjecture, much like Sherlock Holmes weaving together a complete crime story from just some fragmentary evidence. Nevertheless, I have tried to create as seamless a story as possible among the names, dates, and locations which I have gathered, and I hope to have brought to life some of our family members who have walked this earth long before us. I have made my speculations and my guesswork clear in my narrative so that there is room for alternative explanations to my interpretation of certain people, dates and events.

I realized while editing this story that it really is a story-within-a-story. In addition to providing you all with factual and speculative details of our family, I have written of how I obtained, stumbled upon, or was given all the information included here. Multiple sources are responsible for this history.

In addition to utilizing whatever records were available, I have been able to find other genealogical sources of information which have been invaluable. These sources have included:
- Our mother, truly the family historian
- Brother Paul's Michael Colfer story completed in 1991
- National Library of Ireland's online digitized Roman Catholic parish records
- Family History Centers of the Mormon Church (Caldwell and Eatontown)
- Bloomfield, Newark, and Jersey City Public Libraries
- Federal archives at 1 Bowling Green, Manhattan
- New York City Municipal Archives
- New Jersey State Archives
- Neville Colfer

- Ancestry.com
- Several genealogical forums which have connected me to fellow Lipsett, Crowley, and Colfer researchers from all over Ireland, Australia, Italy, and the States
- Third cousins of ours I have uncovered and have emailed, talked to, and/or visited: Marianne (Dunn) Sciuto of North Haven CT; Richard Boehm of Staten Island; Sharon Souther of Old Greenwich, CT; and Kathleen McGowan of Breezy Point, NY
- Bridie Lipsett's notes of family history
- Carla McDonald (Madison, Wisconsin)
- Heather Corbally Bryant, granddaughter of Irene Corbally Kuhn, Grandma Colford's maid of honor
- Mary McGrath, another Lipsett historian whose contact information nephew Liam passed along to me during his last days as a Dublin scholar
- Randy Herschaft, an Associated Press colleague of Paul's who has assisted me in my search
- Randi Koenig, owner of Legacy Genealogy Services whom I met during one of my many visits to the New York City Archives
- Jim Murray, referred to me by Randi, who helped me in my fruitless search for our great-grandmother, Margaret Harvey Dunn's, death certificate
- Amanda Stow, Assistant Archivist at the Rene Kuhn Archives at the University of Wyoming
- Special thanks for my repeated email inquiries of Cyril Newsome (Ireland), Peter Schermerhorn (Massachusetts), Suzanne Watt-Bertoni (Copparo, Italy), Marion Lipsett Barton (Ontario, Canada), Ray Colfer (Ireland), and Mark Colfer (Ireland)
- Recollections of our second cousins:

  Nancy (Colford) Cummings

  Bill Colford

  Ginger (Colford) Miceli

  Thomas Tuzzolino and brother John (Tuzzolino) Lucas

  Michael Colford

  Elinor (Coleman) Sweeney

  Betty (Blewitt) Critchley

  Joan (Downey) Salinas

Barbara (Blewitt) Lowe

- Recollections of second cousins of Mom's and Dad's whom I discovered along the way: Bill and Mabel Sweetnam, retired Dominican Sr. Catherine Dullea, her sister Marie (Dullea) Molony, and Fr. Peter Harvey, retired missionary from the Oblates of St. Francis de Sales

- Recollections of two sisters, 86-year-old Rosemarie Paganelli of Williston Park, NY, and 89-year-old Eileen Kantzler of Bloomington, IL, both nieces of Gertrude (McWilliams) Dunn, Grandma Colford's sister-in-law, her brother Jack's wife

- Online resources such as Griffith's Valuation, the Ireland censuses of 1901 and 1911, and many others which are too numerous to list

- Three Ireland visits, two of which included a bit of family history-gathering from some of the locals in Sligo and Wexford

- Celestine Rafferty at the Wexford County Library

- Countless letters and emails to Wexford parish priests re: their recollections of the Colfer family. I hit the jackpot, I believe, with Fr. James Keogh who directed my queries to a parishioner of his, Mark Colfer, who, I am fairly sure, is our third cousin. (See the section of this narrative which I entitled "*Eureka, Maybe! Possible Current Colfer Cousins.*")

- I also tried to generate other resources of my own. In the spring of 2007, I sent out 64 letters along with a one-page history of our great-grandfather, Michael Colfer, asking for any information about the family. Most of them, 46 in all, went to the Wexford County Colfers whose names I found in the Irish phone book, and the other 18 went to all the Maley families still in the area (Anne Maley is our great-grandmother.). I received several handwritten responses and some email replies as well. However, they were not able to add anything more to the information I already had, but they all wished me well in my search.

- Another long shot I tried was the same mailing to the publicans of two neighboring pubs, the Wheelhouse Bar in Baldwinstown (the townland where Anna Maley was from), and the local pub in Rathangan (the parish where some of our Colfers were baptized). I asked each publican to post the letter in the hopes that a regular customer who was a long-time local resident might see it and contact me with some information. I received a very cordial email response from Denise Murphy from the Wheelhouse Bar posting, and like the other correspondence, she wished me well but was unable to provide anything more than that.

Of course, a special thank you to my wife Jeanne and to my sons, Matthew and Michael, for tolerating my obsession with our story for these many years and many hours of research, writing, and storytelling.

Chapter I

Colfer History

History has it that the *Colfers*, the original version of our name, actually were not native Irishmen but arrived in Ireland on or about May 1st, 1169, when some may have come as part of the Norman invasion or immediately thereafter. The name *"Norman"* was derived from the name *"Northmen"* or *"Norsemen"* after the Viking conquerors of the northern part of France (Normandy); they were a combination of English, Welsh, French, and Danish. The Vikings actually had been in Ireland since the ninth century, long before the time of the Norman invasion. In fact, the name *Wexford* itself is a Norse name, meaning *"sandy harbor."*

Family Tree DNA, a company to whom I sent a swab for a DNA analysis, also puts an exact match between our Colfer line and England; the second closest match was with Ireland, with Germany the third best.

The term *"invasion"* may be a bit misleading, however, since the group that landed actually came at the invitation of Irishman Diarmuid MacMurrough, the King of Leinster, one of the four regions of Ireland. After having been ousted from his throne by Turlough Mor O'Connor, a new self-appointed High King of Ireland, MacMurrough fled to Normandy which was under the control of the British at the time; it was there he sought permission from King Henry II of England to use some of his soldiers to help him regain his kingdom. The king acceded to MacMurrough's request, and in return, MacMurrough pledged an oath of allegiance to Henry.

According to the County Wexford Heritage and Genealogy Center, the invading group sailed from Wales and landed in Bannow, the southeastern corner of County Wexford, that day; the force included *"a small company of 30 Anglo-Norman knights, 60 breast-plated men-at-arms, and 300 skilled archers."* Its leader was Richard de Clare, the 2nd Earl of Pembroke and a Norman Lord (aka: *Strongbow*). The Irish, mostly farmers and tradesmen, offered little resistance, and MacMurrough won back his throne. In return for his assistance, MacMurrough gave Strongbow his daughter, *Aiofe* (pronounced *Ee-fa*), in marriage and named him heir to the Kingdom of Leinster.

It is of little wonder why MacMurrough holds the # 1 spot in *The top 10 most hated people in Irish history*, according to a recent survey. After all, he invited the British into Ireland, and the Irish have been trying to get rid of them ever since.

The invaders and those who followed, including those mercenaries of mixed European heritage who accompanied the Normans, tended to remain in the Wexford area and to intermarry with the indigenous Irish, many of whom were already of Viking blood. They exchanged everything from customs and languages to farming methods and hairstyles, becoming *"more Irish than the Irish themselves."* This new breed of Irish folk in Bannow eventually developed its own unique culture and dialect and became known as the *Yola People*, from the old English phrase, *Ye Olde People*.

The Colfers were part of this group.

Later kings of England, however, made many attempts to stop the intermingling of Norman descendants with the native Irish by passing laws that prohibited their wearing the Irish dress and hairstyle and using their language.

According to Richard Roche, in his article, *County of Ireland - A Corner of Ireland with a Separate Culture,* this combination of visitors along with the pre-existing Wexford inhabitants, the Norsemen, were

> *"a racial mix that was to produce unusual results. The physical characteristics*
> *of tall Celt and stocky Norman merged to produce a people both big and burly.*
> *Celtic waywardness mingled with Norman method and obstinacy to give a hard-working people with a*
> *great capacity for material and cultural endeavor."*

As benign as this so-called invasion might have been, King Henry II became quite concerned that Strongbow might establish a rival Norman stronghold in Ireland and challenge his rule over the United Kingdom. In order to make sure that it did not happen, Henry accompanied a much larger invasion force to Ireland two years later on October 18, 1171, to ensure control over Strongbow. This later invasion had the approval of Pope Adrian IV, the only English pope, who gave Henry the authority to invade Ireland in order to bring the Irish Church under the control of the papacy.

And so 900 years of British rule and persecution of the Irish began.

Another explanation of the Colfer arrival in Ireland is one that derives from legend with a bit of supportive geographical and historical data. In an 1849 article in the *Journal of the Kilkenny Archaeological Society,* Reverend James Graves wrote the following about the Colfers:

> *"Tradition has it that the first of them was drifted out to sea from the*
> *Welsh coast in a goat-skin canoe, and thrown ashore at Bannow."*

Although a bit far-fetched, the canoe arrival story is certainly possible, considering the relatively short distance (70 miles) between the Dyfed area of Wales and Ireland's Bannow peninsula.

Neville Colfer, the real Colfer historian who has given Paul and me helpful Colfer tidbits over the years, has said that a Welsh custom was to set adrift at sea an individual who committed a crime which normally might have called for the death penalty but where there might have been mitigating circumstances, like a lack of intention or extreme provocation. The tribe then would put these folks to sea in order to let the gods decide whether the offenders should live or die. The right winds and currents could indeed have provided an individual with safe passage between these locations.

Another article in this same journal claimed that the Colfers' *"tradition derives from Wales at a very early period."* This version places the Colfers in Ireland before the Norman invasion.

I have heard several different versions of the origin of the Colfer name. An occupational origin has its derivation coming from the word *"calfur,"* then *"calfer,"* referring to a worker or seller of young cattle; the name Colfer then was "someone who worked as a *'calfer.'"* Other origins of surnames referred to physical characteristics or to personal attributes; the reference for *"calfur"* (young calf) was *"strong child."* Another explanation claims that the name comes from the word *"col"* (coal) and refers to people with dark or swarthy characteristics; the name *Collier*, for example, refers to a maker or seller of charcoal. Common variations of the Colfer name were Colford and Coylefer.

Yet Fran and I heard another version from 94-year-old Peter Colfer of Vernegly (pronounced *Ver-ne-lay*), County Wexford, whom we met during our Ireland trip in 2008. He said that among the first groups of people who followed the Normans to Ireland came a young unaccompanied boy who stepped off the boat with a sign hung around his neck with the statement, *"To be **called for**,"* written on it, thus the beginning of the Colfer name. Peter was a charming older gentleman, so I would like to give him "first dibs" on the Colfer explanation, but his version may be a bit more apochryphal than the other ones.

Hilary Murphy, Irish genealogist and author, writes that the precise meaning of the name is unclear, although it does date to early Norman times. The name *Coylerer* is found in early 14th century Irish records, and there was a William *Culpher* in Wexford in 1666. The earliest record of the *Colfer* spelling in Wexford appears as part of a Latin inscription on a slab in a church ruin at Bannow, located just above the protected cove where the Normans landed. The inscription commemorates John Colfer and his wife, Anna, and the engraving has them wearing the garb of a knight and lady; experts determined it to be a 13th - century tombstone.

In perusing the U.S. federal censuses, the first *Colford* to appear was in the 1800 census; he was a George who was living in Charleston, SC. The 1810 census included an Edward *Colfred* in Richland, SC; Edward was the owner of one slave. George W. and William *Colfer* were living in Saddle River, NJ in 1830, and three other *Colfers* appeared in 1840: James C. (Pulaski, VA), John (Talladega, AL), and Moses B. (Randolph, IN). Several more *Colfers* showed up in 1850, perhaps those fleeing the potato famine-ravaged Ireland; their new homes in the States were in Baltimore, MD, Franklin, NY, and Cocke, TN.

For whatever it's worth, there are two *Colford* Avenues, one in Collingswood, NJ, and another in West Chicago, IL. Mom also said that she saw another one somewhere in Staten Island.

Chapter II

Our Colfers

The Colfer surname was one of the most plentiful ones in County Wexford, particularly in the Bannow area. Wexford is the county in the southeastern corner of the country, whereas Bannow is a civil parish consisting of 24 smaller townlands within the larger Roman Catholic Parish known as Carrig-on-Bannow. Bannow is also the name of a separate townland. Griffith's Valuation listed 94 Colfers in Wexford in 1854, with 33 of them found in Bannow alone, along with one *Colferr*.

I exchanged many emails over the years with a Mark Colfer who said that Bannow *"is the real home of the Colfers."* He cited the following entry from Fr. Tom Butler's book, *A Parish and Its People*:

> *"The name **Colfer** is rarely found outside the Bannow area of County Wexford*
> *but it is the most plentiful surname of all Norman names in the area."*

Frank Delaney, in his book, *Ireland: A Novel*, which combines the tale of a *seanachie* (storyteller) with Irish folklore, also confirmed our Norman ties:

> *"What's in a name? You're descended from a Norman or from a family who*
> *came with them if your name is one of these: Prendergast, Cogan, Fitzgerald . . .*
> ***Colfer**, Stafford, Carew, Hayes . . . Down around Wexford you can't throw a stone without hitting a*
> *Devereaux or a Bolger or a **Colfer** or a Codd or a Stafford or a Roche or a Furlong."*

Having such a saturation of one name in one place is a double-edged sword for any genealogist. On the one hand, it places our family in a specific location (Bannow), but on the other hand, it makes it difficult, if not impossible, to determine precisely what family line is ours. Griffith's listed 12 Patrick Colfers, the same given name as our great-great grandfather, living in nine different townlands in our part of County Wexford. One can imagine the near impossibility of determining which of these Patricks is ours. Tom McDonald, a local Wexford historian, did some research for me and said that there were so many Colfers in the parishes of Carrig-on-Bannow and Rathangan that finding our family would not be possible without some additional identifying details.

The Colfer – Maley – Colford Connection

The following section of our story traces four generations of the families of Dad's father:

Patrick and Mary (Dwyer) Colfer
(Our great-great-grandparents)

.
.
.
.
.

Michael Colfer
(Our great-grandfather)

Bryan and Mary (Neil) Maley
(Our great-great-grandparents)

.
.
.
.
.

Anne Maley
(Our great-grandmother)

Michael and Anne (Maley) Colfer
(Our great-grandparents)

.
.
.
.
.

Joseph Colford
(Our grandfather)

Joseph and Agnes (Dunn) Colford
(Our grandparents)

Chapter III

Colfer – Dwyer – Maley Beginnings

Whichever one of these 12 Patrick Colfers is our great-great grandfather would go on to marry Mary Dwyer.

For the longest while we thought that Patrick's and Mary's son, our great-grandfather, Michael Colfer, was from the townland of Ballycullane. Jeanne, Michael, and I paid a visit to the pastor of St. Leonard's Church there, Fr. Laurence O'Connor, during our 2004 trip to look over parish records, but I knew long before that visit that Michael was not in our direct line. This Michael's parents were Richard and Bridget (Finn) Colfer, whereas our Michael's folks were Patrick and Mary (Dwyer) Colfer. Our Michael gave these names to the keeper of the parish register of St. Patrick's Cathedral in Newark when he married our great-grandmother, Anne. I was fortunate to have been able to purchase Fr. O'Connor's book, *The Parish of Tintern*, during our visit; the book essentially is a listing of all the headstone inscriptions in the cemeteries throughout his parish. There are no fewer than 37 Colfers buried in his parish alone.

I have been unsuccessful in locating the marriage record which would have listed the exact home townland of our great-great-grandparents, Patrick and Mary, either because they don't exist in any parish due to shoddy record-keeping, or simply because I have not looked in the right places. The baptismal record of their son Michael, our great-grandfather, also has eluded me; even the paid researchers at the Wexford Heritage and Genealogy Centre could not locate either of these records for me. As I mentioned earlier, these records may be among those burned, lost, or simply locked away forever in the faded and unreadable Carrig-on-Bannow parish register.

There is a parish marriage record for our other great-great-grandparents, Bryan and Mary (Neil) Maley, however. They were married on December 2, 1843, in Rathangan and were to have three children whom I can locate: Anne/Anna (our great-grandmother), James, and Kate. The name *Maley* was probably a derivation of the name *O'Malley* from an earlier generation.

Anne (Maley) Colford, Our Maternal Great-Grandmother

The online parish registers allowed me to confirm some of the records Paul unearthed years ago from Rathangan, a Roman Catholic parish which abuts Carrig-on-Bannow immediately to the east.

Rathangan also is the name of one of the villages that falls within the parish itself. These records include those of our great-grandmother and of at least two great-great-uncles.

The following James is indeed our great-great uncle, Michael's brother, who eventually would be a Newark, NJ, resident; the register had his baptismal record as follows:

James Colfer – "of Patt and Mary Dwyer" – "sponsor Mary Merriman" - baptized July 15, 1835

His was the only Rathangan baptism record for our direct line of Colfers I found (read about him later in this narrative). The only Patrick Colfer I found in the digitized marriage records was a Patrick Colfer who was witness to the nuptials of John Colfer, probably his brother, and Catherine White on the 22nd of October, 1831.

There also was another Colfer, a Patrick *"of Patrick and Mary Goff,"* baptized November 17, 1836. This Mary's surname ruled him out as Michael's brother, however.

Could our Patrick and Mary (Dwyer) Colfer have left Rathangan after the birth of James and moved to the neighboring parish of Carrig-on-Bannow?

Who knows? In fact, we may never know, since the pages of the latter parish register are too faded to read.

The Rathangan register includes the baptism records of our Maley kin:

> *Anne of Brian Maley and Mary Neile* – "*sponsors John Kavanagh and Mary Furlong*" - baptized April 10, 1846 - our great-grandmother
>
> *Catherine of Brian Mealy and Mary Neil* – "*sponsors William Hayes and Mary White*" - baptized March 4, 1844 – our great-great aunt, Anne's sister
>
> *James of Bryan Mayly and Mary Neil* – "*sponsor Phil Kavanagh*" - baptized January 21, 1850 – our great-great uncle, Anne's brother

Despite the missing records of our great-great grandparents' marriage and our great- grandfather Michael's baptism, I consider these Rathangan records to be as close as we will ever get to a "smoking gun" in confirming Rathangan as the place where our Colfers were baptized and where they lived, at least for a time. Great-grandma Anne's home at the time of her birth was Baldwinstown, but by the time of her younger brother, James', birth in 1850, the family had moved right next door to Rathangan itself. These two townlands were just a mile apart, so it would have been very easy for that move to take place. Both of these villages were small and cozy farming communities where everyone knew everyone else. Griffith's lists just nine *occupiers* in Baldwinstown in 1854 and 28 in Rathangan that same year.

Michael eventually gave his birth years to census takers as 1841, 1845, and 1848, but there is reason to believe that 1841 was the most accurate one of the three.

Although brothers Michael and James both left for the States, I believe that Patrick, another *possible* brother, stayed behind and married another Mary (last name unknown), and settled in the townland of Vernegly, just a short distance from Rathangan. (See a further discussion about this Patrick in a later section, *Eureka, Maybe! Possible Current Colfer Cousins*.)

Another Patrick Colfer, born and raised in Rathangan, was *"killed in action"* in France on October 15, 1914, during World War I; he earned both the *Victory Medal* and the *British War Medal* for his actions. I am not sure how this Patrick might be related to us, but surely there is a link somewhere.

Chapter IV

Our Paternal Great-Grandparents
Michael and Anne (Maley) Colfer

There are many reasons why the Irish emigrated from their country to parts unknown during the middle of the 19th century; limited economic opportunities, political repression, and the ravages of the potato famine (1845-49) were just some of them. Given the birthdates of our great-grandfather, Michael (1841), and great-grandmother, Anne (1846), their early childhood years must have seen significant deprivation during the height of the famine. The fungus that devastated the potato crop during that period ushered in the famine which resulted in over a million deaths and in the emigration of one million other Irish folk who left behind their country for good. One estimate claimed that one of every nine inhabitants of Ireland died. It must have been quite a task for families to keep body and soul together.

However, I suspect that another compelling reason for Michael and Anne to depart their homeland years later was the fact that Anne was approximately five months pregnant and unmarried. One can only imagine the disgrace her condition might have created for her family, since the Irish didn't take too kindly to those pregnant and not yet married. Chroniclers of the era wrote of the

"stigma of illegitimacy" and *"the representation of unmarried mothers as immoral and their children as a drain on resources . . . unwed mothers and their infants were an affront to morality . . ."*

Dorothy Haller wrote:

> *"Even family and friends could not be depended on to offer comfort and aid.*
> *If a young woman became pregnant while still living at home, she was forced*
> *to leave in disgrace and move to an area where she was not known."*

Thus was the lot of our Anne, I suppose, and the driving force behind her emigration to the States.

What I have found in practically all of the Catholic parish registers I have surveyed are countless numbers of babies throughout these parishes listed as *"illegitimate"* or as *"elligitimate"* and accompanied by the names of their unmarried parents. Still other parishes preferred the term *"bastard"* next to these babies' names. I suppose that such a designation was something that most families preferred to avoid.

There is a notation in the July 17, 1823, Rathangan parish baptism record that Anne's own mother, Mary (Neal), also was born to unmarried parents, John Neal and Catherine Murphy. However, the parish register did not label her as *"illegitimate"* or as *"bastard,"* but rather as *"spuria,"* a Latin term (*spurius/spuria*) meaning *"false . . . of illegitimate birth."*

Could Mary's unpleasant experiences as an out-of-wedlock child have convinced her own pregnant daughter to leave town? Who knows?

Although unrelated to us, the saddest of all such entries was one I found in the register of a parish in County Clare; it recorded a January 24, 1847, birth accordingly:

> *"Johanna . . . to Joanna Corrigan. This woman being deaf and*
> *dumb and not married could not account for the father of the child."*

Jeez!

Another unrelated entry in the Rathangan baptism register on November 24, 1849, came from an Ann Murphy who recorded (or had recorded) in it the following statement which suggests to me that she was considering a life of celibacy, perhaps in response all those out-of-wedlock children out there. Her statement reads as follows:

> *"This true Catholic Church without which none can be saved, I Anne Murphy, do at this present time freely profess and sincerely hold, and I promise most constantly to retain and profess the same entire and unviolated, with God's assistance to the end of my life."*

Chapter V

Michael and Anne in America

It was on Thursday, July 5, 1866, when Captain William Eves guided his *Ship Atmosphere* into New York harbor. The first page of the ship's manifest included his promise to

"solemnly, sincerely, and truly swear the following . . . that on said list
is truly designated the age, the sex, and the occupation of each of said
passengers, the part of the vessel occupied by each during the passage,
the country to which each belongs, and also the country of which it is
intended by each to become an inhabitant; and said List or Manifest
truly sets forth the number of said passengers who have died on said
voyage, and the names and ages of those who died."

The ship's arrival was a little more than a year after the end of the Civil War and President Lincoln's assassination and one day after the 90th anniversary of the signing of the Declaration of Independence. Inclement weather, however, seemed to have dampened the celebratory spirits in the New York area the day before.

The Jersey City Daily Times reported on a rather sedate July 4th celebration:

"The weather, until toward evening, was propitious, although hot; the
rain clouds gathering in the afternoon, admonished picnic parties to seek

shelter, and indicated what happened, a general postponement of the
exhibition of fireworks until this evening . . . Independence Day never
was noticed in Jersey City. We should think that the greater portion of
our people left town to seek pleasure and to celebrate elsewhere. There
was no programme here for any oration, or assemblage, to draw people
together, and they all sped away by steamboat, yacht and car to all points
of the compass."

Listed on page seven of the *Ship Atmosphere's* 421- passenger manifest were the following names:

Mich Colfer – 25 years of age – Male – Laborer
Kate Mealy – 21 years of age – Female – Spinster
Jas Mealy – 15 years of age - Male – Laborer
Anne Mealy – 19 years of age – Female – Spinster

Great-grandma's surname took on many spelling variations over the years, but it is clear that the above folks were our great-grandfather, Michael Colfer, his future wife, Anne Mealy/Maley, and her two siblings, Kate and James. Both her siblings served as godparents to a number of Michael and Anne's children over the years and as witnesses to their marriage. Included on another page of the ship's manifest was yet another James Maley (*"30 – laborer"*) and a *Brid* (Bridget) Maley (*"30 – spinster"*); this second James was Anne's first cousin, the son of her uncle John *Mayle* and his wife, Mary. Bridget's relationship is unclear, but she probably was another cousin or perhaps an older sister of Anne's. There are six Maleys, including James and Bridget, all buried in Holy Sepulchre cemetery in East Orange, NJ.

At the time of their immigration, ships' manifests recorded little information besides that which I provided here. It wasn't until the Immigration Act of 1891 when the federal government became involved in the process and required that the manifests include much more information, including the travelers' place of origin and the persons whom they were intending to visit in the States. This Act also included the opening of Ellis Island.

I suspect that our great-grandparents' voyage to the States was not without its share of problems for a couple of reasons. First of all, it left from Liverpool, England, not Ireland's own port of Queenstown from which Grandpa Lipsett departed. Practically all emigrants in those days sailed first to Liverpool

27

before taking off for the States. Leaving from there required the travelers to arrive in the city several days before boarding their ship; in addition to making final arrangements for their travel, Michael and his mates had to find a place to stay as well, adding to the expense of their emigration. The available boarding houses there all had a reputation of being just awful, and Liverpool itself was a bawdy, dirty, unsettled port town, rife with scams and hucksters of all kinds just waiting to take advantage of the unwitting and naïve departing Irishmen. How Michael and his companions spent their time there is probably a story unto itself.

Another genealogist mentioned in an email to me that requiring the Irish to sail from Dublin to Liverpool as the first step in their departure was just another way for the English to extract more money from the poor Irish to allow them to leave their homeland.

Second, the name of their boat was *Ship Atmosphere*, and it did not carry the more common Designation of *SS* (steamship), indicating that their ship may have been more of a sailing ship than a true steamship. However, since more than 90% of immigrants arrived at our shores in steamships by 1870, I assume that the *Atmosphere* was one of them, but I have been unable to verify its ship's type. Improvements in steamship travel kept the average voyage length between Ireland and the States from seven to ten days by the time Grandpa Lipsett left in 1904, but the more primitive steamships in 1866 required a crossing time of more like 18 – 21 days. True sailing ships, if indeed the *Atmosphere* was one, took as many as 12 weeks.

Once they arrived in the States, our great-grandparents would have come through Castle Garden, America's first official immigration center/Emigrant Landing Depot which was in operation from 1855 – 1892. Built originally in 1807 as a military fort in preparation for the War of 1812, its later years saw its uses change to an amusement park, then a concert hall, before being turned over to the federal government as a place to process our expanding immigrant flow. Between eight and twelve million souls passed through this first debarkation point located at Battery Park at the very tip of Manhattan.

The feds opened the site specifically for the protection of immigrants. Otherwise, they would have continued to land at some unsupervised location in New York City, only to be put upon by the same type of unscrupulous, predatory folk who stalked them back in Liverpool. Castle Garden provided, among other things, access to railroad tickets, to accurate directions to their destinations, and to a fair exchange rate for their money. After approximately 37 years of our immigrant population passing through here, Ellis Island opened in 1892 and saw to the admittance of our *"huddled masses,"* including Grandpa Lipsett, until 1954. Unfortunately, a fire in 1897 destroyed many of the Castle Garden records.

Michael and Anne's first destination was the Ironbound section of Newark (aka: *Down Neck)*, a rail-locked community closest to Jersey City which was populated largely by Irish and German immigrants; they were to remain there until 1880 when they moved to Jersey City. Michael took up residence in this location to meet up with his older brother, James, who had emigrated from Ireland at least six years before him and settled there.

This four-square-mile section of Newark was considered one of the city's poorest districts at the time. It is now referred to as *New Jersey's Portugal* or as *Little Portugal* for that sizable population now living there.

Reverend F. Schneider Doam presided over the marriage of Michael and Anne a month after their arrival on Saturday, August 11, 1866, in Newark's St. Patrick's Cathedral, although the state record places the date at August 15 due to the four-day delay in reporting it. The parish register included the following entry: *"Michael Colver (24) – laborer – of Patrick and Mary Dwyer and Ann Maily (20) of Bryan Maily and Mary Neil."* Witnesses to their nuptials were Patrick Dillon and Catherine Maily. Anne gave birth to their first child, John *Colfer*, on October 25, two months after the wedding; his sponsors were John Cummings and Catherine Mealy. The baptism took place at St. James Church, a massive Gothic structure that had only recently been completed. John eventually married Sarah Merity; he lived until 1934.

More Colfer children were to follow, but it appears that Anne may have been unclear regarding the actual number of children she had. She told the census-taker in 1900 that she had *11* children, *seven* of whom survived, yet she (or Michael) mentioned to the 1910 census taker that *seven* of her *10* children were still living. However, I am sure that *11* was the correct number. Below are their names after John's as they appeared in parish and state birth records (note the five different spellings of the name from the baptismal records).

James Colfar (September 28, 1868; sponsors: Patrick Dillon and
Mary McConnell; died 10 months later on August 10, 1869;

29

cause of death: *"convulsions"*)

Michael Colfar, Jr. (October 10, 1870 – June 22, 1911; sponsors: James
Meale and Margaret Whalen)

Bernard Colfar (December 9, 1872 – September 21, 1875; sponsors: John
Whelan and Catherine Gartland; cause of death for this three year, four month-old was
"diptheria")

James Colfer (August 29, 1874 – December 18, 1945; sponsors: Richard
Delaney and Mary Meyler)

Thomas Calford (December 19, 1876; sponsors: James Gartland and Mary
Brown; Thomas died in infancy, but death certificate not found)

Peter Colford (February 11, 1878 – February 14, 1878; cause of death for this three-day-old
was *"eclampsia,"* but the Holy Sepulchre Cemetery listing attributed his passing to
"premature birth" and laid him to rest in the *"stillborn plot"*)

Joseph Cholfer (our Grandfather; May 26, 1880 – Nov. 18, 1968)
Married Agnes Dunn and had one child: our father, Joseph, Jr.

Mary Agnes Colford (aka: *Mamie*; August 21, 1883 – November 25, 1958)

Catherine Colford (aka: *Aunt Kate*; May, 1885 – February 15, 1979)

William Patrick Colford (November 26, 1887 – January 29, 1939)

Of the aforementioned 11 children, Bernard is the one who one might *suspect* is not one of them, since the state birth record lists his parents' names as Michael and *Ellen*. However, I am fairly convinced that he indeed was Michael and Anne's son, with his mother's name mistakenly listed as *Ellen*, for several reasons. First of all, there was no Michael and Ellen Colfer couple in any local census records or city directories that I found, and the surnames of his sponsors, *Whalen* and *Gartland*, also appeared as sponsors to two other Colfer siblings. Finally, as has been borne out multiple times in my research, families tended to have children every two years, placing Bernard's birth two years apart from older brother Michael and younger brother James. The other Colfer children also were spaced every two years.

For what it's worth, there was a Bernard Colfer who arrived in New York Harbor on June 18, 1877, aboard the ship, *City of Richmond*. I have not been able to place this 36-year-old *"farmer"* anywhere after his arrival, nor can I attest to his possible relationship to our Michael, but might he be the family member for whom Michael and Anne named their son?

30

Speculation, for sure.

Son James lived only 10 months. The practice of naming another child after one who predeceased him was common, yet the next son born was named *Michael* instead. Michael and Anne apparently waited until the birth of their sixth child before they chose the name *James* again.

What also is interesting in the naming of Michael's and Anne's children is that they did not follow the traditional Irish naming patterns at that time. The common practice was to name the first-born son after the father's father. However, despite the fact that Michael reported his father's given name as Patrick, he did not name any one of his sons after his own father, choosing *John* as his first-born. Of equal interest is the fact that Michael's older brother, James, whose birth record also listed his father's name as Patrick, named his first-born son *John* also. It is highly unusual for both of these brothers not to have followed this naming pattern.

Such a practice might have meant that this "oversight" indicated a rift of sorts between father and son, thus the purposeful refusal to pass on the family patriarch's given name. However, a more likely explanation is what I have experienced myself in my research and what I have learned from other genealogical folk. It was a very common practice for families to identify their members by middle names in order to distinguish them from the more common first names in the family which were passed on over and over again, as per the Irish naming tradition.

For example, if we six Colford brothers followed this practice, all of our first-born sons would have been named Joseph (after Dad's father), thus the likelihood that they may have been known by their middle names in order to distinguish one of the six Josephs from the others. This explanation suggests that our great-great-grandfather may actually have been born Patrick *John*, thus the use of *John* as the name for the two brothers' first-born sons. In keeping with this same traditional practice, Michael's and Anne's first-born daughter, Mary Agnes (aka: *Mamie*) was named after her mother's mother, Mary (Neil), and Mom *was* named after her own mother's mother, Catherine/Katie (Hayes).

Michael's name does not appear in Newark's annual municipal directory until the 1869-70 edition which listed him as a resident at 57 Charlton St. Family names in city directories are missing almost as often as they are listed, so trying to string together consecutive annual listings of the same family can be a challenge. The 1870 census offers a clearer picture, however. Michael, like so many other newcomers, found work as a laborer, doubtless in one of the industries (brewing, tanning, iron works, etc.) that began to locate in the Ironbound section after the Morris Canal and the railroads were completed through the area. Among the trades given by his neighbors in the same census were "*hat trimmer*" and "*smelter.*"

Michael and Anne and their brood moved several times after 57 Charlton, according to the Newark City Directories of the period: 455 ½ Ferry St. (1871-72), 76 Christie St. (1873 - 74), 38 Christie St. (1874 - 76), and 92 Chapel St. (1877 - 79). The 1880 census had Michael and Anne and their four children living at 67 Brill St., a five - family building they shared with the Madden, Lambert, Donahan, and Milligan families, just a short walk from the Passaic River. Michael had been unemployed for two months that year. The family's hopscotching around suggests either a constant search for larger quarters, or perhaps cheaper ones. However, there often were rental incentives created by landlords wanting to fill their apartment vacancies. Families were offered a reduced rent for several months before the rent then would rise to the going rate, so families would take advantage of the reduced fee and then move on to another rental incentive until they had to pay that increased monthly amount.

The Newark City Directories had Michael as *Colfer* in 1870, *Colford* in 1872, then back again to *Colfer* in 1875. However, *Colford* began to appear consistently by the 1878 Directory, even though the first of his 11 children to be baptized as *Colford* was Mary Agnes (Mamie), the ninth born, in 1883. Catherine and William followed with *Colford* as their baptismal surnames in 1885 and 1887, respectively.

When the census taker came to call in 1880, Michael and Anne's youngest child at home was our Grandpa Joseph who was only a few months old. He was the first in the family to be baptized in nearby St. Aloysius Church in Newark. Indeed, his was among the first christenings performed there, then a newly constructed place of worship thanks to the funds donated by the Ballantine Brewery, headquartered just across the street. The church stands on what is now Fleming St., named after the longtime pastor, the Reverend M.A. Fleming, who baptized Grandpa Colford the day he was born, May 26, 1880.

Michael moved his family to Jersey City immediately after the 1880 census, and he had different residences there. The family's first place was on Hoadley Ave. near the Morris Canal; Hoadley was then the name of Boyd Ave., specifically that section of the street that ran below West Side and Mallory Aves. The 1881-82 Jersey City Directory placed Michael at *"Hoadley Ave. n canal,"* whereas the 1883 - 84 Directory had him at *"Hoadley Ave. n Mallory Ave."* They then were at 187 Clendenny Ave. for approximately three years (1884 – 87) before moving briefly to *"Williams Ave. n Miller"* (1888) and then a year later to 280 Virginia Ave. where they remained for almost 16 years. However, the 1900 federal census recorded the house number as 282, not 280 as all the Jersey City Directories did. The 1888, 1889, and 1890 city directories also recorded Michael's name as *Colfred.*

After the family's move to Jersey City, the school-age children attended Public School No. 18, a one-room structure at Yale and Mallory Aves. The newly constructed P.S. 24 on Virginia Ave. eventually replaced it.

Great-grandpa Michael was identified as a *"laborer,"* a *"steelworker,"* and a *"molder"* in the directories over the years. The 1896 directory is the first one to show that sons Michael, Jr., John, and James also were *"laborers."* At that time, the Spaulding - Jennings Steel Company, originally founded by 1890, was in operation nearby, roughly at Grant and Claremont Aves. near the Morris Canal. Its parent company, the Crucible Steel Company of America, absorbed this Jersey City plant in 1900 and expanded it with additional buildings until it was spread over 12 full acres ranging from West Side to Mallory Ave.

A January 4, 1902, article in volume 91 of the trade journal, *Iron and Machinery World*, made the following statement about the plant: *"Tools of every description are to be manufactured and upwards of 2,000 men employed."* Living within just a few short blocks of such a sizable employer must have sat well with our Michael and his family, since the plant provided employment opportunities for all the locals who were just a short walk from their jobs.

Forty three-year-old Michael visited the clerk at the Court of Common Pleas on Communipaw Ave. in Jersey City on January 8, 1885, to file his *Declaration of Intention* (aka: *First Papers*), the first of two steps needed for the granting of U.S. citizenship. Immigrants were able to register their *Intentions* immediately after their arrival; the second step was to complete a *Petition for Naturalization* (aka: *Second* or *Final Papers*), typically done after establishing U.S. residency for three to five years.

Our illiterate great-grandfather signed the requisite papers with an *"X,"* labeled by a witness as *"his mark."* For the purposes of the application, Michael stated that he had come to America on July 3, 1866 (he was off by two days). The text of the document goes on to say that it was his wish to become a U.S. citizen *"and to renounce forever all allegiance and fidelity to the QUEEN OF THE UNITED KINGDOM OF GREAT BRITAIN AND IRELAND, whose subject he had heretofore been."*

A John Roberts was the character witness for Michael that day who claimed that he was *"well acquainted"* with Michael Colford and that he had *"behaved himself as a man of good moral character, attached to the principles and Constitution of the United States, and well-disposed to the good order and happiness of the same."* The court granted Michael citizenship three years later on April 5, 1888.

With Michael's naturalization as a U.S. citizen came Anne's citizenship as well. Once a husband became a citizen, his wife also was granted the same status; nationality laws generally tied a woman's citizenship status to that of her husband's. An immigrant woman also became a U.S. citizen automatically if she married a U.S. citizen. Conversely, a U.S.-born woman lost her citizenship if she married a non-citizen. It wasn't until 1922 with the passage of the Married Women's Act when women were granted citizenship status separate from that of their husbands.

What is interesting to note are the various dates Michael gave to the census takers over the years regarding his birth and his arrival in the States. Although he reported his year of arrival accurately (1866) when he applied for citizenship, he reported in several censuses that his arrival years were 1868 and 1870. However, these variations, along with his many birth years mentioned earlier, are very common, record by record.

Michael (53) and Anne (50) were still at their Virginia Ave. address in 1900 with six of their seven children: Michael, James, Joseph, Mamie, Kate, and William. Their oldest son, 31-year-old John, was off and married by this time; he and his wife Sarah were living at 108 Williams Ave. Father Michael, Michael, Jr., and James said that their occupations were as *"laborer – steel mill."* As for the others, Joseph (our Grandpa) was listed as *"bartender,"* Mamie as *"saleslady (candy),"* and Kate and William both *"at school."*

Our great-grandparents continued to move around the West Bergen section, living at 149 Boyd Ave. for a time (1905 – 1909) before relocating one last time two blocks south to 22 Clarke Ave. where the 1910 census had them renting space in a two-family home along with a German immigrant, 44-year-old Conrad Zimmerman, his 17-year-old daughter Irene, and another *"boarder,"* Marjorie Soper (17).

By this time, the 69-year-old Michael identified his trade as *"own income,"* an indication that he had retired. The only remaining Colford offspring who shared living space with their parents that year was 30-year-old Grandpa, at that time a clerk in City Hall, and Kate (25), listed in the census as *"wrapper – noodle factory."*

Grandpa Colford was the last of Michael's and Anne's children to marry; his sister Kate remained single. He was on the rise as an office-holder in Hague's political organization when he married our grandmother, Agnes (Dunn), in 1919 (her story follows).

Michael passed away at home on December 28, 1916, at the age of 76, a full 51 years after leaving Ireland. The official *Certificate and Record of Death*, however, listed his age as 71; cause of death was *"acute bronchitis"* and the secondary cause, *"arterial stenosis."* He had been treated for the condition since November 6th. The Jersey Journal reported his passing as follows:

> *"The funeral of Michael J. Colford, one of the old-timers in the West Side*
> *section who died last Saturday, was held this morning from his late home,*
> *22 Clark Ave. A requiem mass was offered at St. Aloysius Church . . . he*
> *was one of the first employees of the old steel mill in that section and worked*
> *there for 25 years. He was obliged to retire some years ago because of*
> *advancing years and impaired health."*

The paper also identified him as a member of St. Aloysius' Holy Name Society; sons James and John were *"following the occupation of their father in the steel mills,"* Joseph was *"a clerk in Commissioner Brensinger's office,"* and William was *"a former alderman."* Two daughters also were listed as surviving him.

The attending physician relied upon a *"Mr. Colford"* as his *"Informant"* (possibly Grandpa Colford) in assisting him in completing the death certificate. However, this informant apparently replied, *"Do not know,"* when asked for Michael's date of birth, the names of his parents, and their birthplaces.

Interesting.

Sadly, there is no photograph of Michael Colford known to exist, although we do have one of our great-grandma Anne. Nicholas Villa (aka: *Uncle Nick*), who lived next door to us on Ege Ave. for many years until his death in 1978 at age 74, was 13 years old when Michael died. He remembered Michael when he was an old man. He was tall, Nick said, often wore bib overalls, probably a steelworker's outfit, and liked to tease the neighborhood youngsters by hiding on them behind a tree and jumping out to startle them.

Great-grandma Anne would outlive her husband by 15 years. She died on September 24, 1932. The day before the funeral, the Jersey Journal described the wake thusly:

> *Hundreds of residents of West Bergen visited the Colford home, 307 Virginia Ave., last night to pay their respects and the parlor of the home was filled with floral offerings. Members of Our Lady of Victories Rosary Society filed through first and then members of the Tioga Democratic Club and Auxiliary paid their respects.*

The Sunday, September 25th, edition of *The New York Times* ran the following obit:

MRS. ANNA COLFORD

> *Mrs. Anna Colford, mother of Under Sheriff Joseph Colford of Hudson County, N.J., died yesterday at his home, 418 West Side Avenue, Jersey City, from the infirmities of her age, which was 84. Born in County Wexford, Ireland, she came to this country as a girl and for more than sixty years had resided in the West Bergen section of Jersey City. Surviving are four sons, Joseph, who is chairman of the Hudson County Democratic Committee as well as Under Sheriff; William, John, and James, and two daughters, Mrs. Mary Blewitt and Miss Catherine Colford.*

However, she actually died in the 307 Virginia Ave. home she shared with her two daughters, Mamie Blewitt, a widow herself, unmarried Aunt Kate, and the rest of Mamie's brood. Hertrue age was 86, not 84 as reported in the press, nor "*83 years, 5 months, 23 days,*" her death certificate noted. The cause of death was "*myocarditis – general arteriosclerosis.*"

The whereabouts of Anne's sister Kate over the years is a mystery. I have been unable to find her in any of the Newark City Directories, primarily because they only listed the male heads of households as residents. If she had been living with her brother James or with her sister and brother-in-law, Anne and Michael, her name apparently would not have been included in these books.

Given the added possibilities of a marriage and a change of name, locating her may not be possible.

I thought that I had located Anne's brother, James, but now I think not. The James *Mealey* who I thought was ours married a Bridget Shields on June 15, 1868, in Newark's St. Patrick's Cathedral. A *"hatter,"* according to his marriage record and to other directory listings, he wed a *"seamstress,"* the daughter of Edward and Mary (Peoples) Shields. They were to have three children, Alexander, Joseph, and Kate. He had passed away by 1900 when the census that year listed Bridget as his widow living with 22-year-old Alexander, a *"bookkeeper,"* Katie (19; *"dressmaker"*), and Joseph (17; *"plumber"*). However, this James listed his parents' names as William and Catherine (Keegan), whereas our James' parents were Bryan and Mary (Neil).

Chapter VI

Michael and Anne's Children

Grandpa Colford and His Siblings,
Our Great-Uncles and Great-Aunts

T his section of our story chronicles the lives, as best we know them, of Grandpa Colford and his siblings, according to birth order.

I have been able to locate several Colford second cousins of ours, some of whom have reached out to me and to Paul in the most serendipitous of ways. These cousins include Nancy (Colford) Cummings, Michael Colford, Bill Colford, Tom Tuzzolino, John (Tuzzolino) Lucas, and Ginger (Colford) Miceli. What I have been able to include here are their recollections. The last names as presented below are as they appeared in the parish baptismal records:

John Colfer

Neither Mom nor any one of the second cousins I have talked to have any recollections of the eldest John, so all the information I can provide has been gleaned primarily from census records. John (31) and Sarah Merity (29) were married on April 25, 1899; the couple shared a three-family house at 108 Williams Ave. in Jersey City with the Kelly and Henrihan families, according to the 1900 census. Sarah's parents, James and Sarah, natives of Ireland, lived at 195 Clendenny Ave. with Sarah's 33-year-old brother, Charles. John told the census-taker that he was employed as a *"steel heater."*

The 1906 city directory had John (*"maker – cement stones")* and Sarah eventually joined by her brother Charles (*"checker – tobacco factory")* at 191 Clendenny where they remained for another 20 years. The city directories consistently listed John as a *"steelworker"* in later years, however, obviously in the employ of the Spaulding-Jennings Steel Company. John and Sarah lost an infant son, John, on September 8, 1902; they had no other children. Although she was not working in 1910, Sarah eventually found work as a *"laundress-private family"* (1920) and as a *"janitress – police department"* (1930). By 1926, the couple had relocated to 195 Clendenny. The latter census did not include Charles any longer but listed Sarah's brother, James (67), and his daughter, Marion (26), as living with them.

John passed away on November 25, 1934, at the age of 68, still a resident of 195 Clendenny, but his death certificate had his age as *65* and his date of birth as October 31, 1869, when it actually was three years earlier on August 11, 1866. The cause of death of this *"steel worker"* was *"chronic endocarditis (mitral regurgitation)."* His widow Sarah had moved to 277 Harrison Ave. by 1940 where she continued her work as *"housework – police station."* The 66-year-old widow earned a salary of $1,500 the year before.

Michael Colfar

Our great-grandfather's namesake was the fourth-born and the second surviving child in the family. Second cousins Bill Colford and John Lucas, two of Michael's grandsons, both told me that they had heard that Michael had been a professional boxer for a time. Michael and his wife, Delia (aka: *Daisy*) Mae (McDonough), must have been a memorable couple; he stood six feet, three inches tall, whereas she fell an inch short of five feet. Tom Tuzzolino, another second cousin, described Michael as the *"picture"* of Grandpa Colford.

Michael and Daisy Mae left New Jersey for Reading, PA, around 1906 with their three children, Benny, Joe, and Bill, where Michael found work as a *"foreman – steel works"*; children four and five, Mary (aka: *Mae*) and Howie, were born in PA during that time. The 1910 census placed Michael (38), his 37-year-old wife (whose name was listed as *"Della"*), and their five children at 312 Bern St. in Reading. They had been married for 10 years at that time. Daisy apparently had lost two children, since she reported to the census taker when asked, *"The mother of how many children?"* that the *"Number born"* was *"7"* and the *"Number now living"* was *"5."*

What prompted Michael to head to Pennsylvania for employment as a steelworker when he had been gainfully employed as one in Jersey City is not known. However, one explanation might have to do with a possible friendship he forged with Ernest Judson Poole, a *master mechanic* at Spaulding – Jennings and a resident of 870 Communipaw Ave. with his wife and three children. It was around 1900 when Poole left Jersey City to assume the position of superintendent of the Carpenter Steel Works, another subsidiary of Crucible Steel, in Reading.

Could he have offered a foreman position to Michael, perhaps a promotion of sorts, to lure him and others to PA?

A bit more speculation.

Whatever the reason, Michael worked for only a short time in his adopted state. Although he claimed not to have missed a single day of work in all of 1910, he spent the last *"350 days"* of his life as a patient in the Berks County Tuberculosis Sanitorium before his death on June 22, 1911. Dr. A. M. Rothrock, one of the attending physicians at the Sanitorium, wrote on Michael's death certificate that he had contracted the disease *"At work"* and that the disease *"Began December, 1909."* Although tuberculosis was *"contributory"* to his death, the actual cause was *"Pulmonary Hemorrhage."* Michael Joseph died almost a full year after his July 7, 1910, admission to the institution. His age was listed as *"38 years, 8 months, 10 days,"* but his actual age was 40 years, eight months, 15 days.

Cousin John Lucas (see his story later) said that his grandmother, Daisy Mae, told him that Michael worked in the coal mines for a while before succumbing to the dreaded black lung disease, but this story is not an accurate one. Could a black lung cause of death have been a more acceptable explanation than tuberculosis was? Could he have contracted this ailment due to exposure to steelworks-related environmental toxins?

Probably, but who knows?

Remember that the Department of Labor's Occupational Safety and Health Administration (OSHA) was not yet in existence to oversee and enforce proper workplace safety standards for workers such as Michael.

A young 38-year-old widow, Daisy Mae returned right away with her children to Jersey City; Michael's wake was held in his parents' (our great-grandparents, Michael and Anne's) home at 22 Clarke Ave. The 1920 census later placed Daisy Mae at 78 Williams Ave. with her five children: Benny (18; *"laborer – silk factory"*), Joseph (16; *"laborer – chair factory"*), William (14; *"laborer – silk factory"*), Mae (12), and Howard (10). Daisy found employment as a cleaning lady in St. Aloysius Church.

The 1930 census placed Daisy Mae's family this time at 294 Boyd Ave. Benny is the only one of the five children no longer listed with the rest of the family, undoubtedly out on his own by this time. Other residents with the Colfers included Mae and her husband, Thomas Tuzzolino (22; *"chauffeur"*), and their son John (son Tom would be born six years later). *Delia Daisey* Colford, according to her death certificate, was a resident of 8 Roosevelt Ave. just three years later when she died just before midnight on October 21, 1933. The 58-year-old *"housewife"* succumbed to *"cerebral hemorrhage, essential hypertension, cerebral arteriosclerosis"*; paralysis apparently set in just a couple of days before she passed. Her wake took place in her apartment.

The stories of Michael's and Daisy Mae's five children, all Dad's first cousins, follow, thanks to the recollections provided to me by our second cousins: Benny's son, Bill; Howie's son, Michael; Willie's daughter, Ginger; and Mae's sons, Tom Tuzzolino and John Lucas.

Benjamin (*aka: Benny*). In March of 2004, not long after Dad's death, Paul received an email from a Bill Colford asking if we were related to him. He had seen Dad's obituary in the newspaper and decided to contact Paul. His email reads, in part:

> *"I am 75 years-old now, and one of my many regrets is the lost contact*
> *with family. It surely would be wonderful if we were related, to open a*
> *world that I had lost forever."*

As it turned out, Bill's father was Benny, the oldest child of Michael Colfer, Jr., and Dad's first cousin. Therefore, Bill is our second cousin.

Bill's follow-up email to Paul ended with the following kind comments:

> *"I met your father only once when he was a young man and I was a boy. I remember your grandfather on a number of occasions, always helping out our family. We were not well off and he came to aid many times. He was a good man and from what I have read your father was even better."*

Bill emailed Paul one more time in April of 2004 and told him that he hoped to visit New Jersey from his home in North Carolina that June to meet some of us. However, the visit never materialized. In attempting to complete our story, I tried to reach Bill again, despite the seven years that had passed since his last correspondence with Paul. My email was returned as *"undeliverable,"* and the two phone messages I left for him both went for naught. Just as I was about to piece together the small amount of information I had on Benny, I received an email from Nancy Colford, Bill's daughter, who said that Bill was alive and well and more than happy to provide whatever information he could. I called Bill several times at his Hendersonville, NC, home which he shares with Nancy.

His family story follows:

Benny, only nine years of age when his father died, undoubtedly had to drop out of school at an early age in order to go to work and provide financial support to his widowed mother, Daisy. His status as the oldest of five children made him the responsible one. Unfortunately, Benny never learned to read or write, limiting his job opportunities considerably. It was his *Uncle Joe*, our Grandpa Colford, who was instrumental in getting Benny a job with the county parks department; Benny's work site was Lincoln Park's tennis court, just a short walk from his home at 9 Roosevelt Ave.

Benny married Helen Duffy. Together they had our second cousins, Bill (1928) and two years later, a daughter, Theresa. Bill described the marriage as a troubled one. Helen *"was the boss, always,"* Bill reported, and Benny was the easy-going one. When Bill was 18 years old, Benny and Helen separated and remained apart for approximately three years. However, they were in the process of reconciling when Benny dropped dead of a heart attack at the age of 51 on August 4, 1953, while painting an apartment at 159 Hutton St. in which they were to live. Forced back to work as a widow, Helen took a position as a cook at St. Michael's Rectory in the Hamilton Park area where she also was provided room and board. She returned to the furnished apartment she shared with Theresa during her free time.

According to Bill, a seminal event in the family was the diagnosis of polio in Theresa when she was just two years old. Although Bill described her as ambulatory, she had a spinal deformity which left her with a noticeable hump on her back. The diagnosis changed the family dynamics a great deal. Self-conscious about her appearance, Theresa cut herself off from the outside world. Even our second cousin Michael Colford (son of Howie; his story follows) told me that she hid behind her closed bedroom door during his visits with his father. According to Michael's recollections, *"I think Teresa had some kind of physical or mental disability. She was kept in a dark bedroom located in the back of their apartment."*

Helen also became completely focused on caring for Theresa and on providing for her every whim, to the exclusion of other family members. Bill described the considerable antipathy Theresa felt toward their father, apparently blaming him for her condition and faulting him for being illiterate. According to him, his mother also restricted his own outdoor activities, since Theresa was unable or unwilling to participate in such things herself.

Directly across the street from Benny and his family at 8 Roosevelt Ave. lived Daisy Mae and his four other siblings: Joe, Willie, Mae, and Howie, in addition to Mae's husband, Tom Tuzzolino, and their two sons, Tom and John. However, Bill maintains that his mother did not like the rest of the Colford family, so she decided not to interact with them at all and to restrict Bill's access to them as well. He surmised that his mother, whose own family was fairly well off financially, *"thought she was better than they were."* Although Bill visited his uncles, his aunt, and her children from time-to-time, his mother *"didn't want anything to do with them."*

In several emails I exchanged with our second cousin Michael Colford, he also stated that Benny and his wife *"were kind of distant from the rest of the family. The three brothers and sister were quite close . . . my father Howard, Joseph, William and Mae."* Michael also recalled conversations at his Aunt Mae's and Uncle Tom's household that Benny *"wasn't very responsible and did drink."*

Bill graduated from Our Lady of Victories School and started Snyder High School, but a family move to West Side Ave. near Duncan Ave. required him to switch to Lincoln High School from which he graduated. A two - year army enlistment which he spent in Japan followed. His 53-year-marriage to Janet Smith yielded three children: Michael, Debbi, and Nancy. Before his move to Hendersonville, NC several years ago, Bill and his family spent 24 years in Austin, TX, after a four-year stay in Florida. He enjoyed a successful career as a district sales manager for a number of companies.

The 62-year-old Helen eventually died while sitting in Bill's living room during her visit to his home in Pompton Plains.

As for Theresa, there is little more that even Bill knows about her. The last time he saw her was at their mother's funeral where she sat in the back of the church during Mass and left before he had a chance to speak to her. He described his mother several times as a *"mystery woman"* who kept everything, particularly news about Theresa, to herself. All he knows is that Theresa taught herself to type and managed to support herself with that skill.

As a young boy, I recall seeing from time-to-time a distinctive-looking woman walking through our Ege Ave. neighborhood, sometimes with a young boy. Her appearance always gave me pause, since she had a noticeable hump on her back, and her face and hands were covered with nodules that one now might associate with the disease, neurofibromatosis. I remember trying to keep my distance from her whenever I saw her. I certainly am not saying definitively that she was Theresa, but it certainly is not outside the realm of possibility.

Tracking Theresa is quite problematic without having any direction from Bill as to her general whereabouts. I thought that one Theresa possibility could be the Theresa A. Colfer, born June 12, 1929, (a good match with Bill's recollection), who lived for a time in Kearney. Her death on January 10, 1999, came while she was a resident of Spotswood, NJ. With the help of the staff of the New Jersey Archives, I was able to locate her obituary in an online resource, but this Theresa clearly was not ours.

Unless a person has been deceased for 50 years or more, it is close to impossible to retrieve a copy of a death certificate. The Department of Health requires many levels of documentation of the family relationship before it would consider providing such a document. Therefore, my search for Theresa came to an abrupt end.

Joe. The second oldest in the family, Joe was affectionately referred to as *"Goo – Goo."* The last brother to wed, he married very late in life (late 50s) to Margaret, a widow, apparently somewhat older than he; he had no children of his own. Second cousin Michael said that he was an alcoholic who developed diabetes when he stopped drinking and switched to soda only. His condition cost him an eye, so a glass eye took its place several years before his death. He worked for many years at General Electric in Kearney as an *"oiler – electric company,"* according to the 1940 census.

Willie. The third child, Willie bore the nickname *"Willie the Wisp"*; he stood five feet, eight inches. He and his wife, Muriel (Doerrer), had one child, Muriel Virginia (aka: *Ginger*). Thanks to cousin Tom Tuzzolino, I was able to track down Ginger at the Manchester, NJ, home she shares with her husband, Frank Miceli, also a Jersey City native of Roosevelt Ave. Ginger told me that she preferred her nickname to her given name.

The 1930 census listed Willie as a *"cooper – barrel concern,"* but he eventually worked for Jersey City as a street cleaner. The 1940 census described his position as *"laborer – county"* while he still resided in the Tuzzolino household at 8 Roosevelt Ave. An accomplished baseball player, he was a catcher for a team in the International League, but he played football as well for the Jersey City Trojans alongside his brother, Howie. Ginger recalled seeing pictures of Willie in uniforms for both sports. Willie also was a close friend to Nick Villa. Ginger told me that Grandpa tried to get him a position with the Jersey City Police Department, but he was an inch shy of the five feet, nine inch height requirement. Although eligible for a spot with the fire department, he passed on that opportunity.

According to Ginger, Willie waited until after his mother, Daisy Mae, died before he married in his late 30s. There is an old Irish practice that the son of a widowed mother never married until his mother passed away. Ginger's other recollections of her aunt Mae (see her story below) were of her diminutive stature (size five shoe) and of her weekly Sunday dinners she prepared for her brothers. As cousin Bill also recalled, creamed corn was a staple at each of these gatherings. Ginger added, however, that the creamed corn was always placed in the middle of the mashed potatoes and that her dad was the only one who ate it.

Cousin John Lucas described Willie as his favorite uncle, maintaining that he was always *"nice, quiet, consistently even,"* although he described each of his uncles as *"great, easy-going guys, just regular guys . . . I speak about them to this day."* Willie apparently spent a lot of time at his sister Mae's household, and he would regale John's son, Jack, among others, with baseball stories. Jack used to ask to see Willie's hands, since he *"broke a few knuckles"* during his playing days and had the misshapen hands to show for it. Willie passed away on April 10, 1969.

Mae. The only daughter born to Michael and Daisy Mae was Mae. She was quite petite from all accounts, and she has been described as the *"spitting image"* of her diminutive mother. Mae married Tom Tuzzolino whose Sicilian-born immigrant parents operated a grocery store in downtown Jersey City. Tom was quite the accomplished musician, playing five different instruments and establishing a career for himself as a touring singer and dancer under the stage name of *Tommy Lucas.* He even earned himself a weekly New York-area 30-minute radio show, *Tommy Lucas and His Guitar.* After his traveling days were over, he remained active in the music industry, opening up his own music business on West Side Ave. where he taught multiple instruments to aspiring performers and tuned pianos for the locals and for all the cruise ships that claimed New York Harbor as their home.

Together Mae and Tom had two sons, John and Tom. The 1940 census had Tom (32; *"salesman – dancing school"*) and *Mary* (32), their sons John (12) and Thomas, Jr. (6), and Mae's brothers, Joseph (35) and William (34), at 8 Roosevelt Ave. Their two-bedroom apartment accommodated quite a few people; John told me of how he, his brother, and his uncles Joe, Willie, and Howie all shared the same bed in one bedroom, while the rest of the family occupied the other one. The Storms, Vanderveer, and Farley families were residents of the other three apartments in their building. The Tuzzolinos eventually purchased a home of their own on Jefferson Ave. Mae passed away in April of 1973; both sons described their mother as a remarkable woman, who *"took care of everybody"* while also working at a laundry on West Side Ave.

John, the older of the two sons by six years, changed his last name to *Lucas*, his father's professional music name, for business purposes when he was 21 years of age. Our second cousin now resides in

Williamstown, NJ. During my telephone conversations with John, he was effusive in his praise for his *"Uncle Joe,"* our Grandpa Colford. He claimed that he was always proud of the fact the Grandpa had been so successful, rising to the position of commissioner and to other offices during his years in public service. *"The Colford genes helped me out a lot!"* he told me. With a successful career in banking and finance and as chairman of a hospital board and of the Atlantic City Convention Center Board who had to provide plenty of public speeches, John said that he *"got that from the Colfords . . . gotta be in the genes, right, Joseph?"*

John also followed in his father's footsteps, joining the Air Force after high school and playing the saxophone, clarinet, and flute in its band. John married Patricia Dunn, and together they had a son, John, and three daughters: Laura, Audrey, and Lynn.

Tom Jr. and his wife Frances (Pugliese) currently live in West Babylon, Long Island. Tom was a 1950 Snyder High School graduate, finishing his senior year as a member of the county championship baseball team and earning all-county and all-state honors; his season batting average of .525 earned him the county batting title that year. The Dodgers organization gave him a $500 bonus to play for them, and he spent two years in its minor league system before Uncle Sam called him to serve in the Korean War. His baseball career also may have been cut short due to a severe concussion he suffered after running into the outfield wall during one of his minor league night games. Tom enjoyed a career in the glass business. He and Frances had two children, Philip and Dianne.

Howie. The youngest of Michael's and Daisy Mae's five children, I heard Howie's story from his son, Michael Colford, then of Bound Brook, who called me in March of 2004 after reading Dad's obituary and asked me about our possible family relationship. I was able to track him down several years later at his new residence in Las Vegas, NV. Michael indeed is a second cousin to us. Here is his father's story:

Howie (aka: *Honey*), the shortest in the family at five feet, six inches, seemed to be quite the pugnacious type. In addition to playing semi-pro football for the Jersey City Trojans, Howie also forged a brief career as a boxer, a club fighter known in boxing circles as *Honey Colford*, who was trained and managed by the brother of Mickey Walker, a Jersey-based fighter of some renown who held both the world welterweight and middleweight titles at one time. Howie also sparred with

Mickey Walker himself on two occasions. Although he received some compensation for his fights, it was not enough for Howie to support himself or his mother, so he worked as a pipefitter, first at the Bayonne Naval Base, and then at the Brooklyn Navy Yard where he remained for 38 years until it closed. There were those who felt that he could have been a boxer of some note if he had stayed with the sport.

According to the 1930 census, the 23-year-old Howie was a *"tinsmith helper - repair shop"* who had to drop out of school after the seventh grade to help support his family. I dare say that his brothers also had to leave school quite early in order to go to work to support their widowed mother. Howie married Frances Veronica Gadek and had two children, our second cousins, Michael and Maureen. The 1940 census placed the 29-year-old Howie (*"estimator – navy yard"*), his wife Frances, and our three-month-old cousin Michael at 157 10th St. in Bayonne by this time; the family soon would relocate to the town of Roselle. (Note the six-year difference in his age despite the 10-year gap between the two censuses.)

Howie's and Frances' wedding reception must have been a memorable occasion. Cousin Michael tells me that Howie apparently punched out his wife's younger brother, John, after which a few other guys then jumped him. John would go on to perish in World War II.

Another story had Howie knocking out a much taller man (*"About six feet, three inches,"* Michael recalled) after a few beers and a few rounds of shuffleboard at Paladino's, his favorite hang-out bar in Elizabeth. Ten-year-old Michael was present, and he claimed that several people in the bar assumed that the victim was dead before he eventually was revived.

On yet another occasion, a New York City police officer had to escort Howie to the subway en route to work at the navy yard after he had just finished decking two fellow coffee drinkers at a mobile coffee wagon. A small mob, friends of the two victims, was waiting for Howie before the policeman intervened.

As Michael reported,

> *"I wouldn't put it past him; he wouldn't care if the guy was eight feet tall and he*

got him angry, especially when he had a few beers in him . . . you never knew   when something would agitate him, and before you know, he would be swinging."

Howie passed away on April 14, 1984. Cousin Michael retired and moved from Bound Brook to Las Vegas in 2007 where he resides with his wife, Dora; his son also is Michael, and his two grandchildren, Dylan and Logan, share Michael as middle names. Our cousin Maureen, Michael's younger sister, died on April 30, 2011, at the age of 67. She resided in Linden.

After several years of phone calls and emails between us, Cousin Michael surprised me in July of 2014 with a knock on my door here in Middletown. He decided to stop by during an extended visit to his stepdaughter who lived nearby and to his son who resided in Pennsylvania. We spent an hour-or-so comparing family stories; he is an energetic guy with a great sense of humor. He stopped by again the following summer, this time on his way back home after the funeral of his 42-year-old son who was killed in an automobile accident in his home town in the Poconos just a week earlier.

Our second cousins have all reminisced with me about how easy-going, kind, and gracious their uncles were (Benny, Joe, Willie, and Howie) and the care that their aunt Mae provided for her siblings and their offspring. They also recalled the kindness and support Grandpa Colford gave them all. Grandpa was fairly well known as the one in the family who could be counted on for assistance. Remember that Grandpa had his widowed sister-in-law, Daisy Mae, his widowed sister, Mamie, his widowed mother, Anne, and his unmarried sister, Kate, to look after. He undoubtedly felt some responsibility to provide for them what he could.

James Colfer

Five years older than Grandpa, James was his partner in the tavern business for several years. Members of the Quinn family of Jersey City, long-time neighbors of James and his family, have told me that people always remarked at the different body types James and Grandpa had: Grandpa, with the long and lanky frame, and James with the much stockier, heavier one. The 1900 census listed the 24-year-old James as a *"laborer-steel"* while living with the rest of the Colfords at 282 Virginia Ave. This *"roller-steel mill"* married Anne Reilly on October 30, 1907, at St. Paul's Church, and the couple was in residence at 397 Ocean Ave. by the 1910 census. Their two children, Florence (9) and Virginia

(2½), had arrived by the 1920 census when the family resided at 86 Bostwick Ave.; now James was listed as a *"steel roller-steel company,"* the same occupation he declared on his World War I Draft Registration Card on September 12, 1918. His employer was the Spaulding - Jennings Steel Company at its Grant Ave. location.

It may have been Grandpa who helped James get on the city payroll a few years later, since the 1930 census listed him as a *"laborer-city streets."* Anne and her older daughter, Florence, each worked as a *"typist-law office"* at the time. By 1940 the family had moved to 90 Bostwick Ave. where James worked as an *"inspector – public works"*; his daughters both were secretaries, Florence for an insurance company, and Virginia for *"city hospital."* Anne eventually became involved in politics, serving as a committeewoman at one time. James passed away on December 18, 1945, at the age of 71; Anne followed four years later on November 15, 1949.

Florence never married; she lived with her younger sister and her husband, Harry Ertle, in their Jersey City apartment along with their two daughters, Deidre and Nadine.

Dad apparently was very fond of his Uncle Jim who used to chauffeur him around and be somewhat solicitous of him during his prolonged tuberculosis-related recuperation period (remember that Grandpa Colford never drove).

Joseph Cholfer

Our Grandpa Colford, *"Uncle Joe"* to the many relatives who have contributed to this story, as we all know, maintained a career in politics as one of Frank Hague's commissioners. Before his foray into politics, however, Grandpa was a tavern owner for approximately seven years along with his older brother, James. Their first tavern in 1902 was at 57 Mallory Ave. near Claremont Ave. before they relocated it to 77 Mallory, near Yale Ave., from 1903-06; it moved back again to 57 Mallory (1907-08). An advertisement for *Colford Bros. Saloon* in the 1903 Jersey City Directory noted that the establishment offered *"ales, wines, and liquors and fine cigars"* as well as *"a shuffle board and pool tables."*

The tavern locations were ideal for business; they were no more than two to three blocks from the burgeoning Spaulding – Jennings Steel Company just around the corner. One can only imagine the large numbers of employees stopping in for a few drinks before work or after their shifts were over. At the 77 Mallory site now sits a large storage business, and *City Homes at West Side Station*, a relatively new apartment complex, appears to be where the 57 Mallory tavern once stood. The lone tavern in that area now is *Bayside Tavern* at 80 Mallory, corner of Yale Ave.

Several years ago at a St. Peter's Prep Century Club reception at the Liberty House Restaurant in Jersey City, David Donnelly, an administrator for the Jersey City Board of Education and the grandson of Frank Donnelly, a long-time friend of Grandpa, sought me out, claiming that he had a great story to tell me. He went on to regale me with the following tale his father told him:

> *One night while tending bar at his own establishment, Grandpa Colford had*
> *a request for a drink from one of the locals, a Bob O'Brien. Unfortunately,*
> *O'Brien began his request with, "Hey, Curly!" so our very prematurely bald*
> *Grandpa apparently leaped over the bar and decked him!*

Grandpa, as you recall, was slick bald at a very young age. Donnelly swore to the veracity of this story, and he laughed out loud while delivering it.

What is interesting is that Dad always said that Grandpa Colford was discovered as a possible political candidate when he gave a campaign speech for his brother, William, who was running for alderman at the time. It is safe to assume that this, and other, political speeches took place in the back room of Grandpa's tavern, the typical local gathering place for such campaigns. An observer of one of his addresses grabbed Grandpa, apparently an effective public speaker, and told him that he had a future in politics.

Could this event have prompted Grandpa to leave behind the tavern business and enter the political arena?

Grandpa and James left the bar business in 1908 when Jim took a position in the steel mill and Grandpa began his political career at City Hall as a clerk during the administration of H. Otto Wittpenn, Jersey City's 28th mayor, who served three terms from 1908 to 1913. Wittpenn would later

51

fail in all four attempts in his runs for governor. Grandpa was to remain in public service until 1952 when he retired as a member of the Hudson County Board of Chosen Freeholders, just three years after the Hague *"organization"* (a preferred term to that of the Hague *"machine"*) lost to John V. Kenny and his *"organization."*

Other positions Grandpa held were Director of the Bureau of Motor Bus Transportation (1923- 29), Hudson County Undersheriff and Sheriff (1929 – 39), City Clerk (1939), Clerk/Bureau of Collections, City Commissioner (1940 – 49), Commissioner of the Department of Public Works/Bureau of Water, and County Freeholder (1949 – 52). He also served as Hudson County Democratic Chairman. Grandpa's moves from office to office were not of his own doing, but rather they came at the behest of Hague himself who reassigned Grandpa and others in his organization to newer responsibilities on a regular basis.

In *The Life and Times of Jersey City Mayor Frank Hague*, author Leonard F. Vernon wrote that these constant reassignments were due to Hague's wish *"to prevent them from developing a following among those under them or to give the public the perception of them having a hold on the office."* In other words, it was Hague's way to maintain power and control.

Grandpa also was leader of the city's eighth ward, the Bergen Ward, one of the 12 wards in Jersey City (Mom's Hamilton Park area was in the second ward). Hague chose his ward leaders carefully; their primary job was to deliver the votes each election day and to take care of the issues and concerns of the ward residents (providing jobs, turkeys at Thanksgiving, and a whole host of other assistance). In fact, Hague apparently rated his ward leaders based upon the size of the voter turnouts they provided. Like all ward leaders, Grandpa had to keep Hague informed about the general goings-on in his ward. *"Everything that happened politically in the city went through the ward leader,"* author Tom Fleming, whose own father was the leader of the second ward, stated in *The Life and Times of Frank Hague*.

Friday was the day when he could be found in his West Side Ave. realty office, the *Colford and Crocker Real Estate and General Insurance Company*, at 434 West Side Ave., fielding concerns, complaints, and requests for assistance from his eighth ward constituents. The city directory listed its phone number: *Bergen 9899*. The floor above his office was the location of the local Democratic Party headquarters, the Tioga Club, where Grandpa also could be found on most Fridays.

Grandpa's other business interests included part ownership of the Jersey City Skeeters from 1928 - 1933, a minor league baseball team in the International League whose home field was the 8,500-seat West Side Park located at Culver and West Side Aves., home now to New Jersey City University. He also served as the team's Vice President; among a handful of other part-owners was the aforementioned Frank Donnelly. The Skeeters, named after the abundant mosquitos which inhabited the area, had been around since 1885 and had enjoyed a league championship in 1903 with a record of 92-33, but it usually fared much more poorly than that, finishing in last place in 10 different seasons.

The team suffered three consecutive last-place finishes from 1928-30 and never enjoyed a winning season during Grandpa's ownership. Its aggregate win-loss record during that time was 375-622. The Depression-related low attendance (fewer than 1,000 per game, half of what it had been) and high costs eventually made it difficult for the Skeeters and for many other teams to survive. They then sold the team, and the new owners relocated it to Syracuse for the 1934 season where they re-named it the *Syracuse Chiefs.*

Besides the aforementioned story of Grandpa's altercation with Bob O'Brien in his tavern, another favorite of mine was one Bob Leach, a self-appointed historian of sorts and the chronicler of Hudson County politics, particularly that of the Frank Hague/Grandpa Colford era, told me. As members of the Hudson County Historical and Genealogical Society, Jeanne and I had an opportunity to meet Bob in the fall of 2010 at the society-sponsored day-long conference, *Come Home to History: Celebrating 350 Years of Hudson County's Heritage History Fair*, at Jersey City's Hudson County Community College. Among the speakers and presentations that day was Bob's hosting of his video entitled, "*Invasion of the Reds: Mayor Hague's War on Radicals and Free Speech,*" the story of Hague's heavy-handed ways of keeping "*radicals*" from Jersey City.

When I introduced myself to Bob before his presentation, he greeted me with several stories of Grandpa, but the very first thing he said was that Grandpa always dressed just like Hague: three-piece navy blue suit, starched shirt, and tie. Mom recalls that Grandma Colford would trek over to Manhattan to shop for Grandpa's shirts and ties at Sulka's, a high-priced men's clothier known for its ties and custom shirts. Undoubtedly, Hague also did his shopping there. The obituary for Amos Sulka, its founder, described him as *"Haberdasher to the Upper Crust."*

The other story Bob told which is priceless is the one which I will summarize now:

Bob's own father had been unemployed for a little over a year during the early 1930s. A resident of Grandpa's eighth ward, the older Mr. Leach was one of those rare maverick Republicans in this Democrat-saturated ward. His allegiances undoubtedly were well known to everyone, including Grandpa. As he also continued to do long after his retirement from public service, Grandpa strolled the streets of his ward daily, making his presence known and making himself available to whatever constituents he encountered.

Bob's mother used to badger her job-seeking husband daily to ask Grandpa for a job whenever she saw him walking by; "Go ahead, there's Mr. Colford, go ask him for a job," she would say. After putting it off for many months, the older Mr. Leach finally approached Grandpa on the street and made his need for a job known to him. According to Bob, Grandpa made it clear in no uncertain terms that he had no intention of assisting him in gaining employment. "Why don't you ask your friend, Herbert Hoover, for a job!" Grandpa replied.

Hoover, as you may recall, was the Republican president from 1928-32 who lost a bid for re-election in 1932 to the Democrat Franklin Delano Roosevelt.

I guess the older Mr. Leach must have cast a vote for the wrong candidate.

Just recently I attended a luncheon at the invitation of Tom Schember, a friend and colleague of Dad's who sat on the St. Francis Hospital Board with him for several years. The luncheon was a monthly event of the loosely organized social club, *Hudson South*, composed primarily of former Jersey City octogenarians, all males, now living in the Jersey Shore area. When I introduced myself to one John Donnelly, his eyes grew large as he blurted out, *"Colford? Ah, the Tioga Club!"*

John then told me the following story which he admitted to having told many times over the years every time he heard the name Colford:

"My grandfather, who lived to be 90, was a resident of the old eighth ward. In his later years he was in and out of the Medical Center several times. At

54

the end of one of his stays, my father told him that he owed the hospital $1,283.

Surprised and/or outraged by this charge, my grandfather said to my father,

'Wait . . . give that bill to Joe Colford . . . I'm a lifelong democrat!'"

And so the bill for the fellow eighth-warder went away.

Mary Agnes Colford

Mary Agnes (aka: *Mamie*), three years younger than Grandpa, married George E. Blewitt. By the 1910 census, they had four children at their 18 Ege Ave. address: Mary Edna (aka: *Edna*; 5), Laura (4), George, Jr. (2), and Robert (two months). Another daughter, Catherine, would join the family two years later. However, Mamie was a widow by the time she was 35 years of age when husband George, Sr. (*"produce dealer – vegetables"*) passed away from pneumonia in 1912. The 1920 census placed Mamie (37) at 159 Virginia Ave. with a Kathryn Colford (25; *"storekeeper - stationery"*) who was listed as a *"daughter,"* but it is clear that this Kathryn was Mamie's sister, our Aunt Kate. Her correct age at the time also was 35, not 25 as the census reported. Aunt Kate must have moved into Mamie's household to provide personal and financial support to her widowed sister. I also assume that another resident at this same address was their mother, Anne, since Grandpa was off and married by this time. Mary Edna's name does not appear again in the census records, an indication that she passed away at a very young age. Second cousin Betty (Blewitt) Critchley, Mamie's granddaughter, recalled her death also. Betty has described Mamie as *"always going, never stopping,"* a high-energy woman whose drive and enthusiasm undoubtedly was essential for a young widow trying to raise a family on her own. Mom also spoke of the sharp contrast in temperament between the very effervescent Mamie and her sister, the stern, dour Aunt Kate.

Mamie was living in 307 Virginia Ave. in 1930 with her three adult children (George, Robert, and Catherine), her sister Kate, her mother Anne, and two nieces, daughters of her brother William (his story follows). By the 1940 census, however, Mamie *"Blewytt"* and her son, Robert, were living with Catherine, her youngest child, and her husband, William Downey, in their Gifford Ave. apartment. The Downey's six-year-old daughter, Joan, also was in the household.

Seventy-five-year-old Mamie dropped dead on the sidewalk just outside a beauty parlor on the corner of West Side and Jewett Aves where she had just had her hair done along with Aunt Kate; the date was November 25, 1958. Mom was the one who delivered this news to Grandpa Colford. Below is a brief accounting of Mamie's children, all Dad's first cousins:

Laura. The oldest of the four surviving children (born December 18, 1905), Laura married William Chadwick Coleman, and together they had two children, Elinor (Sweeney) and Bill. Bill, Sr. passed away in August of 1953 after 25 years of marriage, but Laura eventually married again, this time to Emil Boehm. Their marriage lasted another 25 years. I recall the folks hosting Laura and Emil on several occasions; they were a very charming, sweet, and kind couple who always seemed quite the affectionate pair with each other.

George, Jr. I'll always remember George as the one who provided Dad and us with clubhouse passes to the Monmouth Park Racetrack whenever we paid a visit; he had been employed there in retirement in an assortment of positions. He resembled Grandpa: tall, thin, and quite bald.   A very fashionable and sharp dresser, his daughter Betty also described him as *"debonair."* Grandpa also served as one of the ushers at George's September 21, 1935, nuptials to Helen Burnside. The couple had one child, our second cousin, Betty. However, Helen was unable to parent Betty due to some mental health issues, so she and George eventually moved in with Mamie, and it was she who raised Betty.

The 1930 census listed the 22-year-old George as a *"runner – office work."* He also worked for Grandpa while he was Commissioner of Public Works; he then served as secretary to Jersey City's mayor Bernard J. Berry who held office from 1953 – 1957 following the resignation of John V. Kenny. George's next move was to a position in traffic court. According to the 1940 census, George was living with Helen and one-year-old Betty at 29 Bentley Ave. and was employed as a *"field man – house owner loan,"* probably in Grandpa's insurance/real estate business. In fact, George's niece, Joan (Downey), our second cousin, told me that he and Grandma Colford's brother-in-law, Ed Connor, actually were the ones who managed the real estate office. Betty said that her father was Grandpa's *"protégé,"* accompanying him to various political gatherings over the years.

Helen Burnside Blewitt, George's wife, was one of three children, all daughters, of the Scotland-born Robert Hubberthorne Burnside and his wife, Katherine. Robert's own parents were show business people in their native Glasgow, and he established himself as an accomplished actor, director, and playwright here in the States.

Helen lived until the age of 82 before her death in February of 1994. Her *"Last Place of Residence"* was Secaucus, NJ, although she lived for many years in a group home on Bergen Ave. It is probable that she was a resident of the Laurel Hill section of town which housed numerous state-run institutions at the time of her death. She could have been in residence in the Hudson County Hospital for Mental Diseases, later renamed Hudson County Meadowview Hospital.

One must remember that no one talked about such things in those days.

Robert. With all of his siblings off and married, Robert (DOB: February 18, 1910) must have felt somewhat duty-bound to provide for his widowed mother, Mamie, as per the Irish belief that I have made reference to earlier, that an Irish son waited until his widowed mother passed away before marrying. In fact, according to Cousin Betty, Robert *"was supposed to take care of Mamie, so he never told anyone he got married!"* Although he continued to live with Mamie, he managed to keep secret from her and from everyone else the fact that he had married a nurse, Mary (Nagy), with whom he also had a child, Barbara; no one knew of the nuptials nor of the birth! Mary and Barbara lived apart from Robert, first in Jersey City, and then for a short time in New Haven, CT, while he continued to live with Mamie as if he were a single person.

He enlisted in the army on April 15, 1943; the terms of his enlistment were *"for the duration of the war or other emergency, plus six months."* His occupation on the record form was *"clerks, general office,"* and his marital status was *"separated, with dependents."*

He obviously was more honest with his enlistment officer than he was with his own family.

It was only a matter of happenstance that enabled the family to learn of Robert's secret life. Robert apparently developed a bad case of hypertension, the result, as the U.S. military confirmed later, of experimental inoculations the army gave to its enlistees, including Robert. Betty recalled that it was late in 1943 when he was hospitalized with the ailment at Fort Dix; the word went out to Mamie and the family during their stay at George, Jr.'s summer home at Lake Wallenpaupak, PA, that he was dying. Mamie and Aunt Kate made their way to the hospital where, for the first time, they discovered that the nurse who was tending to Robert actually was Mary, his wife. When they asked Mamie to identify herself, she said, *"My name is Mary Blewitt."* The reply, *"But she's already here!"* was her first indication that there was indeed another Mrs. Mary Blewitt in the room.

A surprise, indeed!

Robert recovered, however, and lived another eight years before passing away in 1951 due to ongoing kidney complications from the army's inoculations. A meter reader for the Public Service, he and Mary had another daughter, Mary, but the couple also lost a son who was stillborn. Robert and his family eventually lived for a time with Mamie. According to Cousin Betty, it was after Robert moved out that *"Uncle Joe* (Grandpa Colford) *said he would take care of Mamie."*

Mary and the girls moved to be near her family in Pennsylvania after Robert passed, so Barbara told me that her knowledge of Colford-related family matters was limited. Barbara eventually would marry George Lowe and move to Syracuse, and her sister Mary would marry and relocate to Hawaii.

Catherine. The youngest of the family (DOB: November 27, 1912), Cousin Betty has described Catherine as *"very beautiful."* She also was a very young bride at the age of 19 when she married William Downey (*"assistant manager – public service"*) with whom she had two children, our second cousins Joan (1933) and Bill, Jr. (1941). Their Gifford Ave. home also included mother-in-law Mamie and brother-in-law Robert Blewitt in 1940.

Within a year or two, the Downeys were at 167 Ege Ave., little more than a stone's throw from Dad and 277 Ege; this residence also was the first stopover for her brother George and his daughter, Betty, after it was determined that Helen was unable to provide for them. Cousin Joan told me that her mother and our Dad became very close during his period of convalescence from his tuberculosis scare while confined to his hospital bed on the second floor of 277 Ege. Catherine, Dad's first cousin, would bring him books *"almost every day,"* and they would read together. *"Your father was so very smart!"* Joan told me.

However, Catherine was born with only one functioning kidney, leading to a series of health-related issues over the years. As a result, her mother and her Aunt Kate advised her against visiting Dad, lest she *"catch"* whatever it was they feared Dad had which might further compromise her own frail health. Nevertheless, she refused to heed their advice and continued her visits, Joan recalled.

Dad eventually was the one who taught his cousin Catherine, eight years his senior, to drive. Complications from the birth of her second child, Bill Jr, on June 5, 1941, however, exacerbated her chronic kidney problems. She was only 30 years of age when she passed away in her 167 Ege residence on September 13, 1943, due to kidney failure. Her official cause of death was *"uremia from sub-acute glomerulo nephritis"*; her death certificate also had her name as *"Kathryn."* Bill was only two years of age at the time of his mother's death, Joan a 10-year-old. Husband Bill eventually would remarry and relocate to Lexington Ave; he was to become a high-ranking official for New Jersey Public Service.

Mom and Joan both recall that Dad became a mentor of sorts to Bill, Jr. who would spend hours over a period of years talking with Dad about a variety of issues. It was thought for a while that Bill would enter the seminary, but it was for a brief time only. A Bayonne resident, he spent 34 years in the Hudson County's Prosecutor's Office as the Criminal Justice Planner; two of his three children would go into law enforcement, Bill as a member of the Bayonne PD, and Brian as a NYPD officer. Bill passed away just before I completed our story, and his wife, Patricia Ann, predeceased him by two years. Joan divides her time between her two homes in Allentown, PA, and Florida; her husband, the dentist John Salinas, passed away in 2012.

Catherine Colford

Catherine (aka: *Aunt Kate*) was the only one of the 11 Colfords who never married. I have heard from several sources that she was in love at one time with a gentleman who was a Protestant. When her local Catholic parish priest told her that the union could not exist in the eyes of the Catholic Church, she broke off the relationship completely. Perhaps this sad turn of events accounted for her rather dour demeanor until her death in 1979.

Aunt Kate's benevolent older brother, Joe, always took care of her, staking her at one point to a store at 454 West Side Ave., near the corner of Virginia Ave., and bailing her out after it want "belly-up," according to Mom. She must have had some kind of entrepreneurial spirit, however, since it would appear that her store ownership lasted, as I can best determine from city records, from at least 1915 through 1930. The 1915 – 1918 city directories listed her business as *"cigars,"* but from 1922 through 1926 (the last year of the Jersey City Directory), her business was listed as *"variety."* The 1920 and 1930 federal censuses had her as a *"storekeeper – stationery"* and as a *"clerk – stationery store,"* respectively. Finally, the 1940 census had the 52-year-old Kate employed as an *"investigator-county,"* obviously a position she secured with Grandpa's help.

Interestingly, Aunt Kate had moved in with her widowed sister-in-law, Daisy Mae, and her five children at 78 Williams Ave. sometime before 1922. Daisy's sons, Benny and William, appeared in the 1922-23 city directories as each working as a *"tobacco pipe maker,"* probably both in the employ of their aunt Kate in her store. Second cousin Joan (Downey) Salinas also said that cousins George and Robert Blewitt delivered the newspapers for Aunt Kate.

Aunt Kate's store location has long since been replaced by *"La Primicia,"* a Hispanic restaurant. This current site appears to have been the merging of what we would remember as the old One Hour Martinizing and Sal's Candy Store. I also might add that an Egyptian deli and grocery, *Misty 2*, currently occupies the space once held by our favorite haberdasher, Jack Liebowitz, and *Jesus the Savior*, a religious articles store, now sits where shoemaker Louie Noto once plied his trade.

Her residences changed throughout the years; she lived with her sister, Mamie, and her family for several years in different locations before securing an apartment of her own at 343 Bergen Ave. She lived out the last few years of her life in St. Ann's Home for the Aged where she passed away on February 15, 1979. Mom recalls the many favors Grandpa (who never drove) asked of Dad and of his next-door neighbor, *Buck* Ennis, to drive Kate back to her Bergen Ave. abode after a Sunday dinner at 277 Ege. I remember accompanying Dad as he drove Kate to her apartment on several of these occasions.

Kate was the "spitting image" of Grandpa Colford: tall, lean, and with that same distinctive look of Grandpa's. Second cousin Betty has said that Kate was *"always there for us."* However, Kate also had a rather unpredictable, feisty side. *"She would take a fit"* from time-to-time, Betty claimed, and storm off for no apparent reason. *"You never knew, something would set her off, and she would always go into a snit!"* Betty told the story of Kate's *"snit"* one summer day while staying at their Lake Wallenpaupak retreat. Whatever the trigger was, Kate apparently got up and left with nary an explanation of any kind and returned on her own to Jersey City.

William Colford

About two months into my one-year stay as an assistant professor of psychology at Caldwell College during the 2003-04 school year, I received an email from a Nancy Cummings who worked in Caldwell's Office of the Bursar, claiming that we were indeed cousins. She had seen my name on the campus list of new employees and contacted me. As it turned out, it was true that Nancy was the granddaughter of William Colford, Grandpa Colford's youngest sibling, and his wife Sarah. Anna, Nancy's mom, was Dad's first cousin, making Nancy and us second cousins. We had dinner one night, and Nancy provided me with a copy of a history of her life as a Colford her mother had written. I have summarized for you what her particularly sad story had to say.

The youngest of the Colfords, William (21), a *"bartender,"* married Sarah Howes (20) on March 8, 1908, in a quick ceremony performed in the rectory of St. Aloysius Parish. The young bride was approximately four months pregnant at the time; it is safe to assume that the witnesses were neither friends nor family members, but rather two parish employees of some sort hastily summoned to see the event. Their son George was born five months later on April 18, 1908.

The 1910 census placed the 22-year-old *"bartender-hotel"* with his wife (21; named *"Sadie"* on the census form) and George, not yet two years old, at 357a West Side Ave. William (*"bartender-café"*) and Sarah added two more children by the 1920 census, May (10) and Anna (4); the family had moved to 41 Clarke Ave. by then. William declared on his World War I Draft Registration Card in 1917 that he was employed by *"Fred Butzel of West Side Ave."* as a *"bartender."* His height and build were *"medium,"* his eyes *"gray,"* and his hair *"brown."* William earlier had won the election as alderman for the old eighth ward, but he held office for a short time only, since the alderman form of government was voted out of existence in 1913 and replaced by a five-man city commission.

Sadly, Sarah died on Valentine's Day in 1923 at the age of 36 after an appendix operation; the official cause of death was "*bilateral pyosalpinx* (severe infection of the fallopian tubes) – *pelvic peritonitis.*" Anna was barely seven years of age when her mother died. According to Anna, her maternal grandmother, Caroline, and her aunts Viola and Bertha dropped her and her siblings, May, then 13 years old, and George (15), like a hot potato; they never heard from that side of the family again until 1950 when George saw the obituary of their grandmother Howes in the local newspaper. However, I am unclear what our cousins' relationship was with the other members of the large Howes family which included George, the father, sons George, Alfred, August, and Harry, and daughter Caroline.

Could Sarah's out-of-wedlock pregnancy have been a lingering source of contention between the Howes family and the newlyweds, thus the neglect of the widowed William and his children? Or could William's emerging drinking problem also have been a factor?

One can only speculate.

With no one to care for May and Anna, our great-uncle William placed the girls in St. Francis Home on Central Ave in Union City, a so-called boarding home which Anna described as more like an orphanage; the Franciscan Sisters of the Immaculate Conception operated the facility. It was a common practice in those days for a widowed father to place his young children, particularly daughters, in a facility to be raised by nuns; men alone typically did not raise young girls.

Mom has a vague recollection that perhaps the first stopover for Anna and/or May after their mother's death was at Grandma and Grandpa Colford's Ege Ave. residence; Dad would have been three years old at the time. According to Mom, the arrangement didn't work out as well as hoped; I suppose that the addition of one or two young children was more than 43-year-old Grandpa and 35-year-old Grandma could manage.

May and Anna remained at the Home for five years. May became a surrogate mother to Anna, and she was allowed outside the gates of the home to attend St. Michael's High School. When Anna turned 12 years of age, their Aunt Mamie (Colford) Blewitt agreed to take her and May (18) into her home at 307 Virginia Ave, the same home Grandpa Colford had purchased for her. With the help of Grandma Colford, herself once a telephone operator, May took a job as an operator with New Jersey Bell, earning $14 per week, $10 of which she turned over to Aunt Mamie for room and board. Anna recalled that her years with Mamie were difficult and unpleasant ones. *"But she made our lives miserable (mine anyway),"* she wrote, without elaboration.

When the girls entered Mamie's household in 1928, it must have been a crowded, busy place. In addition to Mamie (45) and the girls, other residents included her sons, George, Jr. (22) and Robert (20), daughter Katherine (17), her sister Katherine (Aunt Kate), and her mother, our great-grandma Anne. It must have required quite an effort for Mamie to have maintained a household with such an extended group of family members which spanned three generations.

Meanwhile, William and George were roomers together at a home on Ege Ave. William had breakfast and dinner each day at Mamie's, but George was on his own. He supported himself with the $15 weekly income he earned at his New York City job with the Cunard Lines.

By 1930, William, for the first time in the records I have seen, was no longer identified as a bartender; the census that year listed the 42-year-old as *"mechanic-police"* and son George (21) as *"clerical - steamship agency."* William died on January 29, 1939, at the age of 51 due to complications after gall bladder surgery. The official cause of death, however, was *"cirrhosis of liver, chronic cholecystitis"* (severe inflammation of the gall bladder). He was a resident of 6 Bergen Ave. at the time of his death. His occupation this time was *"mechanic, county,"* undoubtedly a position Grandpa had a large hand in securing for him. Later that same year George married Vera Goode and moved to Gifford Ave; the couple had no children.

Anna completed grades seven and eight at St. Aloysius School and then went to Lincoln High School where she met her first husband, Ed Smith. They eloped to New York and were married just six months after graduation. Father William and brother George then moved in with the newlyweds at 10 Bergen Ave, and Anna kept house for them all.

Ed and Anna had four children, three girls (Marilyn, Ellen, and Nancy), and one boy, Ed. They also lost another son, Dennis, at eight months of age; he had been born with spina bifida. By this time the family had moved to 90 High St. in Nutley. Ed lost a battle with pancreatic cancer in 1974, but Anna married again in 1978 to Ray Klimaski. May married Fred Hansen in 1935; she passed away just three months after her father. Nancy was to marry Jim Cummings from whom she is now divorced.

To Anna's great credit, she seemed to have come to terms with these adverse childhood conditions. She accepted the fact that her placement in St. Francis Home after the death of her mother was out of financial necessity. She also highlighted the positive aspects of the Home in her recollections of it, particularly the education she received there. Anna felt that it prepared her well, since she eventually graduated from St. Aloysius School third in a class of 50 and with two academic awards as well. Her years there also allowed her to cement her relationship with her sister May.

I discovered that the home where William and son George lived as *"lodgers"* while the girls were at Mamie's was none other than 260 Ege Ave., the same 260 Ege home where Grandpa Lipsett was a *"lodger"* himself for several months in the winter of 1965 before purchasing the home a year later and which eventually was home to both him and to Grandma and Grandpa Colford. Small world, indeed!

The widowed homeowner, Olive Marshall (58), and her son James (22) also were in residence at 260 Ege at that time. Two other *"lodgers,"* John Southwick and John Lee, and a *"boarder,"* William Lowder, a Danish-born *"cabinet maker,"* joined the two Colfords there.

What distinguished *"lodgers"* from *"boarders"* was the additional pay the latter group provided for meals as well as lodging.

Chapter VII

Michael Colfer's Brother

Our Great-Great Uncle James Colfer

Our great-great uncle James, Michael's older brother by six years, was baptized on July 15, 1835, in Rathangan, Ireland. He left Ireland several years before Michael, but I have not found any definitive and verifiable ship's manifest with his name on it. I have found many, many James' with related spellings of the Colfer name: Calford, Colver, Colfar, Colbert, Coffer (31 of them), and Clifford (71 of them). The estimated birth years and the dates of arrival for these James' all match the approximate timelines I know of for our James, but there is no way to discern his actual arrival information from the others. One of the more interesting possibilities was a James *Calford* who arrived in the States on July 17, 1850, aboard the ship named (are you ready?) *Catherine.* This James would have been only 15 when he came, although he told the keeper of the manifest that he was born *"about 1831,"* adding another four years to his age.

Could this James have been our James? Is there really any way to know for sure? Another bit of data that might lead one to speculate that there could be something to this James *Calford* being ours was the fact that on board the ship with him were two *Whalens*, Michael (20) and Patrick (19). Their surname was the same one as James' first wife, Mary Whalen (more of her story later); considering the tendency for the Irish to stay with people in the States they knew from back home, this connection may amount to a bit more than just coincidence. There were several Whelan families listed in the Rathangan parish registers who clearly were neighbors of the Colfers, so perhaps they were not strangers to each other here in the States. There also were three Whalens (Margaret, Ellen, and John), the same given names as those of Mary's siblings, who were godparents to two of Michael's and one of James' children.

Both Michael and James asserted in their parish marriage records here in the States that their parents' names were Patrick and Mary (Dwyer) Colfer; James' Rathangan parish baptismal register also recorded them similarly. However, the names recorded as James' parents in the state record of his second marriage were *John* and Mary. Errors such as these are common in older records, and there is too much other confirming evidence that connects the dots between siblings Michael and James. Besides, as I mentioned earlier in our story, middle names were used quite often in families in order to distinguish one member from another who happened to share a similar first name, thus the mention of both *Patrick* and *John* as the given name for our great-great-grandfather.

It also is interesting to note that James continued with *Colfer* as his surname, whereas Michael's became *Colford* around 1878; two brothers who eventually would live within a few miles of each other in Newark and Jersey City spelled their last names differently.

The first record I have found of James' presence here was in the 1860 federal census which has him living as a *"boarder"* with the Lambert family at 543 Ferry St. in Newark's 12th Ward; another *"boarder,"* George Taylor, was in this home as well. The head of the household was 65-year-old Nicholas, a widower, and his five children: Bridget (26), Mark (28), James (20), Elizabeth (18), and Ellen (12). James' occupation was *"cartman,"* someone who pushed a two-wheeled delivery cart from place to place, dropping off whatever goods the business provided. Four-wheeled carts/wagons were of the horse-drawn variety.

The Lamberts were from the same part of County Wexford as the Colfers, and, in all likelihood, their families were related to our Colfers, or they were simply familiar with each other long before they emigrated. In fact, a Richard Lambert wrote the book, *Loves Greatest Gift . . . Remembrance,* which, like Fr. O'Connor's listing of headstone inscriptions throughout the cemeteries of his parish, his book includes inscriptions throughout his Rathangan parish cemeteries.

There were more Colfer and Lambert family members buried in Rathangan than any other. Griffith's Valuation lists 261 Lamberts in Wexford, including seven with the given name, Nicholas. Surely there was a connection between these families.

James completed the first step in applying for citizenship on June 12, 1860, when he went to the Essex County Court of Common Pleas and filled out the paperwork for his *Declaration of Intention* (aka: *First Papers)*. Immigrants were allowed to complete this first step as soon as they arrived in the States. This date does not really narrow down his arrival date in this country, since it is not known if he applied immediately after he came in 1860 or after having been here for a while.

It was on October 10, 1864, when James was granted citizenship. The witness to his good character at the naturalization ceremony was a Thomas O'Connor who agreed that James had *"behaved himself as a man of good moral character, attached to the principles of the Constitution of the United States, and well-disposed to the good order and happiness of the same."* O'Connor also claimed that he had known that James *"has resided within the United States five years at least, and within the State of New Jersey one year at least."* This record suggests that James was here by the late 1850s.

The most helpful source of information I have found about James was the record of his military service which I was able to retrieve from the National Archives in Washington, DC. Although our James *Colfort* had registered for the draft in June of 1863, as required by Congress' Enrollment Act passed that year, he was never drafted. The intent of the Act was to increase the ranks of the military during the dark days of the Civil War by requiring all men between the ages of 20 and 45 to register, but all married man were deemed ineligible for the draft. James was married for the first time just one month before his registration date, allowing him to be immune to the draft. Another provision of this Act allowed an eligible draftee to pay a substitute a $300 fee to stand in for him.

James's first wife was one Mary Whalen who was not yet two years old when she arrived in the States with her parents, John (31) and Mary (24), on August 20, 1846, aboard the ship *Chester.* The 1850 census places the three Whalens with their first New Jersey-born child, John (3), in Newark's fifth ward. By 1860, the family had grown to include four more children: Ellen (6), Margaret (4), Alice (2), and Peter (four months). They all had moved to 7 Frederick St. in Newark's 12th ward, the same ward as neighbor James; Mary's occupation was listed as *"tailoress."* The spelling of her surname took on many forms in these records: Whelan, Whalen, Walan, and Whalan. This surname also was a very familiar one in the Rathangan parish registers.

Reverend Gervais, the pastor at St. James Church in Newark, presided over the marriage of James (27; *"laborer"*) and Mary (19), approximately six months pregnant at the time, on May 11, 1863. The church register recorded the last names as *Colfar* and *Whalan*; their sponsors were John Mc Loughlin and Margaret O'Shaunessy. I have reason to believe that the newlyweds moved in right away with Mary's parents and the rest of the Whalens at 20 Frederick St.

Two years after his marriage, James enlisted in the Union Army as a private on April 13, 1865, four days after the Civil War ended with the peace treaty signed at Appomattox Courthouse. He was one of 19 *"recruits received"* by Company H of the 9th Infantry Regiment of New Jersey that year; two others had deserted the regiment before their hitch was over.

James' enlistment was undoubtedly not out of bravery nor out of duty to serve, but rather out of the wish to cash in on the bonus which the federal government was giving to new enlistees at that time. His *Volunteer Enlistment* papers recorded the *Local Bounty* for James as $475 for a one-year stint; he received the first installment, a check for $100, the day he enlisted.

James gave his age as *"27"* and his occupation as *"teamster"* when he signed up for service in Newark, even though his enlistment date was just three months from his 30th birthday; his first official roll call was in Camp Perrine in Trenton. James stood *"five feet, eight ¼ inches tall"*; his eyes were *"hazel,"* his hair *"black,"* and his complexion *"florid,"* according to the records. The army provided him with a *"knapsack, haversack, and canteen furnished."* James, of course, like Michael, could neither read nor write, so someone else signed his name for him on his *Volunteer Enlistment* papers; he simply affixed an *"X"* on the signature line alongside which the clerk wrote, *"his mark."* Every record I have found for Michael and James Colfer was signed thusly.

However, his military career was over quickly when his regiment was *"mustered out"* of service on July 12, 1865, while in Greensboro, North Carolina, just three months after his enlistment. His wife Mary was the one who collected a check for $330 as the bounty owed to James when he left the army with an honorable discharge.

There were two other George Taylors, the same name as James' fellow boarder with the Lamberts, who also enlisted in Company H of the 9th Infantry Regiment of New Jersey. I dare say that one of them was indeed one and the same as James' housemate. One enlisted as a sergeant, the other as a private. George the private signed up on October 3, 1861, and earned three promotions up to the rank of First Sergeant. However, he was *"discharged due to wounds"* on August 23, 1864, when he had his right arm amputated after being wounded in the disastrous Union defeat at the battle of Cold Harbor, VA. I am not sure how the other George fared during the period of his enlistment, but is not unreasonable to connect the dots between one of these Georges and James.

James and Mary would soon lose both of their children. Their first, Elizabeth (aka: *Lizzie*), was born on August 5, 1863, just three months after their marriage; the state record, however, simply lists her name as *"Girl"* and the parent as *"James Colfar – laborer."* Elizabeth's godparents were Peter Cousins and Ellen Lambert. What I found interesting was the fact that only the fathers' names were included in these early state birth records.

Their daughter never made it to her third birthday; Lizzie passed away on April 23, 1866, at the age of *"two years, eight months, 18 days."* Her cause of death was *"inflammation."* James, her younger brother, succumbed to *"small pox"* the very next day; both died in their home at 2 Lexington St. in Newark. There is no mention of his age on his official state death certificate, but what was reported on his interment record at Holy Sepulchre Cemetery in East Orange where his entire family was buried was that he lived only *"12 hours."*

Mary herself died a month later on May 30 in her family's home at 20 Frederick St. after only three years of marriage. Her age was *"21 years, two months,"* according to her death certificate; James was almost 31 years of age at the time. Louis J. Wendell, Newark's City Clerk, verified for the federal government Mary's cause of death as *"inflamation of lungs,"* essentially the same malady that claimed the life of her Lizzie. In those days of record-keeping, *"inflamation"* typically referred either to pneumonia or pleurisy, so it may be likely that mother Mary passed this contagious disease along to her young daughter who was unable to combat it.

Could pneumonia also have contributed to the death of young James more so than small pox? After all, being born into a living arrangement rife with such a highly contagious bacteria-borne illness would have put him at high risk of contagion as well.

The *Newark Daily Advertiser* ran an announcement of Mary's death the next day (note the dual spellings of the name):

DIED

Coffer – On the 30th inst., MARY, wife of James Coffee, aged 21 years.

The relatives and friends are cordially invited to attend the funeral at 1½ P.M.

on Friday, 1st inst., from the residence of her father, No. 20 Frederick st.

Interment in the Cemetery of the Holy Sepulchre.

James essentially lost his entire family within one month's time.

Fortunately for us, his very brief army career left behind a rather extensive "paper trail" of personal and other information which has been invaluable. It has provided me with access to much more background material on James than I have had on our great-grandpa Michael.

What helped to create his lengthy military file was the fact that his three months of service made his second wife, Caroline (aka: *Carrie*), eligible for a pension after his death. It was her request for such a pension that required a significant amount of documentation regarding his background. The information which is to follow has been derived directly from these records.

James eventually married for a second time to Caroline *Knecht* Code who was born in Easton, PA, on January 14, 1847, to Prussian-born parents, Peter and Rachel Knecht. She also had been married once before to Irish-born Nicholas Code, another resident of Newark's 12th Ward at 31 Berlin St. The Knechts were at 314 Ferry St. in 1860, just a short distance from the Code family, so these folks must have met somewhere in the neighborhood.

The 1860 census placed the 16-year-old Nicholas, a *"silver plater,"* with his parents, Richard and Catherine, and his two younger brothers, James (13) and John (nine months). Nicholas was drafted into the Union Army's Company I of the 12th Infantry Regiment of New Jersey on February 27, 1865. Although the Civil War would not be over for another month, he saw no action and was mustered out of the service five months later on July 15 at the age of 21.

Nicholas and Carrie married on Christmas Eve, 1865. Although a Protestant at the time of her marriage, the parish record stated that Carrie was *"baptized privately"* by Fr. Gervais at St. James

Church a month later on January 26, 1866. Nicholas still was listed as a *"silver plater,"* and Carrie as a *"tayloress."* Their first child, Catharine, was born on September 9, 1866. However, their marriage, like James' and Mary's, was short-lived; Nicholas died on May 10, 1867.

One of the documents provided to the government to secure Carrie's pension stated that Nicholas *"was killed by the railroad,"* but the official cause of death was *"pyaemia"* (blood poisoning), probably the result of a wound suffered in a work-related accident. His death left Carrie the widowed mother of eight-month-old Catharine and a few months pregnant with their second child. Another daughter, *Mary Francess*, was born on December 3, 1867, seven months after Nicholas' death.

How Carrie supported herself and her two daughters during the 14 months between Nicholas' death and her marriage to James is unclear, but one can assume that Carrie had some motivation to marry again in order to gain financial support for herself and her children. Could she have moved back into the *Knecht* household or into the home of her in-laws, Richard and Catherine *Code*, after her husband's passing?

Only a family historian would know for sure.

James was a widower for a little over two years before marrying Carrie on July 5, 1868 (although the name appears as *Cove* on the parish certificate), two years to the day that his brother and the Maleys arrived in the States. The state marriage record had James' name as *John Colfax*. Reverend Gervais presided over the ceremony again for James, and the witnesses to the marriage at St. James Church were James *Maly* and Catherine *Cove*. At the time of their marriage, Carrie's daughter Catherine was almost two years of age, and *Mary Francess* was only seven months old.

Both of Carrie's daughters from her first marriage are listed in the census records as Colfers, so one can assume that James formally adopted them when he married Carrie. In addition to these two girls, James and Carrie raised three other children of their own:

> John (born October 16, 1869; sponsors: James Maly and Ellen Whalen)
>
> William (born August 10, 1874; sponsors: Michael Colfer and Mary Whitty)
>
> Caroline (born February 5, 1884; sponsors: Mark Lambert and Mary Maguire)

Another child, James (born July 21, 1871; sponsors: Patrick Smith and Catherine *Cody*), lived only one day; cause of death was *"cynanosis."* Unlike his other siblings who were baptized several days after their births, James' baptism was the same day of his birth, an indication that that day was expected to be his last. The state record listed James as the parent again and his occupation this time as *"policeman."*

The family's most consistent residences throughout several city directories were 239 Ferry St. (1869 – 1874) and 138 Jackson St. (1875 – 1909).

James toiled at many jobs, both before and during his 26-year marriage to Carrie. Records have him working as a *"laborer"* (1860, 1866-1869), *"engineer in factory"* (1880), and *"celluloid"* (1878 – 1891). There also were entries in the 1870 federal census and in the 1871 and 1874 through 1877 Newark City Directories that listed his occupation as *"policeman"* or as *"police."* However, Ed Dalley, the curator of the Newark Police Museum whom I contacted, said that there was no record of a James Colfer having been a member of its police force; what he suggested was that perhaps James worked as a custodian of sorts in one of the department's precinct buildings.

James eventually passed away at the age of 57 on December 14, 1894. Dr. J. F. Hagan attributed his official cause of death to *"valvular disease of heart and cirrhosis of the liver,"* and his death certificate put the *"Duration of disease"* at *"three months."* His obituary in the Newark Evening News a day later read thusly:

> *COLFER – On December 14, James, beloved husband of*
> *Carrie Colfer, aged 57 years.*
> *Relatives and friends, also members of St. James Council*
> *No. 39, C.B.L., and the Police Mutual Aid Society, are*
> *kindly invited to attend the funeral from his late residence,*
> *No. 138 Jackson street, on Monday, December 17, at 8:30 A.M.,*
> *to St. James's Church, where a Solemn High Mass of Requiem*
> *will be offered for the repose of his soul. Interment in the*
> *Cemetery of the Holy Sepulchre.*

It was just several weeks after his death when 48-year-old Carrie applied to the Department of the Interior, Bureau of Pensions, for the pension to which she was entitled by virtue of the Pension Act of June 27, 1890. This particular pension was for those widows who could document adherence to the following five requirements:

1. *That the soldier served at least ninety days in the War of the Rebellion and was honorably discharged.*

2. *Proof of soldier's death (death cause need not have been due to Army service).*

3. *That the widow is "without other means of support than her daily labor."*

4. *That Widow was married to soldier prior to June 27, 1890 – date of act.*

5. *That all pensions under this Act commence from date of receipt of application (executed after the passage of Act) in Pension Bureau.*

Carrie, still a resident of 138 Jackson St. at the time, completed the application for the pension on February 21, 1895, in the presence of witnesses to the process, her brother Andrew and a Catherine Roessler. Frederick Gniett was the notary public who applied the seal attesting to the facts of the application.

The pension folk rejected her initial application, however, since she made two errors which apparently gave pause to the bureaucratic paper-pushers who processed it. She stated that she *"was married under the name Carrie Knecht to said James Colfer"* when she actually was Carrie *Code* at the time, and she listed her only child under the age of 16 as *Carrie* Colfer when, in fact, the birth certificate supplied as part of the application had her name as *Caroline* Colfer. The pension act provided an additional two dollars per month to the widow for every child under the age of 16, so this error could have cost Carrie some income.

William Lochran, Commissioner of the Bureau of Pensions, wrote to Carrie's attorney, Thomas L. White of 191 Market St., Newark, on June 26, 1895, to explain his concerns about Carrie's application:

". . . a discrepancy appears relative to the Christian name of the child claimed

for. The claimant, in her declaration alleged the name of said child as Carrie
while the transcript which she furnished from the baptismal records in proof of
its birth shows its name as Caroline.

This discrepancy should be explained under oath by the party in error, the correct
Christian name of the child should be established and competent evidence should
be furnished showing whether the soldier had been previously married and, if he
had been, the fact and date of death or divorce of his former wife should be proved."

Because of these relatively minor glitches, Carrie had to supply additional documentation that Carries *Knecht* and *Code* were one-and-the-same person and that *Carrie* and *Caroline* were equivalent names for her daughter. She also had to verify the date of James' first marriage to Mary and proof of her death. The advantage of this additional paperwork for us was that it provided more documents from which to glean other information about Carrie and James.

Carrie completed an affidavit for the pension folk explaining the Carrie/Caroline confusion:

"I state that the child Carrie was baptized under the name of Caroline but we
always called her Carrie. And I testify that she is the same child mentioned in
my declaration. And is now living and is eleven years old last February. I also
send from Father Cody of the St. James Church his affidavit in regards to the   error."

Father Cody's affidavit also accounted for the error, and he assured the pension department that *"the child is personally known to me, and at school and at home is called 'Carrie', but was entered on the Register of Baptisms in the full form of 'Caroline.'"*

She also cleared up the Knecht/Code confusion:

"When I was married to the late soldier the minister (Father Cody) asked me
my maiden name and I gave him Carrie Knecht. A mistake, it should have
been Carrie Code, the name of my first husband deceased."

It would appear that Carrie had a hard time keeping body and soul together. To document that she was *"without other means of support than her daily labor,"* she wrote the following in her pension application:

> *". . . I also testify that I have no property and no income, and the only means*
> *of support is what my daughters bring me for board which is very little for*
> *they do not have steady work and do not earn on an average over three dollars*
> *a week and they have to clothe themselves out of that. I have two daughters.*
> *So I have hard work to get along."*

A month after completing the *General Affidavit* with this information, Carrie certified again:

> *"I own no property, no real personal or mixed in which I have any pecuniary*
> *interest. and have no income only what my daughters pay me for board and*
> *what I earn by daily labor – I further testify that I have no person legally bound*
> *to support me."*

One of the requirements for the pension application was a personal reference. Carrie's came from Andrew Liebhauser, a *Wholesale and Retail Baker*, who also was one of the pall bearers at the funeral of her first husband, Nicholas. He testified to the following:

> *". . . I certify that she has no property. and the only means of her support is*
> *what her two daughters bring in which is hardly enough to keep her. They*
> *cannot earn more than three or four dollars a week and after they clothe*
> *themselves there is very little left for their board – I know these facts for I*
> *am very well acquainted with the family live a neighbor to them and see*
> *them almost every day."*

Jacob Gerber, an assessor for the city of Newark, also claimed on behalf of Carrie that she *"was not assessed for any real or personal property."*

The many affidavits required of Carrie for the pension kept Notary Public Gniett and attorney White quite busy, since their names appeared on all the documents provided to the pension folk. Attorney White charged the outrageous sum of $10 for processing some of these documents.

Carrie's persistence paid off, since she was awarded the pension, commencing February 28, 1895. Her monthly payment was a whopping eight dollars, with an additional two dollars for young Carrie who was only 11 years of age. This two dollar bonus, however, was to cease on February 4, 1900, the day before Carrie turned 16. Pension laws changed regularly, and Carrie's monthly award kept increasing. The Pension Act of September 8, 1916, saw her award go to $20 per month, and the May 23, 1928, act raised it yet again to $40.

The Pension Act of July 3, 1926, offered the tidy sum of $50 per month, but the clearly-stated requirement for the pension (CAPS and all), according to the form letter sent to Carrie by Winfield Scott, Commissioner of Pensions, was for the widow *"IF SHE WAS THE WIFE OF SUCH SOLDIER, SAILOR, OR MARINE DURING THE PERIOD OF HIS SERVICE IN SAID WAR."*

Carrie, of course, was not married to James during his service; his first wife, Mary, was. Nevertheless, Carrie completed another affidavit claiming that she was indeed married to James during his months of service, but it would appear that her inability to prove her claim ruled her out as eligible for this payment.

Carrie remained at 138 Jackson St. until 1909; the 1910 census reported that she then shared a residence at 384 Lafayette St. with her daughters Catherine (36), Mary Francess (34), and Caroline (26). She moved a year later to 148 Polk St. with Catherine and Mary Francess where she remained until 1917. Her younger daughter, Caroline, married John Gnatz on June 25, 1910, and the couple moved to 267 Elm St. It is this Caroline whom Dad recalled visiting as a child at her later home on Polk St. John and Carrie raised three children: Anita (1912), Paul (1914), and John (1915). I dare say that Dad's visits also included his great-aunt, Carrie, who was around until Dad was nine years of age.

Another resident at 148 Polk St. was the German-born Henry Troeber, a *"harness maker,"* according to multiple Newark City Directories. The 51-year old Henry and 35-year-old Mary Francess must have met at that time; they wed in 1916. It would appear that they had no children. By 1926, the couple had joined Carrie and Catherine at 157 Polk where Carrie had been since 1918.

Carrie remained in this residence until her death on July 31, 1929, at the age of *"80 years, six months, 17 days."* The cause of death was *"myocarditis"* with a contributory factor, *"embolus."* The Newark Evening News ran her obituary the next day:

> *COLFER – On July 31, 1929, Caroline Colfer (nee Knecht), beloved widow*
> *of James Coffer. Relatives and friends are kindly invited to attend the funeral*
> *from her residence, 157 Polk street, on Saturday, August 3 at 8:30 a.m. to*
> *St. James Church. Where, at 9:30 a solemn high mass of requiem will be*
> *offered for the repose of her soul. – Interment in Holy Sepulcher Cemetery.*

The unmarried Catherine was still there sharing this home with her sister and brother-in-law in 1930; her monthly rent to them was a hefty $18. Henry, the homeowner, put the value of the house at $4,000.

Mary Francess, a widow after Henry's passing on October 9, 1937, remained at 157 Polk with her sister Catherine, now working as a *"box maker – card board boxes,"* according to the 1940 census. Considering the fact that Catherine would have been 74 years of age in 1940, any occupation at all is surprising for someone of that age. Living next door to Mary Francess and Catherine at 159 ½ Polk was their sister, Carrie Gnatz, her husband John, and Paul, their 26-year-old son. Catherine passed away on December 30, 1942, at the age of 76; Mary Francess (84) died on that same date nine years later, 1951. The 74-year-old John Gnatz outlived his wife Carrie (65 when she passed on July 31, 1949) by seven years, dying on December 7, 1956.

James' and Carrie's son, John (21), married Catherine Hilliard (20), daughter of William and Catherine (Murray), both Ireland-born, on New Year's Eve, 1890, at St Columba's Church in Newark. This marriage did not last long, however, since *Katie Calford,* the name accorded her in the Holy Sepulchre Cemetery records, passed away just six years later on November 17, 1896; the name on her death certificate was *Catherine Colfer.* In the same cemetery plot lies her four-month-old baby, *Joseph Colford,* who died just four months after his mother on March 3, 1897, in his home at 138 Jackson St. due to *"meningitis and eclampsia"*; he had been ill for three days before he passed.

What is interesting is that the cemetery records list John and Catherine's deceased child as *"Catherine Calford,"* probably a record-keeper's error who mistakenly wrote down Joseph's mother's name instead of his. The official state-issued death certificate, however, definitely has the decedent as *Joseph Colford.*

Also of interest is the fact that John's wife passed away while visiting, or living with, a family at 98 Roebling Place in Brooklyn, NY. Her death certificate listed her cause of death as *"acute nephritis – uraemia"*; the coroner, Dr. A. A. Webber, claimed that she had been ailing for a month before she passed. However, a mystery on her death certificate is the statement that she had been a resident of Brooklyn for *"1 ½ years."*

The 1900 census listed three families living in this three-story home at 98 Roebling, one of whom was an Irish-born couple, Bernard and Bridget Mucklign (probably a misspelling of the name McGlynn). Without any other confirming evidence, it is unclear whether or not Catherine was living with them, and if so, what her relationship was to them. Could she have been there as a resident or as a visitor along with her newborn baby, Joseph? Was she estranged from her husband, thus her retreat, of sorts, to Brooklyn? Or did she simply take ill while visiting the McGlynns?

More unanswered questions.

All I know is that the undertaker, William H. Hamilton, took care of Catherine's funeral and burial at Holy Sepulchre Cemetery. An Anne Hilliard purchased the plot right after Catherine died; Joseph, her son, would be interred in the same plot four months later.

The widower John, a *"plumber"* or *"steamfitter"* in multiple sources, joined the army for the first of his three enlistments sometime in 1898, soon after his son died. He apparently hoped to, or actually did, see action in the Spanish-American War. The *Spanish-American War Volunteers Index to Compiled Military Service Records* had the 29-year-old John as a *"private"* in *"Company H, 1ˢᵗ New Jersey Infantry."*

John enlisted for a second time on January 17, 1899, this time in *Company F, 4ᵗʰ Infantry Regiment.* The enlistment papers listed his height as *"5 feet, 7¼ inches,"* his eyes *"blue,"* his hair *"light brown,"* and his complexion *"ruddy."* He also indicated that he was *"single,"* a suggestion that his wife was indeed deceased. I suspect that he didn't return home between his first and second enlistments, since the 1900 census had him as a resident of the town of San Francisco de Malabon in the Philippine

Islands. John was discharged *"at sea"* on January 16, 1902, with his *"experience of service"* cited as *"good."*

He returned to his widowed mother's home at 138 Jackson St. in Newark for approximately 15 months before enlisting for a third time on April 21, 1903, still in *Company F, 4ᵗʰ Infantry Regiment*. This time, however, the detachment for this *"steamfitter"* was to the *"Engineers"* at the United States Military Academy at West Point. However, it was barely two months later on June 16ᵗʰ when the 34-year-old John succumbed in the Soldiers Hospital there to *"chronic tuberculosis and peritonitis with dense adhesion and obstruction of bowels"*; his rank at the time was something like *"second class private."*

What is interesting is that the 1904 Newark City Directory still listed him along with his mother at 138 Jackson, but this time his occupation was *"USA"* (*A* was for *Army*). Could Carrie just have given the name of her deceased son to the directory-keeper as some means of personal solace? Another item of interest was that it wasn't until June 24, 1931, a full 28 years after his death, that a P. J. McElroy applied to the army for a headstone on John's behalf; it now stands in Holy Sepulchre Cemetery.

John's younger brother, William Patrick, fathered nine children with his wife, Mary (Long), and worked as a Newark policeman in the city's fourth precinct. They married on February 7, 1895, just two months after James' death. The couple lost their first child, also named James, seven months later on September 10, 1895; baby James lived only a *"few hours,"* according to his death certificate, before he died due to *"premature birth."* The 1900 census lists William as a *"polisher,"* but it was on February 15, 1910, when he received his official appointment to the police force. *"Assigned to regular patrol,"* the assignment sheet read. He remained with the Newark police force in the fourth, sixth, and seventh precincts until his retirement on January 4, 1935.

His family moves over the years bordered on the nomadic; the federal census records place them in at least four separate Newark locations, probably because he had to find increasingly larger quarters to accommodate his growing brood: 92 Nichols St. (1895), 206 Jefferson St. (1900), 71 Garden St. (1910), and 381 South Orange Ave. (1930) where his monthly rent was $35.

Ed Dalley, the Newark Police Museum curator who provided me with this information, also told me that William brought on board his son, William Aloysius, to the force. However, his son's August 1,

1928, appointment to the second precinct did not last long. Barely two years later on June 6, 1930, the Department dropped son William from the force. The following notation appeared on his service record:

"Name ordered stricken from the rolls of the Police Division in accordance with General Rule # 40 of the Manual – Absent without leave for 5 days or more."

Must have done his Dad proud, you think?

The younger William had listed himself as a *"machinist"* on his World War I Draft Registration Card for which he applied on September 12, 1918; he and his father completed the necessary paperwork on the same day. The card listed his father as *"tall"* with a *"medium"* build and *"brown"* eyes and hair, whereas son William's height was listed as *"six feet, one and ¾ inches"* with a *"slender"* build, *"brown"* eyes, and *"dark"* hair.

Chapter VIII

Some Other Colfers in the Area

Patrick Colfer

A possible missing piece to the Colfer puzzle was a Patrick Colfer who arrived in New York Harbor aboard the *Harvey Birch* with his wife, *Bird* (Bridget), and their infant daughter, Mary A., on June 1, 1860. The family took up residence in Paterson where Patrick found work as a teamster. I suspect that infant Mary did not survive long, since there was another six-year-old Mary listed in the 1880 census. It was an Irish practice to name a later-born child after a sibling who died. The family raised six children, three boys and three girls.

Our Michael and James may have had a brother Patrick who also was born and baptized in Rathangan around their time. This Paterson Patrick had the year 1834 as his *"estimated birth year"* on the ship's manifest. A difference of two years in these estimations was very, very common, however. I thought at first that this Patrick may have been connected to our Michael and James, but I suspect that that is not true. Mom has said that Dad never spoke of a Paterson connection to his family. I also have other thoughts about our Patrick (see a later section, *Eureka, Maybe! Possible Current Colfer Cousins*).

John and Mary (Purcell) Colfer

John and Mary (Purcell) Colfer were county Wexford-born folk, John in 1810, and Mary, approximately 1822; given the vast number of Colfers in Wexford at that time, however, it is difficult to pinpoint exactly how they were related to us. All I know is that the names Colfer and Purcell both were found in the townland of Vernegley, the location I have mentioned previously which might have been the home of our own direct line of Colfers.

John and Mary were to make their way to the States and marry in Perth Amboy, NJ, on June 4, 1841. They had two children, Mary Penelope (June 25, 1842 – June 23, 1941) and William Henry (August, 1843 – January 7, 1919). However, their mother left behind these two young children when she passed away on August 24, 1846, while still a Perth Amboy resident; John would outlive her by 34 years, dying on May 16, 1880.

Their son William spent almost three years in the Union Army, enlisting on August 15, 1862, along with his future brother-in-law, Peter Wyckoff Voorhees. He served until his honorable discharge for *Distinguished Service* on May 25, 1865, having worked his way up to full corporal in Company A of the 11th New Jersey Volunteer Infantry after having seen considerable action in the Virginia campaign, including Gettysburg, during his years of service. William became eligible for an *"Invalid Pension"* after his discharge because his *"inability to earn a support by manual labor"* was judged to have been due to the wounds he received in battle. He suffered two injuries at the battles of Mine Run and Locust Grove, both Virginia, *"while engaged in fighting the enemy a part of the so called Southern Confederacy,"* he said; the battles took place from November 26-28, 1863. The most serious of the injuries was a mini ball (bullet) which struck him in the right breast; William also told one of the many medical examiners who had to re-examine him every time he applied for a pension increase that he suffered sunstroke at Gettysburg.

Since his lingering medical complications throughout the years were *"not caused by bad or vicious habits,"* typically referring to alcoholism or syphilis, he began collecting his pension around 1890. His first monthly payment was eight dollars, but this figure rose steadily over the years until it reached forty dollars per month at the time of his death on January 7, 1919, at the age of 77. Among the medical issues he attributed to his war injuries were *"rheumatism in left shoulder, disease of the heart, contusion and pain in breast from gunshot wound, hernia both sides, dimness of vision, fainting spells."* He stated in one affidavit that he was *"unable to tell my neighbors at a distance of 15 feet."* William always stated that his date of birth was August 14, 1841, but there was no evidence at all to support this claim. When asked for verification of his age and birthdate for one of his re-applications for a pension increase, he had to go to court to explain the missing documentation. A South River notary public, David Serviss, verified the following:

> *". . . he knows of no public, church, or family record of his birth; his*
> *mother died when this defendant was about two (2) years of age; his*
> *father died about 20 or 25 years ago; he believes from what he has*
> *been told that he was born August 14, 1841 in the city of Perth Amboy,*
> *NJ . . . this defendant is unable to furnish any record of his birth for*
> *the reason that he does not know of any such record or if any such*
> *record exists."*

His residences over the years included Perth Amboy, Baltimore, New Brunswick, and South River where he lived for 38 years. William had been married twice. His first wife, Mary (Everett), died in 1886 after only three years of marriage while they were Baltimore residents; he married a second time on January 19, 1890, to Araminda Baisley in South River's Tabernacle Baptist Church. He had two children with Araminda: William Henry, Jr. (September 11, 1892 – July 8, 1970) and Herbert Voorhees Colfer (January 3, 1894 – January, 1970). Although I have been unable to determine exactly when Araminda passed away, it was prior to 1900 when the census that year listed William as a widower. William lived for a time with his sister Mary Penelope and her husband, the aforementioned Peter Wyckoff Voorhees, but then he lived out the last few years of his life in the Home for Disabled Soldiers (aka: the *Old Soldiers Home*) in Kearny, NJ, before passing away on January 7, 1919. Peter and Mary Penelope had three children together, all daughters: Amanda (1869 – 1944), Edith (July, 1874– 1930), and Nettie (October, 1880 – 1940). None of them would marry.

What is interesting is that there was a woman, Margaret (Colfer) Lavin, who wrote to the Pension Office on December 27, 1923, inquiring if William *"is alive and still drawing a pension."* The relationship of Margaret to William is unknown. However, there were 17 Lavins, including a

Margaret, buried in Holy Sepulchre Cemetery in East Orange, NJ, the same burial place as many of our Colfers, so there must have been a strong connection between these Lavin and Colfer families.

Fr. James/Richard Colfer

A James Colfer from the County Wexford townland of Tinraheen was ordained a Carmelite priest on September 19, 1891, taking the name Richard upon ordination. The 42-year-old Fr. Colfer arrived in the States on July 25, 1909, aboard the *Celtic*. The ship's manifest listed his *"destination"* as *"go join the Carmelite Church."* His actual destination was Transfiguration Parish in Tarrytown, New York, where he spent two years as a parish priest. Fr. Richard Colfer then was charged with bringing a Carmelite presence to the Middletown, NY, area, so he founded and became the first pastor of Our Lady of Mount Carmel there from 1912-19. His assistants were Frs. Paul O'Dwyer and Simon Farrington, but a Fr. Louis McCabe replaced him as pastor when he left and returned to Ireland. Fr. Colfer's Enniscorthy - area home in County Wexford is just a stone's throw from the Bannow/Rathangan area from which our Colfers emigrated.

Before his assignments in the States, he served in Ireland as Prior, as Novice Master, and eventually as President of Terenure College, his alma mater, in Dublin. In 1925, six years after his return to Ireland, he was elected Provincial of the Irish Province. The five-foot, 11-inch Fr. Colfer died on February 1, 1932.

I contacted Fr. Alfred Isacsson, the Provincial Archivist of the Carmelite Order, in the fall of 2004. He provided me with a three-volume history of the Carmelite province of which Our Lady of Mount Carmel was a member parish. Although it offered me more than I needed to know about it all, Fr. Isacsson also sent along a picture of Fr. Richard Colfer taken in 1919.

Pictures are valuable, but they are sorely lacking for our Michael and James.

Chapter IX

Eureka, Maybe!

Possible Current Colfer Cousins

T here are two possible connections to third cousins of ours, a Mark Colfer and a Ray Colfer, which I may have unearthed, along with a possible second cousin to Dad, Peter Colfer.

Mark Colfer. Among the many parish priests I contacted over the years via either snail mail or email was a Fr. James Kehoe of the Church of Mary Immaculate and St. Joseph in the Roman Catholic parish of Carrig-on-Bannow. His church sits directly across the road from *Colfer's Pub*, as short a distance as St. Joseph's Church is from the Lipsett's Mountain Inn in Shancough. No longer owned by a Colfer, the pub is known for its very successful four-day-long annual Carrig Music Festival which attracts as many as 25 music groups and singers every year. Current owner John Murphy began the festival tradition in memory of his late father, Phil.

I might have hit the proverbial jackpot with Fr. Kehoe. Although he could not share much Colfer history as per the request in my letter to him, he did pass along my query to a parishioner, Mark Colfer, who also was researching the Colfers. The first of many emails we exchanged came from Mark on September 14, 2004. It is as close to a "smoking gun" regarding our common connection as there can be. Matching together various names and dates leads me and Mark both to believe that we might share a common great-great-grandfather, Patrick Colfer; among his Patrick's children were two sons, Michael and James. If indeed these brothers were the same ones who emigrated as per the timelines for our Michael and James, this connection would make us third cousins to Mark. The one important but missing bit of data which would confirm this connection to Mark beyond a reasonable doubt would be the name of our common great-great-grandmother, Mary Dwyer; Mark was not sure of her name, however. The home townland for Mark's family of Colfers was Verneglye.

Verneglye residents would have received their sacraments from the church at Bannow rather than Rathangan which is only seven miles away. I contacted Fr. Tom Dalton, the current parish priest at Rathangan, and he told me as much. However, families moved constantly from townland to townland, so some of our Colfers could have been baptized in Bannow as well as in Rathangan. At least I have been able to pinpoint our origins to within a few small square miles in the Bannow/Rathangan area of Wexford.

Ray Colfer. I received an email reply to one of the 46 letters I sent out to all Wexford Colfers from a Ray Colfer on September 19, 2007; Ray is a cousin to Mark. It was quite humorous, on the one hand, and very interesting, on the other. The humorous part of his email reads thusly:

> *"In 1983 I received a similar letter from Paul D. Colford . . . I mislaid Paul's letter. I only came across it recently when I was moving house. I am guessing that Paul D. Colford is related to you as his great grandmother was Anna Meely. If that is the case, perhaps you would pass him a copy of this with my apologies for loosing contact with him."*

So, Paul, 24 years later, consider yourself in receipt of a reply to your letter to Ray!

Snail mail, indeed!

What Ray also stated in his email was that Paul's letter did prompt him to ask his father about his Colfer origins. Another jackpot, perhaps:

> *". . . he said that he had a vague recollection of talk in the family of two great-uncles who went to America in the mid-19th century and were not heard from afterwards. One was named Michael and I have forgotten the name of the other."*

Could these brothers be our Michael and James? If so, then Ray would be another third cousin to us.

Peter Colfer. Jeanne and I and Fran and Denise and the kids took what was, for me, my third trip to Ireland, in the summer of 2008. This time, however, my visit was with some genealogical destinations in mind. During our first 24 hours in the town of Wexford, I called several people whose names and phone numbers I had collected before our departure from the States, most of them folks I had communicated with via email over the years. One of these numbers was that of Noel and Kathleen Colfer, whose daughter, Joanna, answered the phone. When I explained to her the reason for my call, she said very enthusiastically that she would be the best one to take us around to the areas I wanted to visit (Rathangan, Bannow, and Baldwinstown). The next morning Fran and I set out to meet her in the parking lot of the Wheelhouse Bar in the townland of Baldwinstown (our great-grandmother, Anna Maley's, birthplace).

Thanks to the wonders of the GPS system, we were directed by the technology through cow paths and all sorts of highways and byways until we reached our destination and our meeting with Joanna. She was a very charming 26-year-old working as a *garda* (police) who was a die-hard Jon Bon Jovi fan. When I called the day before, she said that she was only available to take us around until noon, since she had a scheduled dentist appointment. However, she was pleased to tell us when we met her that morning that she had cancelled the appointment to accommodate us.

I thought that what she said to me and Fran upon first encountering us that morning was quite telling. She said something that I only had heard through my years in Jersey City, *"I can tell that you are Colfers, because you are so tall."* Her comment supports the notion that the height of the Colfers has been attributed to the Norse/Viking connection in the Norman origins of our family.

Joanna took us around the area. One of our stops was to visit her grandfather, 94-year-old Peter Colfer, at a senior citizens center during his daily stopover for lunch; *"Some soup and a piece of brown bread,"* he requested. Peter was a resident of Vernegly, one of the possible home townlands of our Colfers. Peter loved our visit. He knew that we were looking for a Colfer connection for our families, so he punctuated his comments every few minutes with the question, *"So is what I'm telling you any help to you?"*

Peter recalled for us with great clarity his memories of two uncles of his, Michael and James. However, I suspect that neither of these two Irishmen are our Michael and James. First of all, Peter was very clear that Michael *"was a great dancer,"* so that ruled out any Colfer/Colford I know, and James, he said, never left Ireland for the States. Besides, these two brothers would have been much younger than our Michael and James, although their namesakes from an earlier generation certainly could have been a match. First names always persist through generations as per traditional Irish naming practices.

Our visit with Peter really was heartwarming. He was a very classy, tweed-jacketed, engaging gentleman, and when Joanna offered to take our picture, he took hold of my hand and Fran's and smiled proudly for the camera.

However, as I sit here several years after our visit putting the finishing touches on our story and looking over old notes and new leads, I have reason to believe that this Peter may have been Dad's second cousin. Their grandfathers, Patrick and Michael, could have been brothers, thus the connection. The 1901 census of Ireland places a Patrick Colfer, whose age (68) is almost an exact match with the date of birth for the Patrick of the Rathangan records I discussed earlier, with his wife Mary (60) and 26-year-old son, Peter. Mary was deceased by the 1911 census. These family members also were long-standing residents of Vernegly. The Peter (born 1914) whom we visited could indeed have been Patrick and Mary's grandson, but since definitive proof is hard to come by, considering the state of affairs of Irish genealogical records, this evidence-based suggestion may have to suffice as proof. Joanna's father, Noel, also would be a third cousin to us.

Another of our other Johanna-lead visits that day was to Sinnott's Pub in Duncormick, one of the 13 oldest pubs in all of Ireland. John Sinnott, the publican, is a local historian of sorts and is a friend to all the locals, including Joanna. Our visit to the pub at 10:00 that morning might have made the three gentlemen sitting at the bar sipping bottled Guinness a bit nervous, since Joanna was a *garda*, and the law prohibits pubs from opening their doors until noon. Nevertheless, Joanna turned a benevolent blind eye to these early imbibers.

Our other visits were to St. Mary's Church in Rathangan where our Colfers were baptized and to Colfer's Pub which, unfortunately, was not yet open that day for a pint.

The Dunn – Harvey – Colford Connection

The following section of our story traces four generations of the families of our grandmother,

Margaret Elizabeth (aka: *Agnes*) Colford:

John and Mary (Murphy) Dunn
(Our great-great-grandparents)

.
.
.
.
.

Michael Dunn
(Our great-grandfather)

James and Margaret (Hagan) Harvey
(Our great-great-grandparents)

.
.
.
.
.

Margaret Harvey
(Our great-grandmother)

Michael and Margaret (Harvey) Dunn
(Our great-grandparents)

.
.
.

Margaret Elizabeth (aka: Agnes) Dunn
(Our grandmother)

Joseph and Agnes (Dunn) Colford
(Our grandparents)

Chapter X

Grandma Agnes (Dunn) Colford and Her Family

T he major cause of my delay in completing our story has been my extended search for Grandma Colford's family. The biggest missing piece of all is the death certificate for her mother, our great-grandmother, Margaret (Harvey) Dunn. This record would have yielded helpful information about her family and would have filled in several blanks which continue to haunt our story. However, despite searching through dozens and dozens of death certificates in the New York City Archives for a Margaret Dunn, including those with multiple variations in the spelling of both her first and last names, I have been unsuccessful in locating it. I even scoured the archives for the name *Elizabeth/Lizzie* Dunn, since that name appeared on Grandma Colford's birth certificate for some reason; Elizabeth was her middle name. Parish records are of no use in looking for the dates of one's funeral or death. The death of a Catholic was not considered one of the seven sacraments, so there was no obligation for the parish registers to record them in the same way they recorded baptisms and marriages. It would appear that St. Anthony of Padua, the home parish for our Dunns and Harveys, only began recording funerals and deaths in 1925, long after our great-grandparents had passed away.

Two other genealogical researchers whom I have met at the Archives, Randi Koenig and Jim Murray, also have tried in vain to help me find Margaret's record. One possibility is that her surname on the death certificate had been recorded incorrectly with no resemblance to her real name, thus the near impossibility of ever finding it. Another possible, but not likely, explanation is that the certificate has been lost or destroyed. All I know is that a death certificate had to have existed at one point, since a body cannot be interred without one.

I thought at first that her missing certificate from the city's municipal archives might mean that she simply died in a location outside the five boroughs of New York City. However, I have been able to confirm that she did *not* die in any other location in the state of New York, nor in New Jersey nor Pennsylvania; none of those locations have any death record for a Margaret Dunn who died around her time (late November, 1910). Without having any suggestions as to where her place of death might have been, finding it might be a real long shot.

Information regarding the 23 years between her death (1910) and that of her husband's (1887) also is sorely lacking. All I have in her story are speculations about those years. Margaret's story was a sad one, but I am afraid that we will never know what became of her in her last days. I have been able to uncover the tales of most of her family members, but hers is little more than a cliffhanger at this time.

What also don't help are the family secrets which have kept the truth from us all, particularly the long-told fictional tale of how both of Grandma's parents had died by 1900 when she, Aunt Molly, and their brother Jack all had to fend for themselves and find other living arrangements.

Yet another genealogical dead-end involves finding the townland of origin of our great-grandfather, Michael Dunn. Although Grandma Colford and our Aunt Molly always have said that their parents were the Dunns from county Clare, it has been difficult to prove such a connection. There is reason to believe that either Cork or Roscommon might have been the one.

Nevertheless, the Dunn story which I have been able to piece together is based upon many other records, and it allows for some careful evidence-based speculation regarding most of Grandma's family and perhaps, only perhaps, her mother's demise.

So please read on.

Chapter XI

Grandma Colford's Paternal Grandparents

Our Great-Great Grandparents
John and Mary (Murphy) Dunn

Aunt Molly always claimed that the Dunns were from county Clare, but it is difficult to believe that such was the case. It may be more likely, but not necessarily verifiable, that they were from Cork after leaving Roscommon.

The death certificates for our great-grandfather Michael Dunn and his brother, our great-great-uncle John, recorded the names of their parents as John and Mary (Murphy) Dunn. There is little known about them, however. All I know is that the surname *Murphy* has been the most common name in all of Ireland for the last 100 years, so it is hard to track down our family without a lot more specific identifying information. Griffith's Valuation listed 221 Murphy families in Clare in 1855, but there were only eight Dunns/Dunnes listed there. However, county Cork at that same time included many more Dunn/Dunne families, 364 in all, and over 3,000 Murphys, the most populous name in the county, making it far more likely that Cork was the county from which our Dunns emigrated. There also are many more Dunn/Dunne baptisms and marriages found in Cork parish registers than in Clare's.

I also asked Aunt Molly's daughter, Marie Kelly, of her recall of the Dunn origins. She couldn't remember exactly, but she told me that it *"was a very short name."* So perhaps it indeed was Cork, the shortest name of all Ireland's counties?

Another third cousin of ours whom I came across just recently, Marianne (Dunn) Sciuto of North Haven, CT, told me that her father and grandfather were always very clear that only the Murphy side of our family was from Cork, whereas the Dunns/Dunnes were originally from county Roscommon before relocating to another county somewhere in the midlands. We and Marianne have great-grandfathers who were brothers: ours is Michael Dunn, hers, his older brother John.

Our cousin Marianne found out from a DNA analysis going back four generations that there was a match with our common Murphy ancestors who all were families of miners from Cork. The Beara Peninsula, located at the most southwestern part of the county just below the Kerry and Dingle Peninsulas, was a thriving copper mining area from approximately 1812, when the first of six mines opened, through 1885. The Allihies Mines Company, the largest supplier of copper ore in the world at the time, saw to the operation which, at its peak around 1860, was an employer of as many as 1,600 miners. Villages sprang up throughout the peninsula to accommodate the growing numbers of employees and their families, along with a Roman Catholic Church and a Protestant Chapel. Even the privations of the famine did little to curtail production, since the Allihies Company provided extra food and other provisions to keep the work force well fed and production uninterrupted.

Without any other confirming information, it might not be out of the realm of possibility to speculate that our John Dunn, whether from Roscommon or not, might have traveled from his home county and made his way to Cork's Beara Peninsula for a job there in one of its copper mines. There, perhaps, he met and married our Mary Murphy whose family had been established as a family of miners for some time, thus the beginning of the story that our Dunns may have originated from Cork.

As copper production began to subside, thousands of Irish miners eventually emigrated and made their way to the States to Butte, MT, for guaranteed employment with the Anaconda Copper Mining Company. In fact, job opportunities there were well known throughout Beara. There was a popular expression in the area: *"Don't stop in America, go straight to Butte!"* The number of Irish folk in Butte by 1900 was 12,000, including 77 families of Sullivans who left their village of Castletownbere on the Beara Peninsula for work in the mines.

It is quite likely that some of these Butte transplants were from the Murphy clan as well, so I did a quick scan in the federal census of 1880 for the name Murphy in Butte and found hundreds of them, almost all of them declaring their country of origin as Ireland and their occupations as miners.

Distant relatives of ours, perhaps?

There are some who claim that Butte is the most Irish town in America, with 23.6% of its population declaring Irish heritage compared to only 19.8% in Irish Boston.

Wherever and whenever our great-great-grandparents, John and Mary (Murphy) Dunn, may have met and married may not be known, but they were to go on to have at least four children whom I can verify, since they all left Ireland for the States and settled in New York City. If there were other children who remained in Ireland, I would not know anything about them. These are the ones I know:

> John (1846 – September 13, 1909)
> **Michael (our great-grandfather; 1851 – October 5, 1887)**
> Rachel (1854 - ?)
> Hannah (1856 – October 13, 1938)

It is safe to assume that there were other children, perhaps two or three more, born between John and Michael, since it is highly unlikely that there would be a five-year gap between the two without other births during that time span.

The Dunns came to the Greenwich Village section of Manhattan immediately after their arrival, the section of the city that was a mecca for incoming folk from abroad. By 1875, approximately one third of the Villagers were foreign-born, predominantly Irish, Italian, and German. All that was needed was for one Dunn to let others back home know that the Village was the place to go. Or could its close proximity to Castle Garden have made it a destination of mere convenience?

John, our great-great-uncle, may have been the first Dunn to have come through Castle Garden. He told the census-taker in 1900 that he arrived on our shores in 1870, but I have not been able to confirm this date with any other supporting documentation. On the other hand, his death certificate in 1909 claimed that he had been in the States for *"43 years,"* placing him here for the first time in 1866. As I have mentioned earlier, these recalled dates of births and years of arrival often vary, family member to family member, and year-to-year   Could John have been accompanied to the States by his younger brother Michael, our great-grandfather? My searching through hundreds of ships' manifests over the years did not turn up any *"smoking gun"* which contained the names of both Dunn brothers, if indeed these records had survived the fire that destroyed many of the Castle Garden records.

One glaring possibility for us is that the Michael Dunn (17) who arrived on October 7, 1873, aboard the *Adriatic* along with a Johanna (20) and a Kate Dunn (24) is our Michael. Just several entries below Michael's name on the same manifest were a John (22) and Julia (21) Dunn and Ellen, a one-year-old. Manifests at that time offered no other information other than the travelers' names, ages, and general occupations, so it is unclear whether this Ellen is the daughter of John and Julia, or if John and Julia were indeed married, but who really knows for sure?

There also were several Michael Dunns matching our Michael's age living in the Greenwich Village section of New York in 1870; one, a 22-year-old, was working as a *"clerk (grocery)"* and living on Carmine St. in the Village. However, he was not our Michael, since his mother's name (Ann) with whom he was living did not match our great-great grandmother's name (Mary). This same 1870 census did list another Michael Dunn who *could* be ours; he was a 19-year-old *"laborer"* living in lower Manhattan in the home of William and Jane Kearney, their two children, and two other roomers, Catherine O'Rourke and Johanna Ryan, both *"domestics."* The surname *Kearney* was a common one in Ireland, so it is possible that someone from back home referred Michael to the Kearney household for some temporary lodging. The 1880 census placed another same-age Michael Dunn, a *"porter in store,"* living in Manhattan, although his address was not included in the list of residents.

To complicate matters even more, Michael's 1887 death certificate claimed that he had been in the States for eight years, putting his arrival sometime around 1879. However, there were at least three other Michael Dunns who arrived at Castle Garden between 1878 and 1881, proving yet again how difficult it is to track down such a common name without other corroborating information.

Whichever one of these is our Michael is open to little more than pure speculation.

I also suspect that there was an older brother who settled in the same Greenwich Village area as his siblings. This brother, I believe, had a son William (*"police officer"*) who married a Mary (aka: *Minnie*) O'Keefe and fathered at least two children. William probably was the nephew who was a next-door neighbor to his Uncle John and his family in 1900; William was at 34 Clarkson St., John at 36 Clarkson. I have lost track of William after that date.

Chapter XII

Grandma Colford's Maternal Grandparents

Our Great-Great Grandparents
James and Margaret (Hagan) Harvey

The sleepy farming community of Blackwatertown, a place the Irish government designated a *"small village,"* sits alongside the River Blackwater in the civil parish of Clonfeacle, county Armagh, Northern Ireland. It lies within the townland of Lisbofin, much like the village of Coolaney lies within the townland of Shancough in county Sligo. Its location to a convenient waterway facilitated an active trade in the export of corn and potatoes and in the import of coal, timber, and other goods. An 1837 description of the village placed its population at 528 inhabitants living in a total of 103 houses. One can only imagine that the business of one family was well known to the next and that many a marriage took place among the residents of this small, close-knit community of farmers.

Occupying two of the homes in the village were the Harvey and the Hagan/O'Hagan families, most of whose members were listed as *"agricultural laborers"* in later censuses. Edward and Elizabeth Harvey's son, James, and James and Maryanne Hagan/O'Hagan's daughter, Margaret, would go on to become Grandma's maternal grandparents and our great-great grandparents.

James Harvey and Margaret Hagan/O'Hagan were married on Tuesday morning, May 7, 1844, in County Armagh's St. Jarlath's Church. Despite the preponderance of Protestantism in the north of Ireland, Blackwatertown was heavily Roman Catholic; years later, the census of 1911 reported that

95% of its population declared to be so. Perhaps its Catholic majority was the primary reason why, on February 29, 1976, the Ulster Volunteer Force (UVF), a largely Protestant paramilitary group active during *"The Troubles,"* the period of sectarian violence between Irish Protestants and Catholics, exploded a bomb at St. Jarlath's one Sunday morning during Mass, injuring several parishioners.

Our great-great-grandparents, James and Margaret, were to have 10 children; our great-grandmother Margaret was the seventh born. Their children, six boys and four girls, all were baptized the day they were born; the high infant mortality rate made a delay in the sacrament a risky practice indeed. Their dates of birth include the following:

> Edward (April 27, 1845; an *"algriculture labourer"* stayed in Armagh; he
>   and his wife, Bridget, had three children)
> Mary Ann (October 28, 1847; stayed behind and married John Donnelly
>   and had five children)
> James (September 28, 1850; stayed behind)
> Peter (February 24, 1853; was a Greenwich Village resident by 1872)
> Elisabeth (July 29, 1855; stayed behind and married Peter Fields, a *"baker,"* and had five
>   children)
> John (January 1, 1858; was a Greenwich Village resident by 1880)
> **Margaret (April 25, 1860; our great-grandmother; was a Greenwich**
>   **Village resident by 1881)**
> Thomas (April 5, 1863; arrived in Greenwich Village on October 2, 1882)
> Patrick (August 17, 1865; stayed behind and moved to Glasgow, Scotland)
> Sara Jane (February 25, 1868; was a Greenwich Village resident by 1880)

Peter apparently led the way to the States by 1872. Siblings Margaret, John, Thomas, and Sara Jane also made their way here by 1885. When great-grandmother Margaret arrived on our shores is not known, but it is a safe bet that she emigrated from Ireland after the deaths of her parents. Father James passed away on November 22, 1868, and mother Margaret followed eight years later on February 7, 1876.

Finding our Margaret on a ship's manifest has been a challenge, but a real possibility places a Margaret Harvey arriving aboard the ship *Arizona* on October 25, 1881; also on board with her were two other

Harvey women, Eliza (22) and Elizabeth, a 50-year-old *"spinster."* Although her sister, Elizabeth, stayed behind and married Peter Fields, these other Harvey women who came with Margaret could easily have been relatives from the Blackwatertown area. The timeline of another Margaret Harvey who arrived aboard the *Celtic* on March 13, 1880, also makes her a possible connection to us.

Chapter XIII

Our Great-Grandparents

Michael and Margaret (Harvey) Dunn and Their Children

Although it was very typical for Irish immigrant folk to marry spouses from home whom they knew there, I have realized that the first encounter between our great grandparents, Michael Dunn and Margaret Harvey, may not have been in the old sod at all, but rather right here in New York City. However, without knowing the precise area in Ireland where the Dunns were from, I don't know whether or not there had been previous contact between the Dunn and Harvey families back home.

A possibility is that they first may have met at Greenwich Village's 50 King St. Occupying one of the five basement apartments at that address at the time of the 1880 census were Michael's brother, John (35), his wife Annie (Leonard; 28), their two children, Mary (2) and John (four months), and two Dunn sisters, Hannah (25) and Rachel (27). Great-grandfather Michael was either living on his own nearby or was simply left off the census list due to some clerical error.

In another basement apartment at 50 King lived Margaret's brother, Peter Harvey (27), his wife Mary (Daly; 28), their daughter Jennie (11 months), and his siblings Sarah (12) and John (20). The Norton, Burns, and Lilly families resided in the other three basement apartments. Peter would go on to become a naturalized citizen on November 11, 1880, just a few months after the census taker's June visit to his apartment. This date suggests that he was in the States for at least three to five years before gaining his citizenship.

The average size for a tenement apartment was 350 square feet, and it consisted of one bedroom, a kitchen/cooking area, and a sitting room. A total of 23 people occupied these five cramped basement apartments at 50 King. Margaret's conspicuous absence from this living arrangement suggests to me that she wasn't there until 1881, a year before marrying Michael and just after the 1880 census was taken. It was only upon her arrival here when she may have met her future husband while visiting, or actually living with, her brother Peter.

Perhaps the Margaret Harvey listed in the 1880 census as an 18-year-old *"domestic servant"* in the 76 Bank St. home of Joseph and Sarah Godwin and their four children was our Margaret? Maybe the crowded conditions at her brother Peter's small 50 King St. apartment left her with no room at the inn?

Speculation again, but the fact is that the sheer number of Harveys who emigrated from Ireland to the States makes for a sizable haystack in which to find Margaret's needle.

The only entrance to their 50 King St. residence, considered a *tenement* by the city, was through a basement door in the rear of the building. Birth records and census records always mentioned *"rear"* or *"basement of rear house"* as a means of access to their living quarters. It is interesting to note that this residence today is no longer the four-story tenement where the Dunns resided. In its place now is a 10-story co-op consisting of 57 apartments, with the price of a one bedroom, one bath apartment going for $650,000. The original building once had been designated a *Historic American Building* by the Historic American Building Survey, so I am unsure whether the current 50 King was built around and atop the original one or if it replaced it completely.

Different Dunn and Harvey family members never moved more than two blocks from each other in the Greenwich Village section of New York City over the years; King St., Carmine St., Clarkson St., and Leroy St. were the locations where most Dunns and Harveys could be found. The families also served as godparents for each other's children and as witnesses to their marriages.

It was on a Sunday afternoon, February 19, 1882, when Reverend Leonardus married our great-grandparents, Michael Dunn and Margaret Harvey, in the Church of St. Anthony of Padua on Sullivan St. in the Village; witnesses to the marriage were Margaret's brother, John Harvey, and Michael's sister, Hannorah (Hannah) Dunn. At the time of their wedding, Michael was employed as a *"laborer on steamer docks,"* according to the 1882 NYC Directory. The newlyweds were to join the rest of the crowd at 50 King St. after they married. This same address also was the place where Grandma Colford and her two older siblings, John (aka: *Jack*) and Mary (aka: *Aunt Molly*), would be born between 1882 and 1887.

Michael, like countless other uneducated Irish immigrants, was illiterate, had no special skills, and worked as a day laborer; employment was probably catch-as-catch-can wherein there were as many days without jobs as there were with them. As a *"laborer"* working the docks for several years, he undoubtedly worked the *"shape up"* system of employment, the practice of showing up each morning hoping that that day was the one when the dock foreman might pick him for a job.

The International Longshoreman's Association (ILA) itself declared the shape-up system of employment to be a

> *"cruel, graft-ridden and senseless system of hiring . . . Thousands of*
> *men seeking employment were forced to hang around the piers at all*
> *hours, exposed to every kind of weather. Often, hundreds would report*
> *at a single pier at dawn, stand around for hours, only to be told, 'No*
> *work today,' long after there was any chance of obtaining work elsewhere."*

Such was the life of many an Irish immigrant like our great-grandfather. Income was slim, yet families had nothing else to rely on for sustenance.

Michael and Margaret, 50 King St. residents throughout their marriage, were to have three children during their five short years together:

> John (aka: Jack; December 3, 1882 – February 9, 1945)
> Mary (aka: Aunt Molly; March 17, 1885 – June 23, 1981)
> **Margaret Elizabeth (Agnes; Jan. 23, 1887 – May 22, 1967; our Grandma)**

Michael was only 36 years of age when he entered New York Hospital on Thursday, September 29, 1887. He passed away just six days later on Wednesday, October 5th, due to what Dr. Merriman, the medical examiner, claimed was *"typhoid fever."* His death certificate listed his occupation as "*longshore*" and his length of residence in the States as "*8 years.*" The names of his parents, "*John and Mary Dunn*," also match the names on his brother John's death certificate.

Margaret now found herself the widowed mother of three young children: Jack, the oldest, was not yet five years of age, Molly was only 2 ½ years old, and Grandma, the baby, was barely eight months.

So Grandma never knew her father.

Margaret purchased a Calvary Cemetery plot two days after her husband's death and had him interred there that same day (*Section: 15, Range: 41, Plot: Q, Grave: 9*). Margaret herself would be the next one laid to rest there on December 1, 1910; three other family members would follow: her sister-in-law, Hannah (Dunn) Norris on October 15, 1938; her son, Jack, on February 13, 1945; and her daughter-in-law, Gertrude (McWilliams) Dunn, on January 23, 1987, a full 100 years after the plot's purchase.

If you were Irish and Catholic, chances are that you were going to be interred in Calvary. The cemetery had its first burial on July 31, 1848, just three years after the Board of Trustees of St. Patrick's Cathedral purchased 71 acres of land in Woodside, Queens, to open another cemetery after realizing that the original one on Mulberry St. was almost full. By 1852, there were 50 burials per day, half of them poor Irish under seven years of age; by 1907, the cemetery was home to 850,000 folk. It currently holds over three million interments and is considered the largest cemetery in the United States.

Family lore has always had it that both of our great-grandparents had passed away by 1900; this was true for our Michael, but not for our great-grandmother, Margaret, who outlived him by 23 years.

What became of Margaret and her three children after Michael's death is part of the missing piece to our story.

The richest source of information regarding the fate of the Dunn children has come from the combined storytelling of two sisters, 86-year-old Rosemarie Paganelli of Williston Park, NY, and 89-year-old Eileen Kantzler of Bloomington, IL, nieces of Grandma's brother Jack's wife, Gertrude (McWilliams) Dunn; both sisters were very close to Jack and Gertrude. Through a series of serendipitous circumstances, I first came across Rosemarie's name on Gertrude's 1987 death certificate; she was listed as the "*informant.*" A gentleman by the name of Bob Furtaw whose name I found via the website, *Find a Grave*, sent me a copy of the certificate. Bob had been looking into a possible connection he might have had with Gertrude, so he left his name and contact information on the Calvary Cemetery page of the website. After we exchanged several emails, I received this certificate and other documents from Bob.

I was lucky to have been able to find Rosemarie alive and well. After a very heartwarming and informative telephone conversation with this very charming and energetic woman, she directed me to her sister Eileen whom I also called. Like her younger sister, Eileen also was quite a fount of information about Jack and Gertrude; both women were more than happy to share whatever stories they had.

When I asked Rosemarie and Eileen of any comments our great-uncle Jack might have made about his childhood or his parents, they both claimed that neither Jack nor Gertrude spoke of such things. The observant Rosemarie told me that Jack never talked about his family; "*I always thought that there was a problem there,*" she said. Both sisters agreed, however, that Jack only spoke of his Aunt Hannah (Dunn); Jack "*always said she raised him . . . Jack was brought up by her.*" Eileen was particularly strident in telling me that he "*never mentioned his mother or his father; the only one he ever mentioned was his Aunt Hannah . . . he loved his Aunt Hannah!*"

Aunt Hannah, Michael's sister, also was a long-term resident of one of the basement apartments at 50 King. It would appear that she was instrumental in stepping into the role of caregiver as soon as her brother died. Hannah was to remain single until sometime around 1895 when, at the age of 37, she married a gentleman whose last name was Norris; it would appear that they may have relocated to Brooklyn. However, I have not been able to locate a marriage certificate for them in any of the five boroughs of New York.

Perhaps she was around and available to shoulder the bulk of the child care for Jack, Molly, and Grandma only until she wed? Did she did so as an assistant of sorts to Margaret, or was Margaret completely out of the picture for some reason?

Family secrets?

This may be little more than coincidence, but beginning with the 1887-88 New York City Directory, I found a Margaret Dunn, "wid(ow)-Michael" living at 506 First Ave. in Manhattan with yet another Margaret Dunn, this one a "wid-Edward." If the former Margaret is ours, then it meant that she would have vacated 50 King soon after Michael's death. She was at this same address until at least 1891, after which she *may* be the Margaret (*wid-Michael*) who relocated to 204 West 105th St. by 1894.

The city directories from 1905 to 1910 now had two Margarets, both "*wid – Michael*," living at 181 West 97th St. and 340 East 137th St. in Manhattan. There also were many, many other Margaret Dunns living in the five boroughs of New York City, but without any other supportive data to help us choose which one of them is ours, there is no way to know for sure.

Could she have been the Margaret *Dunne* working as an "*employee – assistant matron*" at the *New York Juvenile Asylum* in 1900? Or the Margaret Dunn in 1905 through 1910 working as a "*servant*" in the home of Daniel and Ellen Kelly at 416 Clinton St. in Brooklyn? Or the one who was an "*inmate*" in Manhattan's *Home for the Aged of the Little Sisters of the Poor in 1910*? These possibilities and many others are all open to pure guesswork as to where she might have been between 1887, the year of Michael's death, and her own demise 23 years later.

It is not unreasonable to think that Margaret may have had to go to work after Michael died, perhaps in a domestic servant position of sorts that included room and board, while Hannah cared for her three children.

When I found her interment date of December 1, 1910, just recently, I thought that, for sure, her death certificate would be right around the proverbial corner. However, it has remained as elusive as ever. As far as I know, as I mentioned earlier, she did not die in New York City nor State, nor in Pennsylvania nor New Jersey, since none of these locations have any death records for her.

What has me stymied ever since I found our Michael's true death certificate this past November, 2015, was what to make of my discovery years ago of another Michael Dunn/Margaret Harvey couple who, I thought for some time, were our kin. This other Michael died an alcoholic in the drunk tank of the poor people's hospital, Charity Hospital, on Blackwell's Island, in 1903. The hospital was able to accommodate 1,200 patients at one time among its 29 separate wards.

Is it likely that our Margaret Harvey would have married again to yet another man by the name of Michael Dunn? Far-fetched, to say the least, but worth noting here in our story. Besides, there were a number of other Margaret Harveys living in the five boroughs of New York, making it more likely that one of them was indeed the wife of, then the widow of, this other Michael Dunn. I have included their tale, *The Other Michael Dunn and Margaret Harvey,* later in the *Footnotes* section of our story.

Sometime prior to 1900 after their parents were out of the picture, 15-year-old Aunt Molly and her siblings *apparently* became residents in the household of their Uncle John and Aunt Anne (Leonard) Dunn at 36 Clarkson St. The census record of 1900 clearly lists Molly as a resident there. She was no longer in school and was working as a *"candy maker,"* so her presence in the household actually brought in some income.

John and Annie's household must have been a busy place. In addition to their five sons, another niece (Catherine Ryan), and three *"roomers,"* John Donovan, John Roberts, and James Reilly, also were living with them. Niece Catherine was the daughter of Annie's sister, Bridget, and her husband, William Ryan. Annie's unmarried sister Mary also had been in residence with the Dunns until her death from pneumonia on December 10, 1897. Add to these residents Jack, Molly, and (perhaps) Grandma, and one can only imagine how busy they all kept homemaker Annie.

I have found no record of Jack having been taken in by an extended family member after his parents were no longer around, despite his assertions that his Aunt Hannah was his primary caregiver. However, Laura Kelly, Aunt Molly's great-granddaughter, told me that Molly was always very clear that Jack went with her to live with Michael's brother John and his wife Annie at 36 Clarkson, but perhaps only after Aunt Hannah's marriage around 1895.

Laura also told me that Molly spoke about her brother Jack quite a bit, but she never really talked about our grandma Agnes being in that home. Molly's daughter, Marie Kelly, always *assumed* that Grandma was with her siblings in their Uncle John's home, but she was never completely certain of it.

What has been the most frustrating part of this story has been not knowing much at all about Grandma's childhood. Molly's personal papers, photos, and related family memorabilia apparently were discarded after her passing, another lost opportunity for completing our story. There also are no such records handed down to us by Grandma or Grandpa.

Could Grandma indeed have been with her siblings Molly and Jack in their Uncle John's household in 1900 with her name excluded from that census due to some census taker's error? Given the closeness of the Dunns and Harveys, one could assume that Uncle John and Aunt Annie never would have split up the family, making it likely that Grandma was with them.

Other circumstantial evidence that supports the uncle John Dunn/Grandma connection came from Grandma's maid of honor, Irene Corbally (aka: *Rene Kuhn* after her marriage to Bert Kuhn), who shared fond memories about Grandma with Paul years ago. He interviewed her while he was working as a journalist for Newsday. Rene was to go onto a distinguished career as a world-renown journalist, broadcaster, war correspondent, author of multiple books, columns, articles, and as host of her own New York area radio program. Her professional exploits are chronicled in Julia Edwards' text, *Women of the World: The Great Foreign Correspondents.*

Her stories suggest to me that Grandma probably was a resident of 36 Clarkson and then 119 Leroy, a home their uncle John purchased soon after the 1900 census was taken, along with Molly and the rest of the Dunns. It would appear from her recollections that the friendship she forged with Grandma came from the considerable amount of time she spent with her in the Leroy St. neighborhood where she was the Dunns' next-door neighbor. She and Rene would have been able to interact very frequently over the years in their common stomping grounds. Rene was Ed and Molly (Dunn) Connor's niece, the daughter of Ed's sister, Josephine. (More on their story later.)

The trajectories of the lives of these two women could not have been more different: Grandma, eventually to be settled in the life of tranquil domesticity, and Rene, established in the international sphere as a world traveler and professional journalist. However, Grandma was almost 12 years older than Rene, so it would appear that her relationship was undoubtedly more of a caregiving one, such as babysitter or nanny of sorts.

Rene Kuhn's records are held in the University of Wyoming. These records include her career papers, articles, books, audio recordings, and photographs, both personal and professional. Amanda Stow, the assistant archivist at the University whom I contacted, exchanged several emails with me regarding my request for articles and photos of Rene's which might be a "smoking gun" to prove her relationship with Grandma. Although Amanda sent me a sweet article written by Rene, *Christmas in Those Days*, which appeared in Gourmet Magazine in 1986 and which chronicled her childhood years with her Connor relatives, it did not mention Grandma by name. Amanda's search through a folder of Rene's photos from 1900-1925 also did not yield any personal ones from Leroy St., which, I hoped, might have pictured Grandma as well. These photos only were those taken of Rene abroad on some of her inter-continental travels. (Read more about Rene in the *Footnotes* section later in our story.)

Please read on for more information about the later years of our great-uncle Jack, our great-aunt Molly, and Grandma.

John. John Francis Dunne, known as *Jack* to his family, was the first of the Dunn children to be born in the *"basement of rear house"* at 50 King St. Reverend Camillus of St. Anthony of Padua baptized him one week after his December 3, 1882, birth. Sponsors/godparents were John Harvey, Margaret's brother, and Annie Dunn, Michael's sister-in-law. Curiously, though, his birth certificate was the only one of the three Dunn children which recorded his surname ending with the letter "e." All other records, birth and otherwise for all family members, spelled it without the "e."

In a letter Marie Kelly wrote to Paul years ago regarding his queries into our family history, she described her Uncle Jack as *"a special favorite of mine"* whose *"stories he would tell us of what happened in the household were really hilarious."* One of these stories which Marie told me during one of my telephone conversations with her had Jack taking into the household a homeless young boy, unbeknownst to his Uncle John or Aunt Annie. His aunt first became aware of this new visitor when she went to wake Jack one morning, only to have this newcomer emerge from under the covers as well!

Later records consistently describe Grandma's brother Jack as a plumber. In fact, he became very active in the local plumbers' union, trekking off every Wednesday night to its meetings. He must have learned the profession along with three of his cousins; his Uncle John's sons, James, Frank, and Joseph, all became plumbers. James apparently rose to the rank of *"master plumber."*

Jack's October 2, 1914, passport application listed the address for the 32-year-old as 38 Morton St. in Greenwich Village and his occupation listed surprisingly as *"salesman."* The destination for his trip was not included on the application, but he did declare, *"I intend to return to the United States within one year with the purpose of residing and performing the duties of citizenship therein."* Attesting to the facts of the application was his friend Samuel Brownwine, the son of Russian immigrants, who had known Jack *"personally for ten years."* The *"DESCRIPTION OF APPLICANT"* on the form placed Jack at *"5 feet, 8 inches"* with a *"pointed"* nose, *"grey"* eyes, a *"small"* mouth, *"chestnut"* hair, and a *"round"* face. The description of his chin, however, was illegible on the application.

I dare say that John's trip was a visit to Ireland, either to take care of some family business there or simply to visit Dunn or Harvey relatives.

Four years later he was residing with his cousin James and his wife Emma (Jacob) and their two daughters, Veronica (6) and Helen (5), at 2551 Hughes St. in Ridgewood, Queens, according to Jack's World War I draft registration card. The 1920 census still had 37-year-old Jack living with his cousin's family, this time at 2537 Hughes St.; by now James and Emma had added a six-month-old son, James Jr., to the mix.

The first indication I found of Jack's marriage to his Boston-born wife, Gertrude (McWilliams), was in the 1925 New York City Directory which had the couple living in a four-family apartment house at 1915 Cornelia St. in Ridgewood, Queens; their marriage was Gertrude's second. There is no New York City record of their marriage, so one might assume that they wed somewhere in the Boston area. The circumstances regarding their first encounter are unclear, but they probably first met somewhere in the Bronx or Brooklyn.

The 1900 census placed Gertrude (10) with her brother George (5) at 61 Jefferson St. in Perth Amboy along with their mother Sarah, stepfather Michael Klimm, and their own daughter, Rose (five months old). By 1910, the family had relocated to 17 Garden St. in Brooklyn, and the Klimms had added two more children, William and Frank, to the household. Twenty-year-old Gertrude, however, was not to be found on that census sheet, either excluded from the ledger by mistake or perhaps simply out on her own by then.

Rosemarie and Eileen, Gertrude's nieces whom I discussed earlier, were very close to Jack and Gertrude; these sisters adored their uncle Jack. Rosemarie described him as "*a great guy – wonderful – nobody like him.*" Eileen echoed the same sentiments, describing him as "*the salt of the earth*" and as "*a very gentle man, a true gentleman.*" She also added that he was "*a very handsome man with a full head of steel-gray hair . . . he had beautiful hands, and he dressed beautifully and loved good clothes.*"

Jack and Gertrude had no children of their own, so they apparently treated Rosemarie and Eileen as if they were their own daughters, taking them on trips which included, among other places, the World's Fair and the Hippodrome in Flushing, NY. Every Sunday the girls also were dinner guests at Jack and Gertrude's place along with their parents, Fred and Rose McAuliffe. (Gertrude and Rose actually were half-sisters; Gertrude was a McWilliams, Rose, a Klimm, their mother's second marriage.)

New Year's Day was their annual visit to Jersey City to visit Jack's siblings, Aunt Molly and Grandma Colford. Dad remembered his Uncle Jack's visits; his recollection was that Grandma was very fond of him. During one of my conversations with Eileen, she started to laugh and said something like, "*Maybe I shouldn't tell you this,*" but my insistence that she share any recollections at all resulted in what she told ne next. Although she maintained that her uncle Jack liked Grandpa Colford, he always said, "*My sister must have been drunk the day she married him!*" Jack considered Grandpa to be a bit on the homely side and very quiet, the latter descriptor a sentiment offered by Rosemarie who also added, "*We used to go there, but from what I could recall, they never wanted too much company.*" She described their visits to Aunt Molly's as being much more fun. Eileen's younger sister also contrasted her visits to Grandma's and Aunt Molly's, claiming, "*But Aunt Molly, we loved going there,*" seemingly feeling more at home there than they did at Grandma and Grandpa's 277 Ege address.

By the 1930 census, Jack and Gertrude had relocated to 60 Hale Ave. in Brooklyn, a two-family home they shared with the McKnight family. Jack (47; "*construction – plumbing*") and his wife (39) paid the homeowner McKnights a monthly rent of $45. They were at 9503 76th St. in Ozone Park, Queens in 1940; they realized a $10 savings in their rent, paying only $35 a month this time to homeowner Fred Werbarg with whom they shared this two-family dwelling. That census described Jack as a "*plumber – building*" and indicated that both he and Gertrude had completed the eighth grade. His 1942 World War II Draft Registration Card listed his place of employment as Port Newark.

A mystery to me is the fact that the information Jack and Gertrude provided for the 1930 census taker indicated that they were married at the ages of 32 and 25, putting their year of marriage at 1915. However, the World War I Draft Registration Card he completed on September 2, 1918, listed his *"Nearest Relative"* as *"James L. Dunn – first cousin,"* not Gertrude. She also was not included with the other family members in the 1920 census. Could their recollections of the year of their marriage have been so inaccurate? Or could there be another reason for the disparity in these years?

By 1945, the 62-year-old Jack and his wife had moved to 1812 Cornelia St. in Ridgewood, Queens. He passed away on February 9th of that year after a month-long hospital stay *("chronic rheumatism and endocarditis – congestive failure, then pneumonia")*. Gertrude attended our folks' wedding three years later and gave a mirror as a gift.

Gertrude outlived Jack by 42 years. After his death, she lived alone for several years in and around Brooklyn in different apartments before moving in with her niece, Eileen, in several places, including Kansas and Illinois; Eileen's husband was a career Air Force officer, thus their frequent changes in locales. Gertrude, who *"could be difficult,"* according to Rosemarie, eventually returned to New York where she chose employment as a caregiver for children in a shelter.

This 97-year-old daughter of Benjamin and Sarah (Woodcock) McWilliams passed away on January 20, 1987, while a patient in Flushing Hospital in Queens, New York. She had been in an assisted living facility for a few years before her death. Mom doesn't recall Grandma ever speaking of her, so it would appear that she lost contact with her sister-in-law not long after our folks' wedding.

I also have been able to track down a third cousin of ours, Richard Boehm and his wife, Matilda, living on Staten Island. Richard is the great-grandson of John and Annie (Leonard) Dunn and the grandson of the aforementioned James Dunn, the cousin with whom our great-uncle Jack lived for a time. I visited with Richard, hoping to hear of some family recollections about the Dunns, specifically our great-grandparents, but Richard had little information besides that of his maternal forebears, Emma Jacob and her kin. His 97-year-old mother Helen who was alive and well and living nearby in a nursing facility at the time of my visit was the five-year-old in the household when our Jack was there in 1920. Helen remembered clearly that Jack was a plumber who suffered some kind of injury while working in the Woolworth Building in New York. The type and extent of his injury, however, were unclear.

What our story is sorely lacking are the recollections of any other living descendants of either our Dunn or our Harvey families who might clarify many of the unanswered questions I have.

Mary. Mary (aka: *Molly*) Dunn was born on St. Patrick's Day in 1885. Her granddaughter, Kathy (Doherty) Honan, told me that St. Patrick's Day was always a double celebration for her and the family. St. Anthony of Padua's Reverend Anacletus baptized her five days later; sponsors were Thomas Harvey, Margaret's brother, and Mary Ann O'Hagan, undoubtedly a first cousin of Margaret's from Blackwatertown. Mary/Molly's middle name in subsequent records, probably chosen at her confirmation, was *Celestine*. Like brother Jack, Mary also was born at 50 King St.

As I mentioned in an earlier section, Molly clearly was in residence in her Uncle John's household by 1900, first at 36 Clarkson St., and then at 119 Leroy St. Next door to Molly and the Dunns at their new location was the Connor family at 117 Leroy. Michael and Johanna (Quinan) Connor were both Irish-born; Michael, president of his own cooperage company, *M. Connor & Sons*, on West Houston St. in Manhattan, emigrated from Ireland in 1855. Their previous addresses were 56 Clarkson St. and 331 West Houston St. Residing with the couple were their children: Margaret, Mary, Thomas, Francis, Edward, and Clarence. The three oldest sons eventually joined their father in his cooperage business, and Clarence, the youngest, was to go to medical school and earn his degree.

The Connors' married daughter Josephine, her husband Patrick Corbally, and their daughter, Irene (2), also were in residence at 117 Leroy. Irene would become close to Grandma and would serve as her maid of honor.

Ed Connor (23) and 19-year-old Molly met as neighbors, eloped, according to family lore, and were married by Reverend Spellman on September 8, 1904, at St. Joseph's Church in Manhattan. However, one might think that being married by a Catholic priest in a Catholic Church flies in the face of an elopement. Perhaps it was more of a planned marriage than an elopement? Or more likely, the marriage took place quickly in the church rectory as a private ceremony, a not uncommon practice at the time.

Witnesses to their marriage were Grandma Colford and Clarence Connor. The newlyweds moved into an apartment at 120 Leroy just across the street from the Connor family soon after their marriage. They then were approximately two years at 109 Leroy before relocating to Jersey City by 1909, first to 209 Virginia Ave and then to 172 Lexington Ave. where they remained for several years. Ed commuted to his employment at his father's cooperage business.

By 1910, Johanna Connor had died, as had Patrick Corbally (a *"liquor dealer"* whose cause of death was *"cirrhosis of liver – nephritis uremia"*); his death at home on March 24, 1910, came just one month before the census taker's visit. Still at 117 Leroy that year were Michael Connor and his single children: Margaret, Mary, Francis, and Clarence, in addition to his widowed daughter, Josephine Corbally, and her children, Irene (12) and Clarence (6).

Ed, a *"manufacturer of cooperage,"* disclosed on his World War I Draft Registration card on September 12, 1918, that he had *"one defective eye (left),"* and it was just two weeks later on September 30 when Edward *Leo* Connor completed his passport application for a trip that would keep him abroad for approximately seven months. Now the 38-year-old, five foot, six- inch *"cooperage dealer"* would be on his way to France and Great Britain along with several of his Knights of Columbus colleagues as members of the K of C's Committee on War Activities' Overseas Department. The purpose of the trip was *"to do the same work abroad that we are now doing in the camps and cantonments of this country,"* apparently a good will trip designed to provide some support for the allied troops serving in the war. Ed would return home aboard the *SS Espagne* on March 13, 1919; he obviously was not present at Grandma and Grandpa's wedding.

I find it interesting the information required for the passport application: his *"high"* forehead, *"small"* mouth, *"oval"* face, *"Roman"* nose, and his *"scar on lower right forearm."*

Eileen Kanzler thought that Ed *"was very nice, but a little strange,"* and her sister, Rosemarie, described him as a *"beaut . . . however they got together, I'll never know! He never spoke above a whisper."*

Ed and Molly had been married for 16 years before having the first of their three children, Bill; Eileen and Marie were to follow. By 1930, the family cooperage business had failed, and Ed, Molly, and their three children left for West Orange where Ed found work in something having to do with "*magazines.*" The 1940 census then had him listed as a "*broker – real estate*" after Grandpa Colford came to his rescue and gave him a job in his realty company. Ed apparently tried out other jobs before finally landing in Grandpa's employ. Mom has said that whenever she saw Ed, he was always with Grandpa.

Ed passed away on June 3, 1958, at the age of 78, and Molly lived to the ripe old age of 96. She died on June 23, 1981, while living with her daughter Marie (Kelly) in Scotch Plains. She lived previously for many years in an apartment just across the street from daughter Eileen (Doherty), her husband Dan, and their children, Dan, Maryellen, and Kathy, on "*upper Ege.*"

Decoration Day, 1919 - Ed Connor, Aunt Molly (his wife), and Grandma Colford

Margaret Elizabeth (aka: Agnes). One of the biggest surprises of my family search was finding out that Grandma's given name was Margaret Elizabeth! Mom and Dad had understood all their lives that her name was Agnes, yet her birth certificate from St. Anthony of Padua and her marriage certificate from St. Aloysius Church in Jersey City where she married Grandpa are clear. She began using Agnes as her preferred name by 1904 when she signed the marriage certificate accordingly as a *witness* to Aunt Molly and Uncle Ed Connor's nuptials on September 8th of that year.

Did she take Agnes as a confirmation name? Or could the nickname "Maggie" from Margaret have morphed into "Aggie", then "Agnes?" Or could there have been a repudiation of her mother's name, a rejection of sorts? After all, Aunt Molly named her daughter *Margaret* Marie after her own mother, following the typical Irish naming tradition.

Unfortunately, Ana, the archivist from St. Anthony of Padua who provided me with all these birth records, said that the parish kept no records of confirmations before 1940, so I could not verify my hypothesis. On the other hand, Grandma always used "*H*" as her middle initial; Mom assumed, but was never told, that the "*H*" was for "*Helen.*" Another more likely explanation is that it was for

Hannah, a name taken at confirmation after her aunt who was instrumental in raising her and her two siblings after her father's death.

What is interesting is that Mom has always said that it was Molly, not Grandma, who was the one who kept close ties with the Harvey relatives over the years. I am not sure what that all means, but it certainly remains one of the mysteries in Grandma's background. Could it be simply what sisters Rosemarie and Eileen claimed, that Molly's household was far more inviting and welcoming than Grandma's was? Or was it Grandma's decision to distance herself from an upsetting past? Or could it be that it was Grandpa himself who wished to keep his wife's past far from his high public profile in local politics?

Another issue open to speculation.

Grandma's date of birth on her St. Anthony of Padua birth certificate is January 23, 1887, a day earlier than the date listed on the state - issued *Birth Return*, but I do take the parish date as the more accurate one of the two. Her mother's name on her parish birth certificate is *Elizabeth*, not Margaret, a relatively minor error. *Elizabeth* also was the given name assigned to Grandma's mother on her marriage certificate to Grandpa, but this error would have been the result of transcribing the St. Anthony of Padua information onto the St. Aloysius parish record. Little more than a clerical error, I am sure, since *Margaret* was the given name listed on her own mother's marriage certificate and on each of the state's birth records of two of her three Dunn children. However, *Elizabeth* Harvey was the name of her mother Grandma provided on her Social Security Application many years later on February 2, 1966.

Interesting, but I also have looked in vain for a death certificate for an *Elizabeth* Dunn, considering that name a distant possibility for our great-grandmother.

Grandma was the third child of Michael and Margaret (Harvey) Dunn to have entered the world at 50 King St. Sponsors M. Whelan and Sarah McGrane, probably her mother's married sister, witnessed Reverend Julius baptize her one week later at St. Anthony of Padua. Sarah may have been the one who married a Thomas McGrane, also from Blackwatertown; the surname McGrane was one of the most common names in that area.

I thought for a while that the 13-year-old *Maggie* Dunn listed as an *"inmate"* in the *St. Joseph's Female Orphan Asylum* on Willoughby St. in Brooklyn in 1900 might have been Grandma who herself was that age. However, Sister Maryellen Blumlein, the Sisters of Charity archivist, did some research for me, and it is clear that she is not our grandmother; this *Maggie's* parents' names were Dennis and Annie. The Sisters of Charity was the order of nuns which operated the St. Joseph's facility.

This other Maggie also had a very difficult time. She, her nine-year-old sister, Nellie, and her younger brother, Timmy, all were placed in orphanages by their parents, the girls in St. Joseph's, and their brother in nearby St. John's. Maggie was eventually claimed two years later by her cousin, a Mrs. McGovern, but Nellie was sent instead to another state facility. Sr. Blumlein reported that Timmy's whereabouts after St. John's were unknown.

By 1905, our 17-year-old Grandma was one of several *"boarders"* in the home of Livinia Radermacher at 1775 Lexington Ave. near 110th St. in Manhattan along with Mary Leonard (44), a relative of her aunt Annie (Leonard) Dunn; *"telephone operator"* was Grandma's occupation. Other occupants in this same home were Livinia's son John (18), Margaret Jacob (40), and her daughter Monica (5). They undoubtedly were relatives of Emma Veronica Jacob who married Grandma's cousin, James Dunn.

Soon after Grandma left, or perhaps just before she left, another family of Dunns arrived in the Radermacher house, now at 72 East 124th St., with *Linnia* listed as a *"boarding house keeper."* The 1910 census listed Anna (22), Theresa (21), *Zeta* (probably Irene; 19), and Margaret (17) among the 10 *"boarders"* there; Mary Leonard was in residence again as well. Given their ages, these Dunns probably were siblings who were joined by 1915 by yet another brother, Joseph (18; *"office clerk"* at first, then *"Pennsylvania railroad watchman,"* then *"salesman – grocer"*), and by the 67-year-old retired father of this family, Andrew Dunn. Like Grandma, the Dunn sisters, Margaret, Theresa, and Anna, all found employment as telephone operators; clearly, a local telephone company office must have been located nearby. Anna would go on to marry Livinia's son John by 1915.

I cannot claim definitively what the relationship was of these new Dunn arrivals to Grandma. Andrew was born in PA, and another daughter of his, Mary, reported on the December 26, 1925, death certificate of this 74-year-old former *"driller – masonry"* that the names of his own mother and father were *"unknown."* Without these names, I cannot make a specific connection with our other line of

Dunns; cousins for sure, though, I dare say. Nevertheless, I have included more information of the Radermacher - Dunn connection in the *Footnotes* section of our story.

Grandma had vacated the Radermacher household by 1909 when she joined Molly and Ed Connor at their 209 Virginia Ave. household in Jersey City. Her 61-year-old Uncle John had passed away by then, succumbing to pneumonia on September 13th of that year. The 1910 census placed Grandma (22; *"stock clerk – drug house"*) with Ed (27; *"cooper – barrels factory"*) and Molly (23) at that same address; Ed continued to commute to his father's business on West Houston St.

The next destination for Grandma and the Connors was 172 Kensington Ave. They were ensconced there in 1915 when Ed was still listed as a *"cooper"* and Grandma listed once again as a *"telephone operator."* It would appear that Grandma's *stock clerk* position was only a temporary one she settled for in Jersey City before she secured another more familiar position at a switchboard somewhere. Grandma, still at the same address with her sister and brother-in-law three years later, was elevated to the position of *"telephone supervisor."* Rene Kuhn recounted for Paul that Grandma often picked her up after her work day was over in Manhattan and took her to visit Ed and Molly in their Jersey City home.

Chapter XIV

Grandma and Grandpa Colford

G randma apparently had an ardent suitor before Grandpa, a fellow by the name of John Patrick Aloysius Cannon. Margaret (Farrant) Sauer, our old neighbor and Our Lady of Victories alum, shared this story with me at Jenny Palecek's wedding and in a follow-up email. John Patrick, always known as *JP*, was Margaret's maternal grandfather, the only child born to Mary (Feeney) Cannon from Knock, County Cork, Ireland, who settled in Hoboken after her arrival in the States. Her husband passed away when JP was just a baby, but she was able to secure a position as a housekeeper in a church rectory. *"So my grandfather grew up an only child in a priest's home,"* Margaret wrote.

JP eventually relocated to St. Joseph's Parish in the Journal Square area of Jersey City. It was at that time when he met Grandma, although the circumstances of their courtship are anyone's guess. Margaret was clear, though, that JP *"was very sweet on her."* He would later go on to marry and father six children. Although fancying himself a construction worker, he seemed to have made a living as a magician, befriending Harry Houdini himself while plying his trade. Frequent trips to Cuba for entertainment purposes in its many hotels kept him away from his wife and six children for long stretches of time, Margaret reported.

So it would appear that Grandma chose a politician over an entertainer?

It was while she was living with Ed and Molly when Grandma met Grandpa. It is likely that they first met while both residents of Virginia Ave., Grandma with the Connors at 209, and Grandpa at 159

Virginia in the home he shared with his mother and Aunt Kate. Mom recalls the story that their first encounter was in a store somewhere. Could it have been the same store owned at that time by Aunt Kate at the corner of Virginia and West Side Aves.? Could she have been instrumental in getting Grandma and Grandpa together? Or could Grandpa simply have met her during one of his regular walks through his own eighth ward?

Some more speculation.

The local newspapers of the time, specifically the Jersey Journal and the Hudson Dispatch, were not inclined to include wedding announcements, so there are no news accounts of Grandma and Grandpa's February 19, 1919, wedding. The headline of the Jersey Journal that day ran a major headline that read:

Attempt to Assassinate Clemenceau
Bullet in Shoulder; Walked Home

(Clemenceau was the Prime Minister of France who was shot while at the Paris Peace Conference; he survived the attack.)

Other front page stories included the daily list of those wounded and killed in any one of many World War I battles as well as a major announcement of the reduction in the fare of the Bergen Ave. jitneys from 10 cents to five cents, excluding Sundays and holidays. Supervision of the jitney service also was handed over to Thomas Maloney, the presiding Deputy Director of Streets and Public Improvement, without an increase in his annual salary of $4,000.

Coincidentally, that same position, *Supervisor, Bureau of Motor Bus Transportation*, would belong to Grandpa Colford by 1923.

An editorial which appeared in this same edition called for Congress to pass the immigration bill designed to halt the flow of immigrants into the States (it eventually passed). *"If it is not passed,"* the editorial continued, *"this country will be overrun and swamped with European pauper labor."*

So how many of our own Irish immigrant pauper laborer forebears would have been told to go home?

On Wednesday, February 19, 1919, at 4:30 p.m., Fr. William Lawlor, an assistant pastor at St. Aloysius Church on West Side Ave., presided over the marriage of Joseph E. Colford and Margaret E. Dunn. The state marriage record had their ages as 38 and 30, respectively. However, Grandma was married a month after her 32nd birthday, hardly a "spring chicken" by the marrying standards of the day, and Grandpa was just three months shy of his 39th birthday. Ships' manifests typically described unmarried young women 16 years of age and older as *"spinsters,"* a suggestion that marrying early surely beat marrying later in life.

The official *Certificate and Record of Marriage* listed Grandpa's occupation as *"Clerk in City Hall"*; the couple's parents' names were listed as *Michael and Anna Meely* and *Michael and Elizabeth Harvey*. Best man was Joseph McGuirk, a friend of Grandpa's who also was involved in Jersey City politics and who would serve as Hudson County Sheriff from 1938-39. I found it a bit unusual that he chose a friend as best man when three of his brothers (John, James, and William) were all alive and well in Jersey City; maid of honor was the aforementioned Irene Corbally, not Aunt Molly for whom Grandma served as maid of honor. Also of interest is the fact that February 19 was the same date as Grandma's parents' nuptials.

Our grandparents' first residence as a married couple was a two-family home at 311 Ege Ave. which they shared with a German-born couple, Herman (*"carpenter – steel mill"*) and Sophia Purnost, and their 12-year-old son, Henry; Grandpa was listed in the 1920 census as a *"clerk – party hall."* There was no occupation listed for Grandma who was already pregnant with Dad. Interestingly, they were still at this same address in 1922, but Grandma's name in the city directory that year listed her as *Margaret*, not Agnes!

While they were looking for a home of their own, there were few to choose from in the sparsely populated Ege Ave. area. The completion of Hudson Boulevard which eventually would spur housing development there was still a few years away.

Grandma and Grandpa found one they liked, 277 Ege Ave., and purchased it in 1924 from Leroy Pettit (*"machinist – ship yard"*) and his wife, May, who had been in the home for five or six years only; they and their nine-month-old, Leroy, Jr., relocated to Belleville after the sale. Renting space from the Pettits at 277 Ege was another couple, Frank and Lena Christenson. Frank was also a *"machinist –*

ship yard," probably a work mate with Leroy, or perhaps his brother-in-law. (Read more about the early days of Ege Ave. in the *Footnotes* section of our story.)

Either Grandpa or Grandma told the census taker in 1930 that their home was worth $8,000, but its value shriveled in size by the 1940 census when it was listed as $4,000. Grandpa (*"city clerk – city hall"*) enjoyed an income of $7,000 the year before. The latter census also indicated that Grandpa had finished four years of high school, Grandma only two. Grandpa and Grandma raised Dad at 277 Ege and remained there until 1966 when they moved across the street to 260 Ege to the recently converted two-family home they were to share with our maternal Grandpa, Frank Lipsett (his story follows).

Grandma Colford and Dad

Grandpa's political junkets and his trips as vice-president of the Jersey City Skeeters with whom he traveled often on road trips kept him far from Ege for days at a time after his marriage to Grandma. One such junket was a two-week trip he took in January of 1937 to San Juan, Puerto Rico; it was clear from the five other Jersey City residents who accompanied him that the purpose of the trip was political in nature. Joining Grandpa (sheriff from 1932 – 35) aboard the ship *Statendam* were Hugh Parle, the Hudson County sheriff at the time, Joseph McGuirk (sheriff from 1938 – 39 and Grandpa's aforementioned best man), Eugene Ertle (sheriff from 1939 – 42), William F. Sullivan (leader of the city's third ward), and Howard Smith (role unknown). Sullivan's son, Frank, was the one who introduced Mom and Dad.

121

While I was researching Grandpa's biography for a writing assignment for Sister Marietta as a 10-year-old fifth-grader at Our Lady of Victories School, Grandma told me in no uncertain terms, *"Grandpa liked to take lots of trips by himself!"* Mom also has said that the reason why Dad chose not to go away to college was the fact that Grandma was often left alone. During that same visit to interview Grandpa about the particulars of his life, he told me to record his year of birth as 1888, making him eight years younger than his actual birth year of 1880. Grandma, however, within earshot of this request, made sure that I recorded the more accurate one of the two.

Grandma's days were shorter than they should have been, since she had no particular health issues besides a touch of arthritis now and then. However, when she exited the rear door of 260 Ege one April day to fetch Grandpa some cough medicine, she slipped on a patch of ice on the rear steps and fell, breaking her ankle. The break resulted in a heavy plaster cast, making her quite unwieldy. In an attempt to care for her at home, Dad provided, among other things, a commode which he placed alongside Grandma's bed. An unsuccessful attempt to move herself from her bed to the commode resulted in a fall to the floor where she had to be helped up by the folks. Knowing Grandma, her pride received more of a jolt than her body did. It then became clear that she was reluctant to ask for help from the folks, lest she inconvenience them, so they decided to place her in Pollock Hospital for the proper medical assistance until her ankle mended.

Grandma remained there for approximately three weeks before dying in her sleep on May 22, 1967, at the age of 80 due to a *"pulmonary embolism – arteriosclerotic heart disease,"* the result, they say, of a prolonged level of inactivity while being bedridden. Current practice for such an injury would have included physical exercise, despite the cast, but such was not the case in 1967. The year of her birth on the death certificate was 1890, but her actual year was 1887, making her 80 years of age when she passed, not 77 as her death certificate indicated.

Grandpa was 88-years old when he passed away. He was nursing a cold that day, November 18, 1968. While sitting in his customary upholstered wing chair by the window at 260 Ege where he kept watch over the goings-on outside, Dad was crouched at Grandpa's feet changing his socks when he turned his head to the side and passed.

Not a bad way to go . . .

Son Joseph married Catherine Lipsett, also an only child, on April 5, 1948.

April 5, 1948 - Grandparents Colford, Mom and Dad

April 5, 1948 - Grandparents Lipsett, Mom and Dad, Fr. Billy Hogan

And then there were eight: Mary, Joseph III, Francis, Paul, Christopher, Peter, Loretta, Brian.

Chapter XV

Some Grandpa Colford Recollections

Long into his retirement, Grandpa continued to be an early riser who walked the streets of his eighth ward as if he were still the ward leader. His strolls down West Side Ave. included visits with his barber friends, Angelo Di Maio and George Tomi, and with the new owners of what was once his realty and insurance business, the *Colford and Crocker Real Estate and General Insurance Company*, at the corner of West Side and Williams Aves. In fact, oftentimes on my way to the A&P for some family victuals, I'd pass his former business and give him a wave just inside the plate glass window where he sat with one or more of the current owners. I can only imagine that a busy realty/insurance business didn't need a daily stopover of an elderly gentleman who just wanted to "chew the fat," as they say, but these folk appeared to be very kind and accommodating to him.

Grandpa's attire always remained constant: three-piece suit, starched shirt and tie, and his fedora, always the fedora which he tipped respectfully to any woman who passed him on the sidewalk. His hands always clutched the lapels of his suit jacket as he walked.

By the time we were all up and getting ready for another day at Our Lady of Victories School, Grandpa already had dropped off on our front porch a copy of the morning newspaper, the *Hudson Dispatch*, with a notation typically written in pencil above the title which included advice for things like, *"cold out . . . wear coat"* or *"raining out."* Of course, the greatest treat of all was the loaf of piping hot bread just out of the oven at Strull's bakery which he dropped off regularly as well.

The name *Colford* always resonated with the old timers I have met in the streets of Jersey City or in the Park Tavern at Communipaw and West Side Aves. over the years; they referred to him as either *Commissioner* Colford or as *Sheriff* Colford. To a person, they were complimentary of Grandpa regarding the many favors he was able to do for their struggling friends or family members. Second cousin Betty (Blewitt) Critchley referred to him as the *"family patriarch"* and to him and Grandma as *"the salt of the earth."*

As recently as 2009, Tom Waddleton, another Jersey City native and a part-time security officer at Georgian Court University, sought me out and told me of the friendship his own father had with our Grandpa Colford; he, too, was high in praise of him. *"And he was honest!"* Tom told me as he repeatedly poked his index finger through the air for emphasis. Second cousin Joan (Downey) Salinas also told me that Grandpa *"took very good care of my grandmother* (Mamie) *and her sister Kate . . . he always had a car and would stop by and have coffee."*

One can only imagine that the many city and county positions held by his siblings and by their children over the years were due to the intercession of Grandpa who was in a position to put them on the payroll. Grandpa also purchased a home at 307 Virginia Ave. for his younger widowed sister, Mamie, and her family. Word has it that when Grandma found out about this real estate deal, she was furious that she was completely unaware of it until after it was completed.

Second cousin Michael also told me the following story of Grandpa's assistance to his family:

> *"When my sister was a young infant, she developed a bad case of eczema. We*
> *lived in Bayonne at the time, and the doctor was located in Newark. Neither my*
> *father nor mother ever drove a car, so your grandfather would send his limo to*
> *take them to the doctors. I can still see that big black limo pulling up to the house."*

Grandpa's driver for years was Charlie McClellan whose wife, Vera, was brother Paul's godmother. He surely was the one who made the trip for Michael's sister.

For all those non-family members reading this story, Joseph, Sr. and his wife, Agnes (Dunn) Colford, had one child, our father, Joseph, Jr. Dad would tell us from time-to-time, *"If you ever go into politics, I'll break your arm!"* He had seen first-hand through Grandpa the fickle friends politics breeds, and he wanted no part of it. However, Dad was approached by a mayoral candidate running on the *Clean Government* slate in the late 1960s who asked him to run alongside him as the city council president, essentially the second-in-command. Dad politely declined the offer; the candidate lost the election.

Chapter XVI

Some Grandma Colford Recollections

G randma was a very gentle, soft-spoken individual, always our ready-made babysitter, who never had to raise her voice to us when bedtime arrived. Her lap was like the ultimate of all easy chairs: soft, inviting, and a great place to begin one's night sleep while listening to a story. She struck a more robust figure than that of her older sister, our Aunt Molly, who presented as a much frailer individual.

Grandma also was the consummate worrier. Oftentimes we would hear the rap of her ring through the lace curtains of the front window of her 277 Ege home to warn us kids playing in the street there to desist fighting or to play more carefully: the best of intentions, to be sure, but a bit overbearing for us young kids. In fact, I remember Dad calling her one day after Paul complained of her breaking up one of his fights and telling her, *"Aggie, if you see him lying in a pool of blood, leave him alone . . . they'll work it out themselves!"* Mom said that that request left a slight chill in the air for several days between 277 and 262 Ege.

There was one Saturday night when I was taking my weekly bath (no shower, just a bathtub in those days) as a 12 or 13-year-old when babysitter Grandma must have thought that I had taken too long, so she opened the bathroom door and exclaimed something like, *"Oh! I thought that something had happened to you!"*

I was never a vegetable-eater, so whenever I had lunch at 277, Grandma always made sure she piled high for me a plateful of iceberg lettuce which accompanied my sandwich. And whenever I visited Grandma, she had me relieve myself, if needed, in a porcelain pot in the kitchen, rather than risk me falling down the stairs on the way to or from her second-floor bathroom.

When I did happen to gain access to the upstairs, my first stop was to Dad's former bedroom, still equipped with the hospital bed he used for recuperative purposes while recovering from his tuberculosis scare as a St. Peter's College senior. The bed was curiously very high for someone my age, but the hand cranks at the foot of the bed which elevated the head and feet were always a blast to operate. I also recall the mattress itself being much firmer than the ones on which I was used to sleeping. (Dad, as you recall, had a spot on his lung detected on an x-ray when he went to enlist after the attack on Pearl Harbor. Doctors' orders were for bed rest, thus the hospital bed.)

Grandma's annual Thanksgiving task was to cook the turkey and prepare her distinctive giblet gravy which we transported from 277 to 262 Ege in our little red wagon, while Mom prepared all the other side dishes. And her pot roast always greeted us the day we all returned from Monmouth Beach after our summer stay there; she also had chilled daiquiris awaiting the folks.

That Grandma spoke not at all of her childhood remembrances speaks volumes. How she weathered the storms of a troubled family is known only to her.

Did her Aunt Hannah replace her mother altogether as caregiver after her father passed away, or did she just assist our great-grandmother in raising her children?

Grandma survived, I suppose, carrying those tales with her with nary a mention of them to anyone. The story of her mother's last years undoubtedly is part of some distant relative's oral tradition, but I have not been able to find that person.

One day, perhaps, I'll track that person down . . .

Chapter XVII

Other Dunn and Harvey Siblings

Grandma's Aunts and Uncles and Our Great-Great-Aunts and Uncles

*J**ohn Dunn.*** According to census records, our great-great-uncle John emigrated from Ireland in 1870, and his wife-to-be, Annie Leonard, followed three years later. She arrived as a 20-year-old aboard the ship *Olympus* on April 23, 1873, along with several other Leonards: Catherine (24), John (18), Anne (20), Bridget (11), and another 14-year-old female whose name was illegible on the ship's manifest. I know that some were siblings, but perhaps some were cousins also. John and Annie married in the Church of St. Anthony of Padua on January 28, 1877. The couple raised five children of their own, all boys: John, Jr., William, James, Frank, and Joseph.

They also lost four other children, their only two daughters and two other sons. Catharine, the first born, lived only *"two years, 11 months,"* according to her death certificate, before succumbing to *"tubercular meningitis – convulsions"* on August 19, 1880. Eddie was just a year old when he passed on July 20, 1886, due to *"pneumonia lobular – asthenia,"* and Michael Francis lived for only *"two years, 10 months"* before a three-day bout with *"diphtheria laryngitis – asphyxia"* claimed him on New Year's Eve, 1892. Mary, the second born, suffered for two weeks with spinal meningitis before dying at home at 36 Clarkson on March 14, 1894; unlike her three siblings who predeceased her, she made it to adolescence, passing away at the age of *"16 years, four months, 11 days."*

John, a *"foreman," "laborer,"* and *"stevedore"* for a time, eventually owned two taverns. When his family was living at 36 Clarkson, John's first one was at 324 Spring St.; by the turn of the century, he had relocated his business to 419 West 48th St. A year later (1901-02), he added a second liquor business at 154 Christopher St., right after he and his family moved to a home he purchased at 119 Leroy St. where they remained for many years. Two of John's sons, John, Jr. and William, must have joined their father in the business, since each was listed as a *"bar keeper"* in the 1900 census. John Jr.'s own store location was 439 W 40th St. The other three sons all became plumbers.

John passed away at the age of 61 on September 13, 1909, at 11:30 p.m. after suffering for a week with pneumonia. His widow, Annie, was at 119 Leroy the following year with her sons John (*"bartender – saloon"*) and William (now a *"policeman – bicycle"*) along with two servants and six boarders: four longshoremen, a bartender, and an engineer. Apparently, Annie had to pay the mortgage and keep body and soul together with the income generated by these guests' monthly fees.

Annie lost her sight in her later years, but the age at which it happened and its cause are not known. At the time of her death on April 29, 1921 (*"chronic endocarditis – general oedema"*), her son, Joseph (*"plumber – plumber shop"*) and his wife, Mary (Callahan), had moved into 119 Leroy with their four children. Joining them were Mary's mother and brother, Edward (*"laborer – steamship company"*), and Charles Smith, a *"lodger,"* who was a *"laborer – livery stable."* The 1930 census placed Joseph (*"steamfitter – building"*) and Mary, now with seven children, and Mary's live-in mother and brother, at 203-02 202nd Street in St. Albans, Queens; they all were at the same address 10 years later when that census listed Joseph as a *"bartender – bar and grill."*

Hannah (Dunn) Norris. As I mentioned earlier, Hannah was the aunt who stepped in to help when her brother, Michael, died, leaving Margaret the widowed mother of three young children. Our great-uncle Jack credited her with raising him; undoubtedly, she raised siblings Molly and Grandma Agnes as well. The mystery remains, however, whether she only *assisted* Margaret in childcare or if she shouldered the bulk of this responsibility in the absence of Margaret. Based upon the recollections of the aforementioned sisters, Rosemarie and Eileen, the latter explanation would appear to be the more viable interpretation of events.

There is no marriage certificate in the New York City Archives for Hannah and anyone whose last name was Norris, so they may have wed elsewhere. The 1930 census places an *Anna* Norris, a 72-year-old widow, living with her brother-in-law, William Norris, at 1349 First Ave. in Manhattan. She told the census-taker at that time that she was 37 years old when she married, putting her year of marriage at around 1895. Not sufficient proof to suggest that she was our Hannah, but certainly a possibility.

Regardless of the year of their marriage, one might assume that it was around that time when Jack, Molly, and Grandma left Hannah's care to move in with their Uncle John and Aunt Anne at 36 Clarkson St. Hannah was laid to rest on October 15, 1938, at the age of 80 in the Calvary Cemetery plot purchased by her sister-in-law, our great-grandmother Margaret Dunn.

Rachel Dunn. I have been unsuccessful in locating any New York City marriage or death documentation for Rachel; her fate is unknown. Could she have returned to Ireland? Or simply moved out of the area?

Peter Harvey. Much of the information I have found about Peter, another great-great-uncle of ours, has been courtesy of Sharon Souther of New Greenwich, CT. She is the great-granddaughter of John Harvey, our Margaret's brother, making us indeed third cousins. She and I have exchanged many phone calls and emails these last few years, and we finally met in the NYC Municipal Archives in March of 2015.

As mentioned earlier in this narrative, Peter Harvey and his wife, Mary (Daly), were at 50 King St. in 1880 along with Jennie, their 11-month-old, and Peter's siblings, Sarah and John. Jennie died at home at 2:00 p.m. on June 12, 1880, just nine days after the census taker left; cause of death was *"cholera infantum – asthenia."* Her age on the death certificate was *"10 months, 23 days."* Seventeen months later Mary gave birth to their second child, James, on November 15, 1881, but he was only seven months old when Mary herself passed away at 50 King at 1:00 p.m. on June 23, 1882. Cause of death was *"phthisis pulmonalis* (aka: tuberculosis) - *exhaustion."* Peter, the widowed father of a young child, had to fend for himself as a single parent. Of course, in such cases these folk would seek out another spouse to help raise the children, but Peter had other family members living with him who could help out in the meantime.

According to Peter's grandson, Fr. Peter Harvey of the order of the Oblates of St. Francis de Sales (more on him later), Peter contacted an old girlfriend, Jane Kelly, back in Blackwatertown and asked her to join him here in the States. The Harvey and Kelly families literally lived next door to each other on Drumcullen Road in their village, so their connection must have been a longstanding one. Jane obliged and came to the States to become Peter's second wife. They wed approximately two years after Mary's death, and they had seven children together, four sons and three daughters. However, Peter's child, James, was just *"five years, five months old"* when he passed away late the night of November 7, 1885, within a year of his marriage to Jane. The cause of death which he suffered with for three days was *"membranous croup – exhaustion."* Peter and his new wife now were residing at 29 Clarkson St.

Jane predeceased Peter by five years, passing away on December 1, 1932; the 84-year-old Peter followed on July 1, 1937, while residing with three of his children and two granddaughters at 245 East 196th Street in the Bronx. The death certificate listed the cause of death of this *"retired stevedore"* as *"coronary heart disease – coronary closure; contributory: nephritis."*

I was able to contact the Fr. Peter Harvey I mentioned earlier due to Mom's uncanny recall of past names, dates, and events. She mentioned once that Dad drove Grandma and Aunt Molly to Philadelphia one day to attend the first Mass of two of her Harvey kin (Dad's second cousins and Grandma's nephews) as members of a Catholic order of missionary priests known as the White Fathers. I was unsure what order of missionaries the White Fathers referred to, since a Fr. Francois Richard whom I contacted emailed me that the expression *White Fathers* was a name given to many orders of missionaries.

However, I eventually found 81-year-old Fr. Peter Harvey of the order of the Oblates of St. Francis de Sales (OSFS), a missionary order of priests located in the Wilmington, DE/Philadelphia province. Peter is one of three Harvey brothers who all joined the Oblates. Dad, Grandma, and Molly would have attended his first Mass and that of his brother, James, in 1960. I have spoken with Fr. Peter twice; he is a charming, sharp-as-a-tack gentleman who had a great recall of facts and dates about his grandparents, but he knew nothing of our great-grandmother Margaret. Fr. Harvey is now living in the OSFS retirement community in Delaware, but he spent 38 years as a missionary in South Africa. He told me how strange it was to have been there during the years of apartheid.

133

His older brother, John Xavier Harvey, was ordained an Oblate father three years earlier in 1957. He was one of 12 Oblates named in a lawsuit brought against the all-male, Oblate-run Salesianum School in Wilmington, DE, by 39 survivors of childhood sexual abuse. The lawsuit, finally settled in 2011, involved accusations of abuse that occurred between 1955 and 1991 at the school; the older Fr. Harvey had been assigned there soon after his ordination. In addition to paying out $23.6 million to the victims in the settlement, the Oblates also agreed to make public the names of the 12 members of the order who were involved in the abuse.

Fr. John Xavier Harvey died in 1971, so he was not around to see his name made public.

John Harvey and His Family. (Our cousin Sharon Souther also has contributed much of the information in this section.) After the 1880 census placed John's residence at 50 King St. with his older brother Peter and his family, the 1900 census had our great-great-uncle John, this *"laborer,"* at 815 Greenwich St. with his wife Annie (Kelly) and their four children; the couple also lost three other children. They were to have three more children after 1900, however. Annie claimed that she arrived in the States in 1886, six years after John. The Church of the Holy Innocents was where the couple wed on February 8, 1891. What is of interest is that Annie also was a Kelly from Blackwatertown and the younger sister of Peter's second wife, Jane. So the two Harvey brothers married sisters from home.

John and Annie always seemed to have followed Peter and Jane from place to place; the latter couple had always been very supportive of their younger relations. John did not make it to the 1910 census, however, passing away at the age of 50, on March 1, 1908, while a resident of 22 Little West 12th St. in the West Village section of Manhattan. He was sick for five days with *"acute lumber pneumonia"* before *"heart failure"* contributed to his death which left Annie with the responsibility of raising seven children on her own: Mary, James, Anna, Thomas, Elizabeth (aka: *Lily*), Jane Veronica (aka: *Jennie*), and John. (These children are all Grandma Colford's first cousins and our great-aunts and great-uncles.) In order to provide them with shelter of some kind, Annie took a position as a *"janitress"* at 826 Amsterdam Ave. shortly after John's death; this arrangement undoubtedly provided her and her children with a place to stay and an income of sorts for her.

Annie outlived her husband by six years, but her passing on October 20, 1914, due to "*carcinoma of stomach*" after a hospital stay of several months, also meant the end of the family's living arrangement at 826 Amsterdam. Sons James (21) and Thomas (17) and their sister, Anna (19), were old enough to have been on their own by the time both parents had passed, but their four other siblings were scattered to different caregivers. Their Uncle Peter and Aunt Jane only took in the unmarried girls, Mary (23) and Lily (13), since there was little room left in their home for anyone else. The two youngest, siblings Jennie (11; Sharon's grandmother) and John (9), were sent to the Sisters of Charity-run Roman Catholic Orphan Asylum (RCOA) in the Bronx where they were listed as "*inmates.*" They entered just after Christmas, 1914, and they were to remain there until they turned 15 years of age, Jennie in 1918, after three years there, and John, two years later.

Sharon tells the story of how the boys and girls were separated in the orphanage, and when they were allowed outside, Jennie and John would meet and hold hands through an opening in the fence that kept them apart. Sharon also was clear that her grandmother received great care there and that she maintained close contact with one Sister of Charity in particular, Sister Agnes de Chantel, long after her days at RCOA were over, in fact, until Sister Agnes passed away in 1942.

Sister Anna found herself pregnant, so she married quickly the ne'er-do-well, Henry (aka: *Harry*) Crook, a name Sharon told me was as befitting a surname as there could be, on November 4, 1911; the couple lived with Annie until her death from stomach cancer three years later. Harry and Anna had three children together, all sons: John, Harry, and Edward. After a residence in Long Island City, the family spent approximately 12 years in Irvington, NJ, where the 34-year-old Anna passed away on January 27, 1929.

However, the circumstances of Anna's death and burial are quite mysterious. The coroner ruled her death "*suicide by shooting .38 caliber revolver wounds of chest and abdomen penetrating lungs – hemothorax, shock*"; secondary cause of death was "*manic depressive psychosis,*" a remarkable "out of the blue" diagnosis for someone to make who did not know her in life. Claiming that she shot herself *twice* with a handgun, once in the stomach, then again in the chest, is quite a stretch. Harry was "*a bad guy,*" Cousin Sharon said, so she is convinced that it would not be much of a stretch to think that somehow he beguiled the coroner to get him to conclude that Anna's gunshot wounds were self-inflicted. He also gave misleading and inaccurate background information about his wife to the coroner, making it close to impossible to find out where she was laid to rest. Harry also earned a prominent place for himself in Matthew Linderoth's master's thesis-turned book, *Prohibition at the North Jersey Shore: Gangsters on Vacation.* He became involved in one crooked scam after another, with gambling, racketeering, and bootlegging tops on his list. (Read about him and his family in more detail in the *Footnotes* section of our story.)

John's son, James', 1918 World War I draft registration card had his date of birth as February 1, 1893. Although he claimed that he had *"no family"* at that time, he actually was married to Irene (Lamb) but was referring to the fact that both his parents were deceased. The two married on January 29, 1917, but had no children.

James was employed as a *"truck driver"* at Washington Market in Manhattan for most of his adult life. His World War II draft registration card listed him as *"unemployed"* at his 501 W 42nd St. address, and this 49-year-old indicated that the person *"who will always know your address"* was his landlord, a *"Mr. Lang."* James' unemployment was due to a chronic heart condition which left him unable to work for some time; it also led to his death at Bellevue Hospital on May 22, 1943, at the age of 50. It would appear that a friend of his, undoubtedly the aforementioned Mr. Lang, afforded him and Irene some living space, since he was without an income.

Two other sons of John and Annie (Kelly) Harvey, Thomas and John, also have interesting stories to tell. Thomas could be found soon after his mother's death living with his sister Anna and Harry Crook at their Long Island City residence. A brief stint as an enlistee with the New York National Guard provided him with a government-sponsored place to stay, and he also lived briefly with his sister Mary and her husband, John Bresler, with whom he remained very close. According to his 1918 World War I draft registration card, Thomas was working for the American Can Company, a converted munitions factory, in a job he apparently found help in getting from his uncle John Xavier Harvey (Peter Harvey's son) who himself was a lifetime employee of the same company. Thomas gave his date of birth as April 12, 1897, and his place of employment as Edgewater, NJ.

He then would marry Juliana Frances Thompson on August 3, 1919, at the Church of the Holy Name of Jesus in Manhattan. Their only child, Edward Joseph, born a year later, lived barely six weeks before passing away due to *"marasmus"* (severe malnutrition) caused by *"pyloric stenosis,"* a congenital problem with the digestive system which prevents the processing of food. Their marriage ended soon after, since Thomas blamed his wife for the death of their son. By 1925, Julia had returned to live with her mother, and Thomas was back to living from pillar to post, as they say. The 1930 census placed this *"elevator operator"* as a *"roomer"* at 219 West 104th St. in Manhattan, and he held the same position while a resident of 348 Bloomfield Ave. in Bloomfield, NJ, some years later. Without any confirming evidence, it would appear that Thomas died between 1970 and 1972.

Brother John was the lost soul of the family. He was in and out of jail most of his adult life, serving time in both the Sing Sing Correctional Facility and in the Clinton Correctional Facility in Dannemora, NY, for robbery and for other crimes, including concealing firearms, violating parole, and felonious assault. His older brother James and his wife, Irene (Lamb), took him in after his stay in the orphanage and tried to rein him in, but that was not to be. Interestingly, Irene herself also was an orphan who spent several years as an *"inmate"* in the St. Joseph's Female Orphan Asylum, so it is easy to see how she and her husband were sensitive to John's plight and how they tried time and again to keep him on the straight and narrow, to no avail. The 1925 city directory placed John, a *"driver,"* living with brother James, a *"truck driver,"* his wife Irene, and her brother Harold, a *"chauffeur,"* at 511 West 41st St. It would appear that James probably was able to help John obtain a job similar to his own.

John's arrest record placing him in Sing Sing one more time on December 28, 1928, for *"Robbery 3d,"* claimed that his *"Criminal Acts Attributed to"*, of all things, *"lack of parental supervision."* He had been using the names *Joe Lamb* and *Joe Gallagher* as aliases; the former one at the time of this arrest was the maiden name of his sister-in-law, Irene. This incarceration was not his first, perhaps the reason why Judge Otto handed out a rather harsh sentence, *"10 years, 116 days,"* making him eligible for parole on January 20, 1937. The Sing Sing *"RECEIVING BLOTTER"* had the 24-year-old *"laborer"* as having finished the seventh grade and as being a regular church-goer; he also asserted in the record that his *"nearest relative"* was his brother James. When arrested this time, the police apparently *"recovered $25.00"* from him, perhaps all that was left from his most recent heist. He was able to leave only *"$2.30"* with Sing Sing's Chief Clerk's Office, however, before he entered a cell one more time. When the police picked him up, John reported that he had been working for nine weeks at $25.00 per week and that he had been a resident of 453 West 56th St. in Manhattan. The 1930 census still placed John at Sing Sing State Prison where he was a *"helper – knit shop."*

At the age of 50, John left prison for the last time in 1955 when he appeared to have turned his life around, finding a position in the iron workers' union and becoming active in Democratic politics on the West Side of Manhattan as a member of the Chelsea Democrats. He died on Christmas Day, 1972,

137

without ever having reconciled with his family; his closest family connection was his older brother, James, who passed away in 1943 while John was still incarcerated. The individual who saw to his funeral arrangements was not even a family member, but an Edward Burns listed simply as a *"friend"* on his death certificate. Sadly, John was the one whom nobody talked about in the family, the proverbial *"black sheep,"* as they say.

As for the other Harvey sisters: after she left the orphanage, Jennie lived for a time with her sister, Anna, and her husband, Harry Crook, and then with her sister, Lily, and her husband. She later would go on to marry John McCarthy on February 18, 1928; their marriage would last 56 years before he passed away at the age of 92 on May 31, 1984. Jennie lived another five years before her death on September 15, 1989. Lily married Charles Frederick Utz on March 1, 1919; she died at the age of 45 on March 28, 1946, after a long battle with diabetes, and sister Mary, the eldest of the Harvey daughters and the wife of John Bresler, died on April 29, 1966, at the age of 75.

Thomas Harvey. Other than the fact that he served as Aunt Molly's godfather, I have not found any other information about this other great-great-uncle of ours, brother of our great-grandma Margaret.

Sara Jane Harvey. All I know of the youngest of Margaret's nine siblings and grandma's godmother is that she probably married Thomas McGrane, undoubtedly another immigrant from Blackwatertown, since his surname was one of the most common ones in that area.

The Lipsett Connection

The following section of our story traces five generations of the families of Mom's father,

Francis Andrew (aka: Frank) Lipsett:

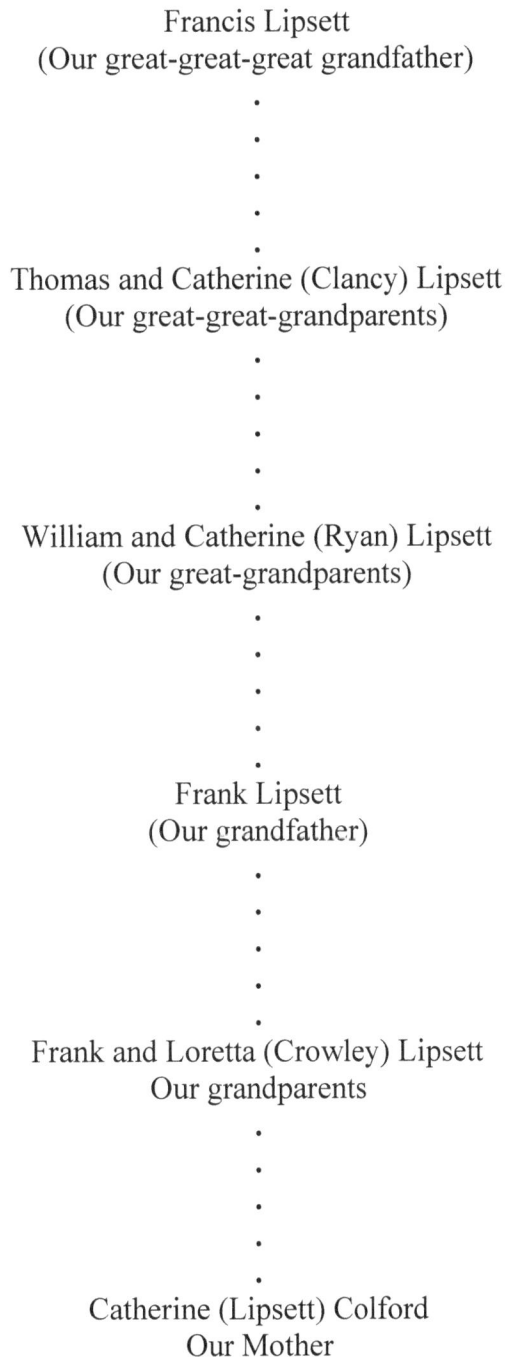

Francis Lipsett
(Our great-great-great grandfather)

.
.
.
.

Thomas and Catherine (Clancy) Lipsett
(Our great-great-grandparents)

.
.
.
.

William and Catherine (Ryan) Lipsett
(Our great-grandparents)

.
.
.
.

Frank Lipsett
(Our grandfather)

.
.
.
.

Frank and Loretta (Crowley) Lipsett
Our grandparents

.
.
.
.

Catherine (Lipsett) Colford
Our Mother

Chapter XVIII

Lipsett Beginnings

Our Lipsett cousins believe that the family originated in France and was of French Huguenot stock, those Calvinist Protestants who belonged to the Protestant Reformed Church of France; it is likely that the name may have been *Lipsette* at that time. History provides some support for this belief, since the Huguenots fled France in great numbers soon after King Louis XIV began his persecution of the group in 1685 when he declared Protestantism illegal and ordered them all to convert to Catholicism. His efforts to see to this conversion were brutal. Estimates vary, but between 200,000 and 500,000 of them eventually left France to escape this persecution and made off for foreign lands, primarily those throughout Europe, but also those as far away as South Africa.

Approximately 10,000 of them landed in Ireland, and most of them settled in the northern part of the country in counties such as Donegal and Sligo. It would appear that our early Lipsetts may have been part of this migration, but I have been unable to verify this Huguenot connection. Lucy Gwynn of *The Huguenot Society of Great Britain and Ireland* could not find for me the name Lipsett or any related variations in the surname index of the Huguenot churches in the United Kingdom or Ireland. She added, though, that this missing piece did not necessarily suggest that Lipsett was *not* a Huguenot name, since there were Huguenots who just did not worship at Huguenot churches, thus perhaps why the surname is missing from their rosters.

Mom has always said that Lilian (stage name: *Billie*), the daughter of Grandpa's brother, Richard, was a dancer of sorts and was due to make a trip with her troupe to the States under the last name of

Lipsette. Yet another explanation of the name has it as an Anglicized form of either the German or Jewish *Lipsitz* or *Lipschutz*, names also located primarily in County Donegal.

The Lipsett name was a common one in Donegal, the northwestern - most county in the Republic which borders Sligo to the north. The very first Lipsett we know of in the area of Coolaney is our great-great-great grandfather, Francis (1765-1835), the one who arrived from Northern Ireland and obtained a land lease for property in Coolaney in 1783. He was one of three Coolaney residents that year who leased their land from, and became tenants of, the estate of Charles O'Hara, the last in a long line of O'Haras going back generations to Cormac O'Hara, the first one to have been granted all the Coolaney-area land in 1578. The number of acres Francis leased and the price he paid for them remain a mystery, however. By 1858, Francis' son, Thomas *Lepsey*, our great-great-grandfather, was the only *Lipsett* to be found in Sligo, and one of only 17 *"occupiers"* in Shancough (pronounced *Shan-coo*) that year. County Donegal counted 72 Lipsetts as residents that same year.

In addition to Thomas (1795 – March 24, 1885), Francis had two other children, our great-great-great-uncles Robert (1795- March 24, 1885) and John.

Thomas, a strict protestant like his father before him, married the Roman Catholic Catherine (Kate) Clancy (1815-1890). The couple's original plan for a family business was to sell general articles only, since they were hesitant to peddle whiskey. However, a Captain Heather convinced them of the merits of entering the tavern business, and he even interceded for the couple with the town council to get them a charter/license to sell the bubbly. The Heather family members were landowners of some renown in the area, having recently purchased the estate of a Captain Meredith Thompson at public auction. Thomas' business was not without competition, however, since there were four holders of *"retail spirit licenses"* in Coolaney by 1837; it is a safe bet that he was one of the four. Among the brands Thomas sold was *Lipsey's Old Irish Whiskey.*

Thomas and Kate had seven children:

> John Francis (1838 – September 13, 1906; died in Albury, New
>   South Wales, Australia; husband of Elizabeth Wallace
>   and father of 10 children, eight of whom survived)
> **William (1839- January 12, 1922; our great-grandfather)**

Patrick (1840 – March 24, 1885; joined the Royal Irish
Constabulary (RIC; aka: *police*)

Thomas (1842 - ? Joined the RIC)

Arthur (1844 - died in Australia, date unknown)

Mary (1845 – ? Married and had a daughter whose married name
was Brindley; lived in Dublin)

Ellen (1848- April 19, 1937; married Thomas Galligan, a publican,
but had no children)

The story is told that Kate had Thomas converted to Catholicism on his death bed on March 24, 1885. Brother Paul reported from his own research that the protestant minister, appalled at the conversion, said to Kate at the time of Thomas' death, "*You've poisoned him!*"

Our great-grandfather, William, a "*farmer and publican,*" married Catherine (Kate) Ryan (1855-1917), 17 years his junior, and fathered 11 children with her, eight sons and three daughters. She was from the nearby townland of Rathglass, daughter of Thomas, a shopkeeper, and Anne (Hopkins). The St. Joseph's parish register in Coolaney lists the 11 Lipsetts accordingly:

Thomas (January 12, 1874 – 1892)

William John (February 16, 1876 – September 2, 1954)

James (July 14, 1877 - ?, in England)

Marianne (June 28, 1879 – June 6, 1903)

Patrick J. (October 11, 1881 – December 29, 1906)

Robert (August 20, 1883 – September 27, 1953)

Richard P. (April 30, 1885 – Spring, 1951 in Suffolk, England)

Frank (May 30, 1888 – November 26, 1969; our grandfather)
(Sponsors: William and Mrs. McNamara)

Kate Ellen (September 23, 1890 – April 27, 1956)

Lily Maria (April 22, 1892 – late 1970s)

Thomas M. (August 4, 1894 – March 26, 1937)

Great-grandparents William and
Kate (Ryan/Rynne) Lipsett

Great-grandparents Lipsett with their
children outside the pub (W. Lipsett)

Under William's watch, the family business grew, and what eventually became *William Lipsett's Pub* later was changed to the *Mountain Inn* by Bridie Lipsett, the wife of Liam Lipsett, Sr., grandson of William and son of Robert. Bridie apparently did not take very well to the original name of the pub.

Throughout his life, Grandpa thought that his birthdate was January 3rd, 1888. It wasn't until he applied for a passport for a return trip to Ireland in the summer of 1954 at the age of 66 when he discovered that his true birthdate was May 30 of that year! He was almost five months younger than ever he thought!

Grandpa's siblings' stories follow.

Chapter XIX

Grandpa Lipsett's Siblings

Our Great-Uncles and Great-Aunts

***T**homas.* The oldest child of the 11 Lipsetts and the namesake of his father's father, as per the Irish naming tradition, Thomas died at home in 1892 at the age of 18 while a seminary student. Genealogist Joseph Buggy wrote that having a priest in an Irish family, particularly in 19th and 20th Irish society, was something to aspire to and was a proud symbol of social status. Other researchers have told me that having a son a priest was a sign of a family's financial success, since it could afford to have a son in the priesthood and not need him around to work the farm or the family business, an indication that family fortunes were good. There also is an old Irish saying that refers to a family's pride in having *"a bull in the yard and a son in the priesthood."*

I wonder if father William put any pressure on any of his other Lipsett sons to follow in Thomas' footsteps and take his place in the seminary after his death.

Who knows?

William John. The next in line would go on to marry Kate Agnes Keenan, a teacher, in the winter of 1908 and have one son, Patrick, and one daughter, Annetta Maria Nuala (pronounced *Noola*; DOB: February 6, 1910), although her preferred name always was simply *Nuala*. I am unclear about Patrick's marital status, but his sister married a John Joseph Droughton in 1935 and had two sons,

Donald (1937) and Derek (1946). Grandpa's brother also would become a publican himself and operate a pub of his own in nearby Ballymote. He passed away on September 2, 1954, at the age of 78, just two months after Grandpa Lipsett's visit.

Brother William John Lipsett and Family

James. Approximately 11 years older than Grandpa, James left for London, England around 1901 and joined the British army; he enlisted in the Irish Guards, an infantry division of the army, on January 20, 1902. The Guards were a special unit of the British Army's Foot Guards formed on April 1, 1900, by Queen Victoria *"in response to the many courageous actions performed by soldiers of the Irish Regiment in the Second Boer War."* Perhaps this newly-formed regimental unit was widely advertised throughout Ireland, enticing James and others to enlist.

Prior to the outbreak of World War I, however, the Guards remained stationed in the United Kingdom (UK) for 14 years, performing mostly ceremonial duties. They then were deployed to fight in France just eight days after the UK declared war on Germany in 1914. James did not see combat during his service, since his 12-year hitch was over just before the War began.

James reported his age as *"22 years, six months"* and his *"trade or calling"* as *"barman"* on the enlistment papers, and he said that his original parish was *"St. Mary's, near the town of Sligo."* He signed up for *"Short Service,"* a stint that made him pension-eligible. He was expected to complete the following requirements:

"3 years with the Colours and 9 years in the Reserve, or, if the man

completes his 3 years' service with the Colours while beyond the seas,

then for a further period, not exceeding one year, with the Colours,

and the remainder of the 12 years in the Reserves."

Sergeant Draper was the officer who met with James and informed him of what to expect as the terms of his enlistment. Later than same day, January 20, 1902, James had a physical examination after which a lieutenant colonel declared him *"fit"* for service. This five foot, eight-inch Lipsett weighed in at 148 pounds; his complexion was *"fresh,"* his eyes *"brown,"* and his hair *"black."* His *"chest minimum"* was *"34 inches,"* but its *"maximum expansion"* was *"36 inches."* A vaccination several days later completed his medical clearance.

As a member of the First Irish Guards Regiment, James received his assignment to the Caterham Barracks (aka: *The Guards' Depot*) in Surrey, approximately 30 miles from London. The largest army depot in the UK at the time, it served as a training facility and as the primary depot for the Foot Guards Regiments.

There are notations in his service record indicating that the training he experienced may have gotten the better of him. Below are the four hospitalizations he had in Caterham Hospital, three of which were in his second year of active duty:

> January 6 – 13, 1903 (8 days): *"inflammation of sheath of tendon . . . transient synovitis* (inflammation) *of ankle probably from strain"*

> August 3 – 10, 1903 (8 days): *"inflammation gland"*; treatment: *"tooth armored. formentation* (a poultice, a hot medicated compress) *. . . recovery"*

> November 21 – December 31, 1903 (41 days): *"hernia,"* initially *"fixed with truss, right"* on November 17 prior to the hospital stay

> January 21 – February 13, 1904 (24 days): *"wound scalp . . . formentations – clear."* He then was *"examined and found fit for transfer to Army reserve."*

146

James also ran afoul of the army's code of conduct while a reservist. He was *"convicted by Court . . . of wilfull damage and sentenced to one month H.L.* (hard labor) *in prison."* He served 28 days in the brig, November 11 – December 9, 1911, after which he was *"Returned to Army Reserves."* There were no details offered in his record about the location or the type of *"damage"* for which he was responsible, so one can only speculate.

A drunken brawl, perhaps?

James' 12-year service commitment (three years active duty, nine years reserves) ended on January 19, 1914, when he was discharged as a private in *"The termination of first period of engagement."* His discharge came just a month after he was *"Examined and found unfit for section ?* (the section type is illegible on his record)" on December 22, 1913.

According to Grandpa Lipsett and to other Lipsett folk, James changed his name to Ryan, his mother's maiden name, after his move to England. Perhaps the name change was intended to be a message to his father? Was his leaving an acrimonious one for him? For the family? Or could it simply have been an idle threat designed to upset his father? Grandpa always claimed that his father *"was a tough man,"* and he often told the story that he and his siblings had to say the rosary every night, and, if they were not kneeling up straight enough, *"You got the cane!"*

Despite this lingering age-old Lipsett-to-Ryan name change story, I have not been able to verify it. His 1914 British army discharge papers still had the 37-year-old James listed as Lipsett, not Ryan. One would think that he would have changed his name long before then, but who knows? Perhaps his reported name change to Ryan had never been done officially or had not been accomplished until after many years after his discharge?

More speculation.

Grandpa corresponded with his brother James, but he had to send his cards and letters in care of their brother, Richard, who also was a London resident. The brothers actually were cohabiting, since the 1911 census of the United Kingdom had James living with his brother and his wife Sophie (although her given name was Matilda Sophia) along with their children, Edwin Morris and Lilian Josephine.

147

All were residents of a three-room *"flat"* in the London district of Camberwell on Artichoke Place, community of Stobart Mansions. The occupation listed for this *"single . . . brother"* was *"grocer's assistant."*

Without having access to any other information about James, I have lost track of him in his later years; where he spent the rest of his days and when he passed away are a mystery. He was the sole sibling of Grandpa Lipsett's whose final days I have been unable to document. All I know is that Mom recalls Grandpa corresponding with James while she was a young girl, so he was around, at least, through the 1920s. Perhaps he emigrated from London at some point, or perhaps he finally changed his name to Ryan, making the whereabouts of a name as common as James Ryan close to impossible to find. I also have found no record that would have documented a marriage for him at any time.

Marianne. The first-born Lipsett daughter married a local Coolaney resident, a celebrity of sorts, Dominick Gilhawley, in the summer of 1902. This *"grocer and spirit merchant"* from the village also served in the elected position (1899) of *"district councillor"* to represent the Coolaney area folk on the Sligo County Council. It was barely a year into their marriage, however, when Marianne died during childbirth along with her only child, Kathleen. The date was June 6, 1903, just three weeks before her 24th birthday.

Dominick would marry again a year later in the summer of 1904, this time to another resident of the village, Margaret Brennan. Luck was not on his side, though, since a Christmas Eve fire destroyed a good part of his business later that year. Dominick himself passed away on January 2, 1908, at the age of only 38; he and Margaret had no children together. The business was sold to a Gerry O'Grady, but Margaret must have struck out on her own or simply worked for the new owners of the business, since the 1911 census listed this *"widow"* as a *"shop keeper."*

Patrick. Seven years Grandpa's senior, Patrick left Ireland aboard the ship *Majestic* on September 14, 1899; the ship's *"master,"* Edward J. Smith, documented his manifest as consisting of 533 adults, 30 children ages one to 12, and nine infants. Patrick awaited Grandpa as a roommate in Jersey City; he never married and had no children. (Read about his tragic story later in the section, *Grandpa Lipsett's Trip to America*.)

Grandpa Lipsett's brother
Patrick

Robert. As the oldest (and only) son remaining in Ireland, he was the logical inheritor of the family business, William Lipsett's Pub. Robert had been married twice. His first wife, Evelyn (McDermott), died on January 19, 1918, within two years of their 1916 marriage and just three weeks after the birth of their only child, Maureen (December 30, 1917). It was our cousin Maureen who would marry George Jenkinson in 1951 and move to the States seven years later where she enjoyed a distinguished career as a nurse in New York City.

Six months after Evelyn's death, Robert married again, this time to Margaret Rynn (aka: *Aunt Peg*), with whom he had one son, William (aka: *Liam*) Joseph. Son Liam would go on to see to the continuing fortunes of the Mountain Inn; he and his wife, Bridie, had eight children, those cousins whom we have met over the years: Rita, Robert, Mary, Anne, Imelda, Liam, Oliver, and Dominic. Coincidentally, John McDermott, Evelyn's brother, would marry Robert's sister Kate Ellen, making our cousins Maureen and Fr. Robert "double cousins." Robert passed away at the age of 70 on September 27, 1953.

Grandpa Lipsett's brother
Bob

Richard Philip (aka: Dick). The second of the Lipsett brothers to relocate to London, Richard left Ireland soon after the 1901 Ireland census which still having him living with his parents and his siblings in Shancough. By 1902 he was a resident in Zetland Arms in the Kensington section of London where he would go on to marry Matilda Sophia Davis (aka: *Sophie*) in the spring of 1906 and father two children with her, Edwin Morris (DOB: March 8, 1909) and Lilian Josephine (DOB: April 22, 1911). Brother James came to live with Richard and his family after his active army duty was over. The 1911 census of the United Kingdom had this mixed family living in the aforementioned three-room "*flat*" in the London district of Camberwell. Richard was working as an "*engineer, hot water fitter,*" according to the census.

After James' departure from their home for whatever reason, Richard and his family could be found for many years at 170 Meeting House Lane in London. Richard passed away in the spring of 1951 at the age of 66 in Suffolk, England; Sophie predeceased him by nine years, dying on June, 1942, at the age of 63.

The 66-year-old Edwin passed away in December of 1975, whereas Lillie lived until the age of 84 before dying in March of 1996. I cannot confirm a marriage for Edwin, but his sister had married a man by the name of Snowdon (first name unknown) with whom she had at least two children, daughters Mavis (1936) and June (1940).

Brothers Bob (L) and Dick and Dick's daughter Lillie

Grandpa Frank A. Lipsett

Francis Andrew. Grandpa's story follows.

Kate Ellen (aka: Kitty). Kitty married John McDermott of Riverstown in 1915. The couple operated a pub in Ballina, a

150

gift to them from Kate's brother, Robert. Together they had four sons: Dermot (September 8, 1917 – December 3, 1964), Sean (December, 1918 – 1947), Brendan (April, 1923 - ?), and Robert (December 27, 1927 – January 2, 1989).

Their youngest son we know as Fr. Robert who was ordained a priest in the Order of the Oblates of Mary Immaculate in Kilkenny, Ireland in 1952. His first assignments were in Texas (Brownsville, then Midland) before he was incarnated in the Bridgeport, CT, diocese; he soon settled into his final appointment as pastor of the Church of the Sacred Heart in Byram, CT, in 1966.

Kitty (Lipsett) McDermott, Fr. Robert's mother

The story goes that Kitty's husband John was not the most ambitious of Irishmen. Other Lipsett researchers have said that he "*had gone to America to make a fortune, but returned home penniless.*" Mom recalls that John was a house guest at 20 West Hamilton Place for approximately 18 months when she was a young teenage girl. Grandpa was able to get him a job as a night watchman with the railroad, but John made it clear that he would not work on a Sunday, despite Grandpa's seven-day-per-week schedule his whole working life. John also took his bedroom slippers to work with him, obviously to make for a more comfortable workplace.

Grandpa's patience wore thin over time with his brother-in-law and his work habits, particularly as he envisioned his sister Kitty back home in Ireland with the responsibilities of raising four sons on her own and keeping the family pub going. Mom recalled that Grandma Lipsett regularly sent clothing and other provisions to Kitty while her husband was a resident of 20 West Hamilton Place.

Fr. Robert was more than aware of his ne'er-do-well father. In fact, it was he who told the story of his father's accounting for his lack of money when he returned to Ireland. John claimed that he had had a pile of cash in his hand when a strong gust of wind came and blew it all away while he was on the dock awaiting his ship home!

Kitty died on April 27, 1956, at the age of 65; John predeceased her by three years.

Lily Maria *(aka: Aunt Lillie*). After a period of eight years in the States (1912-1920) with Grandpa Lipsett, she returned to Ireland and settled in county Armagh where she married Maurice Gillen and had six children: Mannix, Frank, Lilian, Rosaleen, Kathleen, and Alice. They all eventually moved to Leamington Spa, England, a small town just a short train ride from London. (More details about Lillie follow later in the section, *Grandpa Lipsett: The Jersey City Years*.)

Grandpa's sister Lillie (Lipsett) Gillen

Thomas Michael. Like his sister Lillie, he would leave Ireland in 1912 to meet up with Grandpa at his Jersey City address where he would remain until his death in 1937. (The details of his time in the States will follow in the section, *Grandpa Lipsett: The Jersey City Years*.)

Chapter XX

Grandpa Lipsett's Trip to America

How long before Grandpa's departure did he plan it? Was there one precipitating factor that had him put his plan in motion? And, of course, had he confided to anyone in his family about his plans to leave?

Perhaps there was just nothing to hold him there any longer. After all, his position in his family afforded him little chance for advancement; the laws of primogeniture involved the custom of land inheritance whereby the family's entire estate passed to the eldest son. Primogeniture was designed to maintain the political and social status of the Norman barons and to weaken Irish families by forcing the younger sons to leave the family home to go in search of their own lands and livelihoods. In short, Grandpa never would have been the owner of the family business, and he would have worked all his life for his older brother, Robert, instead. *"There was nothing left there for me,"* he told Mom when she inquired of the reasons for his departure.

Perhaps the news one day of the recently constructed, ponderous *SS Cedric* had spread throughout the land among those considering leaving. Built in the Belfast shipyards in 1903, it was the largest steamship ever built, in fact, the largest ship in the world at that time. Like other steamships, the *Cedric* was designed for regular trans-Atlantic crossings delivering scores of emigrating folk to life in America. It carried 742 passengers on its first voyage, February 9, 1903, from Liverpool, England, to New York, completing the trip in only eight days. Its two funnels and four masts helped it travel the 2,889 mile trip at the speed of 17 knots per hour.

Its size would soon pale in comparison with the launch of the Titanic just eight years later.

Grandpa could have heard from the newspapers or from a local shipping agent that the *Cedric* had been cleared to leave Liverpool, so he could have timed his own departure from his townland of Shancough to coincide with the ship's arrival in the port of Queenstown (now called *Cobh*, pronounced *Cove*), thus avoiding an overnight stay in port. This point of departure for Irish emigrants was the single most important port of emigration; more than a third of the six million Irish folk who left home between 1848 and 1950 left from Queenstown.

I have always heard the story told that Grandpa, the eighth child of the 11 Lipsetts, had been charged with taking the equivalent of $16 into town on the family's horse-drawn wagon to purchase some flour for the family business, William Lipsett's Pub. His destination for the transaction undoubtedly was the village of Coolaney, just a mile or so from his home. Grandpa took with him a friend, probably confiding in him that he was leaving Ireland for good and asking him to return the wagon to the family.

When I visited the last remaining of Grandpa's siblings, Aunt Lillie of Leamington Spa, England, in the summer of 1975, she told me of the day she arrived home to the sound of her mother's sobbing. Mother Kate showed her Grandpa's note informing her that he was leaving Ireland behind for good; "*She was so very upset!*" Lillie claimed.

Grandpa was to leave behind his parents, William and Kate (Ryan) Lipsett (although her name is recorded as Rynne in the parish register), and five of his nine surviving siblings: brothers William John, Robert, and Thomas Michael, and sisters Kate Ellen and Lily Maria.

Grandpa's departure reduced by one the population of the townland of Shancough. A mere 237 acres in size, the 1901 census placed the number of Shancough residents at 57; the residents of the village of Coolaney numbered 197 that same year.

There are approximately 20 townlands scattered throughout Ireland that go by the name *Rockfield*. The one that sits alongside Shancough has been associated with the location of the Lipsetts and of the Mountain Inn, although I have seen both names used interchangeably as the family's residence.

The first leg of Grandpa's emigration began with a train ride from the now-defunct Leyney Station in Coolaney, destination Queenstown, County Cork, and eventually America. He was lucky to have had such a convenient mode of travel; the Collooney to Claremorris (County Mayo) railway connection and the local Leyney Station officially opened on October 1, 1895. In his book, *Killoran and Coolaney: A Local History,* historian Michael Farry wrote:

"The station for Coolaney was called Leyney because of
the similarity of the names Collooney and Coolaney."

(Leyney is one of the six County Sligo subdivisions known as baronies which contain both Coolaney and Collooney within its borders.)

A decades-long call for construction of the railway line reached a crescendo in 1890 when another potato blight decimated the crop that year, leaving most of the locals unemployed; it was the worst crop failure since the year known as *"black '47"* of *"an gorta mor"* (aka: *the great hunger*, the potato famine of 1845-1849). The railway project eventually provided 700-800 of the local folk with gainful employment.

This railway connection was the missing piece in the rail system known as the Western Rail Corridor which connected Limerick with Sligo. It was dubbed *"The Burma Road,"* named after the infamous road built as a supply line by prisoners of war for Japanese forces during World War II. The Sligo version was so named because of the difficult terrain through which the railway ran; bogland and rocky landscapes required considerable engineering skill for its construction.

This connection, and with it Coolaney's Leyney Station, was closed to passenger traffic on June 15, 1963, but the line remained open only to freight transport until its final closure on October 30, 1975. For some reason, this section of railway is the only one that has been dismantled, but there is currently a movement afoot to re-open it in an effort to increase tourism in that part of Sligo.

It would appear that Grandpa could have taken the train from Coolaney's Leyney Station to Queenstown with only two changes, one at Limerick Junction and the last one at Cork City. He could have arrived at his destination in just a matter of hours.

It was early in the morning of Saturday, August 6, 1904, when our grandfather, 16-year-old Francis Andrew (aka: *Frank*) Lipsett, awaited the *SS Cedric* of the White Star Line along with 268 of his fellow countrymen. The ship left Liverpool, England for Queenstown the day before, already carrying approximately 1,168 passengers, many of whom were US citizens returning home, with the remainder consisting of travelers from all over Europe. Grandpa was one of the locals who ascended the ramp and boarded the ship upon its arrival that morning. Those who took their places in steerage class numbered 210, and another 59 enjoyed *Second-Cabin Passenger* status. This trip was one of the eight the *Cedric* made that year. Its final voyage was on September 5, 1931, after which it was broken up for scrap metal in Scotland.

Grandpa was not to return again to Ireland until the summer of 1954, a full 50 years after his departure.

Grandpa traveled steerage, the lowest passenger class available, named for its location at the lowest level of the ship near the steering mechanism and the cargo hold; less common names for this accommodation were "'*tween decks*," "*emigrant class*," and "*third class.*" Steerage was the cheapest of all fares; the cost of his ticket was approximately thirty dollars which he admitted on the ship's manifest that he paid for himself. Second class passengers paid approximately double the price of the steerage tickets. Other common practices were for the emigrants' "*sponsors*" in the States to pre-pay tickets for the travelers in advance of their departure. Could Grandpa's brother Patrick, already settled in Jersey City, have pre-paid the ticket for him?

Not according to Grandpa.

Mom always told the story of Grandpa's recollections of the trip across the Atlantic, of the upper deck's *Second Cabin Passengers'* and of the *Saloon* or *First Cabin Passengers'* bemused reactions at the party atmosphere created by the Irish steerage folk who traveled below their lofty decks. Music, singing, and dancing created a good "*craic*" (pronounced *crack*, a joyful atmosphere), and Grandpa was, no doubt, a great contributor to these festive gatherings. According to Mom, Grandpa was one of those Irish musicians who was asked to perform at local gatherings here in the States. Traditional Irish musicians still gather for planned and spontaneous get-togethers known as *seisiuns* (sessions) to perform music from the old sod.

While helping Grandpa pack up his wares at 20 West Hamilton Place in 1965 in preparation for his move to 260 Ege, I recall opening a case which contained what Grandpa referred to as a "*button box*" (aka: a *button accordion*), a concertina-type/miniature accordion, which he apparently had put to good use in his days as a party invitee. The bellows had long since dried out, and they were cracked and beyond use, but the nostalgia was priceless. However, there is no longer a trace of it, since Grandpa obviously discarded it in his haste to make way for his move uptown. Mom always said that he had a gift not only for music but also for Irish step dancing for which he won several "cups" in dance competitions along with his brother, Thomas Michael. Grandpa's classic golden oak player piano, along with its 102 piano rolls, also left his possession before his move, having been handed over to a neighbor who wheeled it down the middle of West Hamilton Place to its new location. Mom can vouch for the number of rolls, since one of her chores as a young child was to dust them off from time to time.

On page 25 of the *SS Cedric's* 26-page manifest nestled between the names John Stinson, a 26-year-old laborer, and Mary Jennings, a 39-year-old housewife, was the following Grandpa Lipsett information recorded on the page's 22 columns:

No. on List: **13197**
Name in Full: **Frank Lipsett**
Age: **19** (but Grandpa had turned only 16 just two months before he
boarded the ship to leave; either there was mistake in recording his age
on the manifest or, more likely, he gave himself an additional three years
to gain some advantage in traveling)
Sex: **M**
Married or Single: **S**
Calling or Occupation: **Labr** (laborer)
Able to Read, Write: **Yes; Yes**
Nationality: **Ireland**
Race or People: **Irish**
Last Residence: **Coolaney**
Final Destination: **Jersey City**
Whether Having a Ticket to Such Final Destination: **Yes**
By Whom Was Passage Paid: **Self**
Whether in Possession of $50, and if Less, How Much? **$30.**
Whether ever before in the United States, and if so, when and where? **No**
Whether going to join a relative or friend, and if so, what relative or friend, and his name and complete address: **bro 654 Grand St, Jersey City**
Ever in Prison or Almshouse or supported by charity. If yes, state which: **No**
Whether a Polygamist: **No**
Whether an Anarchist: **No**

Whether under Contract, expressed or implied to Labor in the United States: <u>**No**</u>
Condition of Health, Mental and Physical: <u>**Good**</u>
Deformed or Crippled, Nature, length of time, and cause: <u>**No**</u>

No other passengers listed Coolaney as their *Last Residence*, nor were there any other nearby townlands listed as the *Last Residence* of any of the other Queenstown boarders.

One can only conclude that Grandpa indeed was a lone traveler.

The "*bro*" recorded as the relative or friend whom Grandpa was planning to join was his older brother, Patrick, who had been in the States since September of 1899. Like countless other Irish immigrants, Patrick worked for the railroad, serving as a brakeman for the Pennsylvania Railroad. Seven years older than Grandpa and the fifth-born of the Lipsett children and fourth-born son, Patrick's surname usually appeared as *Lipsey*.

Grandpa and the *SS Cedric* arrived in New York Harbor on Sunday, August 14, just eight days after leaving Queenstown. The first and second class passengers disembarked first at either the Hudson or East River piers where they passed through customs with just a cursory inspection and were free to go. Grandpa and his fellow steerage folk, however, boarded a barge which took them all on the final step to Ellis Island itself where they had to undergo several hours of medical and legal inspections at the Great Hall Registry Room. Most of that time, however, was spent in waiting to be called forward.

By the time Grandpa set off for the States, steamship companies were held responsible for inspecting their own potential passengers before they boarded ship in their home ports in order to be able to exclude the sick and the infirm from the trip. Since these companies were held financially responsible for payment of the return trip for those deemed unacceptable by the immigration folk at Ellis Island, it was to their advantage to cull from the larger group those individuals who probably would not make it through inspection in the States. In other words, allowing the sick or the infirm aboard ship in the first place and then having to return them to their home port could cost them money.

In an attempt to comply with this relatively new directive, the Cedric's commanding officer, H.J. Haddock, had asked the ship's surgeon, a Dr. J.H. Bell, to make "*a personal examination of each of the aliens names herein . . . relative to the mental and physical condition of such aliens*" as part of the steamship's responsibility for inspecting its own passengers.

Apparently, Dr. Bell had certified that he had done so and that he had *"made a personal examination of each of the aliens names herein"* and had passed muster on Grandpa Lipsett.

The follow-up medical examinations which Grandpa faced next at the port of arrival, however, were quite paltry, at best: *"It was estimated that a total of six seconds was spent on each immigrant inspected on the 'Line.'"*

The *Line Inspection* referred to the practice of the U.S. Public Health Inspectors observing the immigrants climbing the stairs to the main hall; they were particularly interested in looking for signs of physical stress, defective posture, and an unusual gait or weakness. In order to keep these inspections orderly, the flight of stairs to the second floor was divided into 12 lanes, thus enabling the inspectors to make a "thorough" evaluation of the ascendants as they climbed. The inspectors prided themselves on their ability to make snap diagnoses regarding an illness or disability among the arrivals. Those suspected of being of questionable health had their clothing marked with chalk and were detained for a more in-depth examination.

In *Ellis Island: Gateway to the American Dream*, Pamela Reeves wrote:

> *"The chalk marks were coded – B for back, C for conjunctivitis, Ct for trachoma, E for eyes, Ft for feet, G for goiter, H for heart, K for hernia, L for lameness, N for neck, P for physical and lungs, Pg for pregnancy, Sc for scalp, S for senility, X for mental retardation, and a circled K for insanity. On average, fifteen to twenty percent of the immigrants were marked for further examination."*

Of course, many an immigrant either removed the chalked item of clothing or turned it inside-out to avoid closer scrutiny. However, despite the fearfulness among the arrivals that they might not make it through all these inspections, only about two percent of immigrants were told to return to their countries of origin throughout Ellis Island's years of operation. In 1907, for example, only 13,064 immigrants were told to return to their home countries out of a total of 1,285,349 Ellis Island arrivals that year, a mere one percent of the total.

Another medical officer greeted the immigrants at the end of this line and did nothing but inspect their eyes for signs of a dreaded contagious disease called *trachoma* which, if left untreated, could result in blindness. These doctors used their bare fingers or metal buttonhooks to peel back the arrivals' eyelids to look for the presence of the disease. Considering the lack of sterile instruments and the cleanliness of the hands of the inspectors during the exam, there probably was a greater chance of spreading the disease through the examination itself than there was in typical transmission throughout the general immigrant population. A detected case of trachoma would result in immigrants being sent back home, as would a case of *favus*, a contagious scalp disease, among other ailments.

Although Grandpa undoubtedly passed these so-called inspections, he did not leave Ellis Island that day; the Immigration Department detained him overnight and listed him in its *Record of Detained Alien Passengers*. Brother Patrick now was listed as 650 Grand St, not 654 as the *Cedric* manifest claimed.

Immigrants who exhibited some of the aforementioned medical complications were detained for observation for days or weeks, whereas others remained on the island if the contact person named on the ship's manifest was not available for some reason. Ellis Island also had a policy not to release minor children without an adult present to claim them. Although our minor 16-year-old Grandpa claimed to be 19, the immigration officials must have seen through this ruse and insisted that he remain there until Patrick came to retrieve him. Grandpa's *Cause of Detention* was a simple notation, *"To bro."* Perhaps Patrick was not able to leave work to vouch for his younger brother until the day after his arrival.

Inspector Green released Grandpa to Patrick the next day on Monday, the 15th of August, at 10:20 a.m.; the *Disposition* recorded on the *Record* the next day was simply, *"Bro Patrick, 650 Grand St."* Grandpa apparently fared well during his day-long detention, having been provided *"breakfast, dinner, and supper."*

Grandpa's years with Patrick did not last as long as he undoubtedly had hoped. He had been with his older brother for a little over two years when Patrick suffered a fatal railroad injury late one night in the railroad yard of the Harsimus Cove Station in Jersey City; his 1906 death certificate listed the cause of death as due to *"accidental RR injuries."* Undertaker J.J. Shannon & Co. of 482 Communipaw Ave. saw to the wake and the burial at Holy Name Cemetery.

The *Annual Statements of the Railroad and Canal Companies of the State of New Jersey of 1906* and the *New Jersey Bureau of Statistics of Labor and Industries* that same year provided accounts of his injury; the former reported:

> *December 20 – Patrick J. Lipsey, struck by train at Harsimus Cove,*
> *Jersey City, N.J. - conductor - engineman.*

The latter, the following:

> *Patrick Lipsey, a switchman on the Pennsylvania Railroad, was*
> *struck on the tracks at Jersey City, and had his right arm cut off*
> *near the shoulder.*

The *Evening Journal* of Friday, December 21, 1906, ran the following news article, although it referred to the loss of a different arm:

KNOCKED DOWN BY ENGINE – LOSES ARM

> *Patrick Litsey, 25 years old, of 605 Grand Street, while at work*
> *in the yards of the Pennsylvania Railroad Company at Greene*
> *and First Streets last night at 8 o'clock was knocked down by*
> *a drill engine and had his left arm cut off at the shoulder. He*
> *was removed to St. Francis Hospital in an ambulance wagon.*

Another newspaper account of his accident appeared in *The Observer of Hudson County* the day after the event, December 21. If ever there were a comic side to tragedy, this undoubtedly was it. And so the story goes (spelling, grammar, and layout all as it appeared in press):

CONFUSION CAUSED BY FIND OF AN ARM
Had Belonged to Brakeman Who Had

Been Injured and Was Forgotten in Yard

Patrick Litsey, employed as a brakeman for the Pennsylvania Railroad, had

his arm completely severed from his body last night inmaking a flying couple

of two cars in the Greene street yards. He wastaken to St. Francis Hospital

where he is now in a dangerous condition. In the hurry to take Litsey to the

hospital, while placing him in the ambulance, the men forgot to pick up the

man's arm. An hour afterwards one of the brakemen who happened to be in

the place where the accident happened to see it, and not knowing of it, thought

some one else had lost an arm and was laying about the yard. In haste he

hurried to the yard-master and informed him of the gruesome find. The

yardmaster, not thinking at the time of the Litsey accident, called up the

Second Precinct police station to Sergeant Foley, who was on the desk, and

told him to send the patrol to Green street, that there was an accident there.

Down the patrol went in a hurry. As soon as it reached the placeall they

found was a large crowd of brakemen standing around an arm. Some were

busy with their lanterns, looking for the body that belonged tothe arm, when

one brakeman who was a companion of Litsey recognized the color of

the sleeve.

The patrol returned without an occupant.

One can only imagine the anguish for Grandpa in caring for his dying brother all through the Christmas season. Patrick lost his arm on Thursday, December 20, and passed away nine days later. Surviving such a catastrophic injury for that long in an era without antibiotics must have been quite a test of his will and physical strength; the development of penicillin was still 21 years away.

Perhaps a tough Irishman, as they say?

Patrick's obituary appeared in the 1906 New Year's Eve edition of the *Evening Journal*:

LIPSEY – On Saturday, Dec. 29, 1906, Patrick, the beloved son

of William and Catherine Lipsey, aged 23 years and 8 months.

162

Relatives and friends, also International Brotherhood of Stationary
Firemen, Local No. 196, of Jersey City, are respectfully invited to
attend the funeral from the residence of Mr. James Cunningham,
340 Woodward Street, on Wednesday, Jan. 2, 1907, at 9 a.m.
thence to St. Patrick's Church where a solemn high mass of requiem
will be offered for the happy repose of his soul.

The loss of Patrick left Grandpa without his primary supporter and benefactor. Mom has always recalled the kindness of one Jennie Cunningham who took Grandpa under her wing, as it were, and helped him in the immediate aftermath of Patrick's tragic death, making funeral arrangements, securing a burial plot, and helping him with a variety of other tasks.

Jennie was the same Jennie who was married to James Cunningham of the Woodward Street location mentioned in Patrick's obituary; both Jennie and James were Irish-born. The mother of two daughters, Mary (7) and Martha (6), Jennie would have been 23 years of age when Grandpa was left Patrick-less at the age of 18. Jennie maintained contact with Grandpa over the years. In fact, Jennie's daughter, Mary (Cunningham) Talke, stood alongside Mom by the casket at Grandpa's wake in 1969, acting as if her loss were the equivalent of Mom's, as she recalled.

Chapter XXI

The Coolaney–Bloomfield–Graham Connection

For reasons unbeknownst to me, the town of Bloomfield, New Jersey became the destination for a number of emigrating Coolaney - area families.

One family in particular was the Graham family.

The first indication of a Lipsett - Bloomfield - Graham connection appeared when William John, Grandpa's older brother by 10 years, named *Patk* (Patrick) *Graham* of Bloomfield as the *"destination"* noted on his ship's manifest. William John arrived at Ellis Island aboard the *SS Oceanic* from Queenstown on August 1, 1900, four years before Grandpa and a year after Patrick; the ship's manifest also listed him as a *"clerk"* from *"Cooloney"* who came with $30 on his person. He returned to Ireland aboard the *Umbria* three months later on November 3, 1900. One can only assume that he filled in the Shancough Lipsetts on the goings-on among the Bloomfield Grahams when he returned.

The Graham and Lipsett families apparently enjoyed a close relationship over the years in Coolaney. Mom recalls clearly that one of the daughters, Catherine, worked for the Lipsetts in the family pub business, perhaps *"corking bottles of stout,"* like Aunt Lillie said she did as a child. Patrick (56) and Winnie (Gallagher) Greahan (56) of the nearby townlands of Carrownbanny and Knockadoo left Ireland in the spring of 1891 and arrived in the States on May 7 aboard the ship, *City of New York*. Their surname, *Greahan,* was spelled as such in the St. Joseph Church's parish register, but it apparently was the Protestant version of the name that appeared as *Graham* in other records, immigration and otherwise.

Accompanying Patrick and Winnie were three of their six children, Martin (18), Bridget (11), and Winnie (listed as nine years of age on the ship's manifest, but she actually was 13 years old, born December 1, 1878, according to the St. Joseph parish records). Older sisters Mary, Ellen (aka: *Nellie*), and Catherine traveled separately to Bloomfield. Another sister, Anna, appeared in the Coolaney Civil Register but in no immigration records that I could find; she reappeared later in the Bloomfield Directories.

Grandpa was only three years of age when the Grahams left Coolaney for good.

During our Ireland visit in the summer of 2004, I inquired of the Sligo locals of their recollections of the Graham family. There was ne'er a memory of any Graham family in the area in the recent past, as I was told. I spoke by phone with Delia Coleman, the elderly mother of a Mountain Inn regular and the unofficial local historian, who told me that she had no recollection of any Graham family in the area during her time. John McMaster, the rector of the local Protestant parish of the Church of Ireland, also exchanged letters with me and wrote, *"There are no Grahams living around this area since I came to live here over 52 years ago."*

Perhaps the Grahams of this story were the last ones to have left the Coolaney area for the States.

It would appear that the Grahams were financially comfortable. Cousin Mary Lipsett took me and Jeanne to visit what she claimed was the Graham home in the townland of Knockadoo during our 2004 Ireland visit. What we saw were the crumbling remains of a homestead which consisted of a main house and two other smaller buildings in the rear of the property, a surprisingly ample piece of land. The Grahams also purchased a home, 117 Orchard Street, in Bloomfield soon after their arrival. They remained for many years in their home on this very wide, tree-lined residential street until it was passed down to or purchased by daughter Nellie and her husband, Frank Hillock. The Hillocks remained there until 1954 when Nellie passed away, and Frank moved in with his daughter and son-in-law, William and Margaret Nice, in Montclair. The house remained vacant until purchased by one John Molinski in 1957.

The Mount Olivet cemetery caretaker, Tom Gaughan, also told me when I visited the Graham family cemetery plot that the section of the cemetery where it was located was reserved for the more well-to-do families who were able to afford larger monuments for the deceased; he described it as a place which *"used to be for the elite in the cemetery."*

All federal census records and the annual Bloomfield Directories consistently listed mother Winifred and daughters Catherine, Nellie, Mary, and Winifred as *"weavers"* and *"dressmakers."* Father Patrick was a *"laborer,"* and Martin, the only son, was a *"brakeman,"* according to these same records. Catherine reported in the 1910 federal census that she worked in a *"woolen mill."*

Other Coolaney-area transplants to Bloomfield included the Grahams' cousins, the Kerins family, of the nearby townland of Carrownbanny; four of the seven Kerins children, James, Mary, Ellen, and John, all made their way here and moved in with the Grahams on Orchard St. John, the second born and oldest son of Patrick and Ellen, did not fare well, however. This 19-year-old arrived in the States on August 24, 1905, and died just two years later on June 5, 1907. He suffered the same fate as Patrick Lipsett, with his death due to *"accidental R.R. injuries"* suffered at the Erie Railroad's Pavonia Ave. station in Jersey City; in all likelihood, he was a workmate alongside Grandpa Lipsett.

I have included here the sad story of his death which was the front page article of the June 5th edition of the *Evening Journal*:

DIED WITH HIS MOTHER'S NAME ON HIS LIPS
Pathetic Scene Following an Accident in
The Erie Passenger Depot Today
WOMEN CONSOLING ANGELS TO VICTIM

While Erie Railroad passengers were rushing to and from trains
in the depot at the foot of Pavonia Avenue at 11 o'clock this morning a
force of men were hard at work releasing Patrick Kilday, 23 years old,
of 12 Porter Street, this city, and John Kerins, 21 years old, of 117
Orchard Street, Bloomfield, from underneath the whales of a passenger
coach.
Both men were at work at the trucks of the car when more cars sent
down the track to make up the train smashed into the one under which they

were working. They had been warned of the approach of the other cars and
were hastening to get out from under when the impact came. Kilday had
his left leg cut off close to the thigh and Kerins was almost cut in two. An
ambulance took Kilday to St. Francis Hospital and Kerins was carried into
the baggage room. He was absolutely conscious, but, realizing his condition,
asked for a priest. As he was carried to the scene of the accident some women
passengers waiting for trains offered gentle services which were accepted.
Others prayed for him. A message sent to St. Michael's rectory on Ninth
Street brought Rev. Father James A. Kelly along in a great hurry. He was
none too soon. Kerins was conscious, but rapidly dying. His face lit up
with a smile as the priest approached. The bystanders doffed their hats and
withdrew while the dying man made his last confession. Father Kelly's
eyes were moist as he bade farewell to the young man. The clergyman
had hardly left the baggage room when the end came. Kerins died with
his mother's name on his lips. The waiting ambulance went away empty
and the morgue wagon took its place.

The front page of the same newspaper the next day reported that Patrick Kilday had passed away after the loss of his leg. The article questioned whose responsibility the accident was and added that the "*Erie people*" were conducting an investigation into it. It also claimed, "*Men accustomed to this kind of work are supposed to know of the danger and keep their eyes open.*"

Kerins is buried in the Graham family cemetery plot.

Chapter XXII

Winnie Graham

It was Winifred (aka: *Winnie*) Graham, the namesake of her mother, who intrigued me when Aunt Lillie first mentioned her name to me in the summer of 1975 when she said that Grandpa had been married to her before he married our grandmother, Loretta (Crowley) Lipsett. Fate was kind to me the year I taught at Caldwell College, just a stone's throw from Bloomfield, since I was able to enjoy convenient access to the library's Bloomfield City Directories and the archived microfilm records of the local newspapers.

At the suggestion of Emil Pappalardo, the archivist at the Church of the Sacred Heart in Bloomfield, I contacted the local Catholic school, Sacred Heart, hoping to find some records for any of the Grahams, assuming that Irish immigrant families typically enrolled their children in the local Catholic school. In a bit of genealogical luck, the school principal, our old friend, Valerie Oliva, answered the phone when I called. Not 20 minutes after ending my conversation with her and explaining the reason for my call, Valerie called back to tell me that she found the original Sister Rose Genevieve's High School 1893-1896 Roll Book, a record that included one Winnie Graham, beginning with the September, 1894, roll. One also can assume that she would have registered for school for the 1891-92, 1892-93, and 1893-94 school years as well, but I have not been able to find these roll books.

Although it was unclear what the ages were of her classmates, all Irish with the names Hayes, Moran, Mullaney, Honan, O'Hara, Dunigan, Quinn, O'Haire, Callahan, and Moran, Winnie may have been considerably older than they were. Many records list her age as approximately five years younger than she was; however, at the start of the 1894-95 school year, she would have been 16 years, eight months old.

According to the Roll Book, Winnie missed only 13 days in the 1894-95 school year. She returned to school the following September without several of her former classmates; William Hayes, Edward Moran, William O'Hara, and Michael and Teresa Dunigan were all missing. The Roll Book listed names differently this time; they were grouped as *Seniors, First Grade,* and *Second Grade.* Winnie was included among the last group with Rosie Idle, Mamie Glennon, and Philip Sugelkin, by whatever the criterion was at that time: age? achievement level?

The subjects Winnie studied that year included Catechism, Spelling, Grammar, Geography, History, and Science; she also received grades for Lessons, Exercises, and Conduct. However, she appeared to have attended school the next year only until the end of the first full week of November, 1895. Besides a half-day the following Friday, there were no more notations in the roll book about her attendance, not even an *"a"* for *"absent,"* through the end of that school year. That November week appeared to have been the time of her last formal schooling. She apparently left school to provide some financial assistance to her family with her skills as a dressmaker.

Winnie made her confirmation along with her sister, Bridget, and 17 other confirmands at Sacred Heart two years earlier on April 23, 1893; Reverend Bishop Wigger presided over the sacrament. Winifred took the name *Evangeline* and Bridget, *Elizabeth.* Older sister Catherine made her confirmation two years earlier on April 5, 1891, and took the name *Loretta.*

Chapter XXIII

Grandpa and Winnie (Graham) Lipsett

Exactly when Grandpa met Winnie for the first time is not known. It is probably safe to assume, however, that he had been "*keeping company*" with her during his two years with Patrick in Jersey City. I suspect that this was so, since one of the posed professional photographs I have of Patrick was taken in the *Vollmer Photo Atelier* in Bloomfield; if Patrick frequented the Graham family there, perhaps as a suitor of one of the sisters, might not Grandpa have been equally as enthralled with one of them? Grandpa also has left us with several posed portrait pictures over the years, perhaps those taken along with Patrick. Mom always said that Grandpa liked to have such studio pictures taken of him; "*I think he posed for a picture every time he parted his hair!*" she claimed.

Nevertheless, Grandpa married Winifred Graham on Wednesday morning, January 22, 1908, just one year after Patrick's death. The Church of the Sacred Heart's parish register, however, recorded the marriage as having taken place between *Thomas* A. Lipsett and Winifred E. Graham, although the official state record had the name as *Francis A.* Lipsett, a "*laborer*." Their ages were recorded as 22 and 25 years of age, respectively, even though Grandpa was still five months shy of his 20th birthday, and Winnie was 29 years of age. The "*Witnesses*" (best man and maid of honor) were Patrick McGlone and Anna Riley. Reverend Father Joseph Nardiello performed the ceremony.

The January 23, 1908, edition of the Newark Evening News carried the wedding announcement and added, "*A wedding breakfast followed at the home of the bride, in Orchard Street.*"

The local Bloomfield newspaper, *The Sunday Call*, carried the following notice three days later:

> *"The wedding of Miss Winifred Graham, daughter of Mr. and Mrs. P.*
> *Graham, of Orchard Street, and Frank Lifsitt, took place in the Church of*
> *the Sacred Heart Wednesday morning. The ceremony was performed by*
> *the Rev. Joseph Nardiello. Miss Anna Reilly as bridesmaid and Frederick*
> *McGlore was best man. A wedding breakfast followed."*

Best man was Patrick McGlone from the townland of Carrowkeel in County Sligo who made at least two trips between Ireland and the States. Records of his first visit place him at 103 Woodward St. in Jersey City, the same street as the Cunningham residence which held the wake for Patrick. He was joined there on April 17, 1902, by his sister, Kate (19), and his brother, Michael (20). The ship's manifest from his August 21, 1907, arrival aboard the *Oceanic* (the same ship that transported William John) indicated that he had been in Jersey City once before. Listed as a *"saloon keeper,"* his destination this time was to 6<u>??</u> Grand Street, Jersey City (exact address obscured on manifest).

Could he have been returning to stay with Grandpa at his 654 Grand Street address? Could he have returned to provide some support to Grandpa, just eight months after Patrick's death? Could he have been a bartender/saloon keeper at William Lipsett's pub, soon to be known as the *Mountain Inn*? And, of course, the ultimate speculation: could Patrick McGlone have been the friend who returned the horse-drawn wagon to the Lipsett family the day Grandpa left Shancough?

Probably, but one can only speculate.

Mom remembers meeting Patrick McGlone as a young child at the wake for his daughter, Elizabeth, who was killed in an automobile accident while forging a career as a singer with the Peter Van Steeden Orchestra.

Sadly, Grandpa's marriage to Winnie lasted only 45 days. It was on Saturday, March 7, 1908, when Winnie succumbed to what the coroner, Dr. J. D. Moore, certified as a *"cerebral hemorrhage."* However, Michael O'Boyle of the O'Boyle Funeral Home in Bloomfield told me that such a cause of death was typically a "catch-all" diagnosis attributed to many ailments that were not well understood by the physicians at the time. In fact, Winnie's sister, Ellen (aka: *Nellie*), had the same cause of death attributed to her when she passed away in March of 1954. Through a series of connections, I contacted

O'Boyle in the hopes of finding records of Winnie's wake which a Peter Quinn presided over; however, the Quinn Funeral Home had long since been sold to a Mike Murray, and those records were not to be found, O'Boyle concluded.

Winnie died in the "*garret*," a third-floor apartment in the 2 East Liberty St. home of Owen Mullaney, which she and Grandpa shared as newlyweds Owen soon would soon go on to marry Winnie's sister, Catherine.

The cause of Winnie's death might best be determined by the description of her symptoms during her last days as documented in the March 8, 1908, edition of *The Sunday Call:*

YOUNG BRIDE OF FEW WEEKS
DIES AFTER BRIEF ILLNESS

Mrs. Winifred Lipsett, wife of Francis Lipsett, and daughter of Mr. and Mrs. Patrick Graham, of 117 Orchard Street, Bloomfield, died in her home, 2 Liberty Street, that town, early yesterday morning. She was stricken with paralysis about ten days ago, and that, together with an attack of pneumonia, was the cause of her death. Six weeks ago the young woman, who has a large circle of friends, became the bride of Mr. Lipsett in the Church of the Sacred Heart, Bloomfield. Funeral services will be held in the same church on Tuesday morning and will be conducted by the Rev. Joseph M. Nardiello. The interment will be in Mt. Olivet Cemetery. The young woman's brother, Martin, died some time ago from injuries received on the Erie Railroad, where he was employed as a conductor.

It would appear from the symptoms described in the article that polio may have been the cause. However, this same edition of the newspaper also reported that scarlet fever was prevalent in the area, citing 41 new cases the week before.

The *Newark Evening News* the next day ran the following obituary:

LIPSETT – Suddenly, at Bloomfield, on March 7, 1908. Winifred Graham, wife of Francis Lipsett. Relatives and friends are kindly invited to attend the

funeral from the residence of her father, Patrick Graham, 117 Orchard Street,

on Tuesday, March 10, at 8:30 a.m.; thence to the Church of the Sacred Heart,

where a Solemn High Mass of Requiem will be offered for the repose of her soul.

Interment at Mt. Olivet. New York papers please copy.

The tragic death of Winifred was neither the first nor the last for the Graham family. Patrick, Winnie's father, died just 18 days later on March 25, 1908, at the age of 68; cause of death was "*accident: burned to death*" at his home at 117 Orchard St. Unfortunately, the edition of the local newspaper that would have documented this story in some detail had been lost or damaged and never converted to microfilm, according to one of the Bloomfield librarians. Therefore, I have no details of this tragedy.

Two years earlier, Winifred's younger brother, Martin, the only son, died at the age of 34 due to a work-related accident ("*struck by truck*"). The December 29, 1906, edition of the *Bloomfield Citizen* reported that Martin was "*employed as a freight train conductor*" and that he was "*the only son of Patrick Graham of Orchard Street. Several weeks ago he was injured at Forest Hill and was taken to the hospital.*" The article also referred to the "*large attendance at the funeral*" and to his membership in "*the Catholic Lyceum, the Catholic Benevolent Legion and the Brotherhood of Railroad Trainmen.*"

It borders on the eerie that Martin died within 48 hours of Patrick Lipsett due to railroad-related injuries.

The Graham grave monument at Mount Olivet Cemetery in Bloomfield reads:

Patrick Graham
1840-1908

Winifred Graham
1839-1916

Martin Graham
1874-1906

Winifred Lipsett
1884-1908

Chapter XXIV

Grandpa Lipsett After Winnie

Grandpa remained close to the Graham family after Winnie's death. The 1910 federal census placed him as a "*boarder*" at 9 Vine Street in Bloomfield with Michael and Anna (Graham) Sexton and their sons, Joseph and James; Anna was Winnie's younger sister. Joining Grandpa in the same Sexton home was Catherine (aka: *Kate*) Graham, "*sister-in-law*," another one of Winnie's sisters. Grandpa's occupation was "*foreman – railroad terminal*," according to the census report.

Grandpa also served as the best man at the wedding of Francis Aloysius Hillock, a widower, and Nellie Theresa Graham on May 6, 1914; Mom remembers that Hillock "*always had an umbrella, even when it wasn't raining.*" Owen Joseph Mullaney and Catherine Loretta Graham also wed that day along with Francis and Nellie in a double wedding ceremony; best man for the Mullaney wedding was Patrick Finnerty. Bloomfield's *Independent Press* of May 8, 1914, reported the following:

Double Wedding This Week

Two sisters, residents of this town, at a double wedding ceremony Wednesday   morning at the Church of the Sacred Heart. Miss Catherine L. Graham was married to Owen J. Mulraney of Montclair and Miss Nellie Graham became the bride of Frank A, Hillock, also of Montclair. The ceremony was performed by Rev. Charles J. Tischler, assistant rector, at a nuptial mass, and was attended by many relatives and friends. Following the ceremony a wedding breakfast was held at the home of the sisters, 117 Orchard St.

Grandpa and his second wife, our Grandma Loretta (Crowley) Lipsett, also stayed close to the Graham family, and they took Mom for many visits to the remaining Grahams over the years. Mom recalls seeing *"Uncle Jimmy Sexton,"* among others, during these visits. In fact, some of the first folks whom Grandpa and Grandma took her to visit soon after she was born were the Grahams of Bloomfield. She tells the story of how she was transported in a laundry basket to the Graham home during one of her early visits.

Mom also has fond memories of visiting Winnie's older sister, Catherine/Kate (Graham) Mullaney, at 2 East Liberty Street, and chasing chickens around her backyard and collecting eggs from the coops. Catherine/Kate married Owen Mullaney, a widower with five children: four sons and one daughter. Sixty-four-year-old Owen passed away on March 22, 1928, after 14 years of marriage.

Little did Mom know that this home where she played often was the very same home where Winnie died. Owen Mullaney owned the residence and apparently rented the third floor apartment to Grandpa and Winnie.

Mom visited Catherine often, both with her parents and by herself. The bus which she took dropped her off just one block from her home, so the commute was an easy one for a young single woman to make. Mom's relationship with Catherine lasted until her death on February 9, 1960, at the age of 89. Catherine's heirs were limited; the local paper reported that she was *"survived only by a nephew, James P. Sexton of Bloomfield."*

She said to Mom at one point, *"If anything happens to me, see my lawyer."* Mom then recalls seeing in the Newark Star Ledger an announcement that she had been left approximately $1,200 by Catherine/Kate in her will. Catherine also gave Mom a gold brooch which she claimed had been a wedding gift to her mother from President Ulysses S. Grant for whom she worked. I am unclear as to how accurate this story is, but I will continue to investigate it.

Mom never really knew who these Bloomfield folks were during her many visits there. She simply assumed that they were all friends of Grandpa Lipsett's from Ireland. In fact, she didn't know anything at all of Grandpa's marriage to Winnie until she was 13 years of age. Her uncle Thomas Michael's wife-to-be, Marion O'Connell, asked Grandpa one day if Mom *"knew about Winnie."* Fearing that Marion might be the one to "spill the beans," Grandpa and Grandma sat Mom down and told her. When I asked Mom what her reaction was to this news, she replied, *"I cried; nobody knows what it's like to have nobody to talk to!"* A fellow genealogist shared this same story with me. She said that she, too, learned of her father's first marriage for the first time as a young 13-year-old. *"Families never talked about such things in those days,"* she claimed.

The frustrating part of my Graham search is that the trail grew cold quickly. There were no photographs to be found, and I suspect that, among the several photo albums that Grandpa discarded while cleaning house preparatory to his move to us at 260 Ege, were photos of Winnie and her family. I was able to locate only one surviving Graham kin in the area; Frank and Nellie (Graham) Hillock, the couple for whom Grandpa Lipsett served as best man, had two daughters, Margaret and Frances. Margaret married William Nice, and it was their son, Bill, whom I found in Montclair. Bill shared some memories of his visits to the Hillocks at 117 Orchard St. and to a *"Jimmy,"* obviously Jimmy Sexton, son of Michael and Anna (Graham) Sexton. He described Nellie as being *"reclusive"* and Frank as being more fun, playing alongside Bill among the chickens he kept in his backyard. Bill thought that his brother Frank might have some family pictures, but Frank told me that he thought that Bill had whatever pictures of the Grahams or Hillocks existed.

Frances, the Hillocks' other daughter, married Carl Sloan and relocated to Portland, Oregon. Frank Nice told me that his wife had tried in vain to contact the Sloans and their three daughters several years ago. Neither of Anna (Graham) Sexton's two sons married, Martin Graham died before he married, and Catherine (Graham) Mullaney had five step-children. Frank also said that Mary, the other Graham sister, moved to Florida but never married. Thus, without pictures of any kind or additional Graham descendants to contact, the Graham
trail ends here.

Chapter XXV

Grandpa Lipsett: The Jersey City Years

Most municipalities throughout the state published annual city directories, interim population counts between the 10-year federal censuses; however, the Jersey City Directories ended in 1925. Whether apochryphal or not, the story is told that Frank Hague, the mayor of Jersey City from 1917 to 1947, discontinued the Directories in order to put an end to the official accounting of Jersey City residents so that there was no way to verify the actual number of eligible voters in each election cycle.

Cynthia Harris, the Department Supervisor of the New Jersey Room of the Jersey City Public Library, also said that the census-taking of Jersey City residents during the years of the Jersey City Directory yielded less-than-exact information *"through neglect, laziness, or drunkenness."* This explanation may account for the fact that the Jersey City Directories which do exist and which are housed in the New Jersey Room only mention Grandpa's brother, Patrick, in the 1901-1902 edition. His name appeared at that time as *"Patrick Lipsett, fireman, 656 Grand."* (Note: the *"fireman"* notation actually referred to a *"stationary fireman,"* a railroad employee who was charged with stoking with coal the boilers of fire engines or of other *"stationary"* buildings' boilers.)

There is probably no way of knowing how often Grandpa corresponded with his family back home. Perhaps letters received from his parents and siblings were among the photo albums and other materials that he threw in the trash at the time of his move uptown with us. I thought, perhaps, that our Lipsett cousins might have copies of Grandpa's missives in some steamer trunk there, but cousin

Imelda (Lipsett) Fitzgerald checked for me and said that there were no such records in the Lipsett possession. Mom recalls that grandpa's brother, William John, always addressed his letters to Grandpa as "*Esquire.*"

Grandpa was not without family visitors. Siblings Lillie and Thomas Michael arrived at Grandpa's Jersey City address, 204 Ninth Street, within six months of each other in 1912. Lillie came on January 28th aboard the *Celtic*, and Thomas Michael followed seven months later on July 3rd as a passenger on the *Majestic*. Unlike Grandpa who paid his own way, his father paid for Thomas' passage to America.

They were the youngest of Grandpa's 10 siblings; Lillie would turn 20 years of age three months after her arrival, and Thomas Michael was one month shy of his 18th birthday. Accompanying Lillie on her voyage to the States were two Coolaney - area neighbors of hers, Beatrice Gannon (27) of Knockadoo and Thomas Gallagher (25) of Carrownbanny, probably mother Winifred's grand-nephew. These townlands were the same ones from which Patrick and Winifred Graham came.

Lillie apparently left behind in Coolaney an avid suitor, Andy Durkin, who was heartbroken at her departure. He eventually married another Lilian, but this marriage was an unhappy one, according to family lore.

According to immigration records, Lillie returned to Ireland eight years later on May 28, 1920. Although she listed herself as a "*domestic*" on her ship's manifest and worked in such a capacity in the States, Mom always tells of how Lillie thought that such work was beneath her, thus her dwindling interest in it after a few short years. There was no mention of Lillie's address in any of the Jersey City Directories, so it may be that she resided, not with Grandpa, but with another family for whom she worked as a nanny or domestic. One might think that she worked in such a capacity in the Bloomfield area, perhaps being assisted in gaining employment by the Graham family. However, there is no record of a Lillie Lipsett in any of the Bloomfield Directories from 1912-20.

Before she returned home, Lillie met Grandpa's future wife, Loretta Crowley, and undoubtedly attended their wedding, since she didn't leave until two years after their April 30, 1918, nuptials. Lillie recalled for Paul during his summer visit with her in 1973 that she found Loretta to be "*lovely, simply lovely.*" She also told him that Katie Hayes Crowley, our maternal great-grandmother, had invited Lillie to stay with her and her children, Loretta, Denis, and Clara, in their Manhattan abode (the

Crowley story follows), rather than have her remain with her unmarried brothers Frank and Thomas Michael in Jersey City, considering her arrangement to be more befitting a single lady. If that were true, perhaps her employment as a nanny/domestic was in Manhattan rather than in New Jersey. Lillie returned to Ireland before the 1920 census would have verified her residence, but other New York City directories might have placed her in one location after her initial stay with Grandpa.

Mom also tells the story that when Grandpa went to visit Lillie at her place of employment, her employers told her that Grandpa had to enter the residence through the servants' quarters in the rear of the building. Lillie asserted, *"No brother of mine will go through the servants' quarters."* She also bragged about how proud she felt walking down the street with her very handsome brother Frank.

Lillie returned to Ireland and eventually married John Maurice Gillen from Northern Ireland's County Armagh. They had six children together: Frank, Mannix, Rosaleen, Lillian, Kathleen, and Alice. Considering what they felt was a dearth of eligible Catholic men for their daughters to marry in the largely Protestant Northern Ireland, the family moved to Leamington Spa, England, where Rosaleen still resides.

Thomas Michael, on the other hand, lived with Grandpa continually from his 1912 arrival until his marriage in 1936 at the age of 41. His only absence was for approximately two years (1918 – 1919) when he was on active duty with the U.S. Army, having enlisted as an army private and spending his time at Fort Benjamin Harrison in Lawrence, IND. The fort took in 10,000 recruits in 1918 as engineers (aka: *"railroad specialists"*), apparently Thomas' first official training in the railroad life.

Uncle Tom Lipsett

He and Grandpa, as required by law, both had completed their World War I Draft Registration Cards at Jersey City's second precinct on June 5, 1917. Grandpa was a *"Trainman"* for the *"Erie R.R. Co.,"* and Thomas Michael was a *"Clerk"* for the *"Wells Fargo Co."* Thomas was away for Mom's christening in 1919, although he was her godfather; her uncle Denis stood in for him. Thomas Michael appeared again as a resident with Grandpa in the 1920 Jersey City Directory.

Grandpa, a railroader himself, was considered a civilian employee of the army, as per the service he and others provided for the country. World War I had approximately

2,000 German prisoners of war (POWs) transported from the east coast to army camps at Fort Douglas, Utah, and Fort McPherson, GA. World War II, however, had 425,000 POWs sent to 700 different detention camps throughout the country, all of them far from the east coast. Grandpa was one of those railroad men who helped with the transport of POWs, thus his employee status with the army.

Grandpa always told the story of how shocked the German POWs were during the Second World War when they stepped off the trains in Jersey City and saw the New York skyline for the first time; they had been told by the German higher-ups that their air force had bombed and had leveled all of New York City!

Grandpa Lipsett on Duty

Despite Grandpa's and Thomas Michael's extended living arrangement, there was a major rift that developed between the two brothers. Thomas Michael intended to marry his girlfriend, Marion O'Connell, and he told Grandpa that he and Marion expected to remain as a married couple at 20 West Hamilton Place. He apparently recoiled at what he viewed as a rebuff when Grandpa told him that he could no longer stay there as a married person and that he would have to find his own living quarters with his new wife. *"When you're married, you go with your wife!"* Grandpa said.

As a result, he didn't tell Grandpa of his upcoming nuptials to Marion until the private ceremony was over. He may have told our great-grandma Katie of his plans, but her promise of confidentiality kept news of the wedding a secret, save for a suggestion or two to Grandpa that something was about to happen. Fr. Leroy McWilliams, the pastor of St. Michael's, married the couple on August 3, 1936, in the parish rectory. As one can imagine, Grandpa and Grandma Lipsett were hurt that they knew nothing of his wedding plans beforehand. Not only did Thomas Michael keep his nuptials private, but he also ceased all contact with his brother.

Thomas Michael and his bride moved to an apartment on Glenwood Avenue within a stone's throw of St. Peter's College. After a few months, a Mr. Jelly, Marion's uncle and a water meter reader who knew of the rift between Grandpa and his brother, told Grandpa during one of his official visits to 20 West Hamilton that Thomas Michael was in poor health. His health actually had been failing for several years. Grandpa also had to rely on Mr. Jelly to tell him where his brother was living at the time; he immediately took Grandma and Mom with him and went to Thomas Michael's apartment where Grandpa *"closed his eyes,"* according to Mom. Whatever words were exchanged between Grandpa and his brother during this ultimate of all rapprochements will never be known. His five-year struggle with *"pulmonary tuberculosis"* is what led to his passing on Good Friday, March 26, 1937, just eight months after his wedding.

The wake for Thomas Michael, the *"beloved husband of Marion (nee O'Connell),"* was at the Joseph Introcaso Funeral Home at 141 Brunswick Street. As an army veteran, he was entitled to a free headstone from the War Department which Marion ordered two weeks later and had shipped to 351 Virginia Ave. Placement of the gravestone at Holy Cross Cemetery in North Arlington was to be at her expense, however. A recorded version of Taps was played at his graveside.

Neither Grandpa nor Grandma ever heard from Marion again. However, neither was very fond of her.

Grandpa's brother William John's appearances in the States are not entirely clear. His older brother visited here for the first time in 1900 as noted earlier, four years before Grandpa came. However, there is a record of him returning in the winter of 1906 with Bloomfield as his destination once again; this time he came through Halifax aboard the *SS Parisian.* Mom tells an interesting story that Grandpa was watching the marchers in a political parade on Montgomery Street in Jersey City one day when he was surprised to see William John marching. The date of this parade encounter is unclear, however. There was another visit of his when he claimed on the passenger record that he had been living *"two years in Jersey City."* If he was not staying in Bloomfield with the Grahams, then who might he have been living with in Jersey City, if not Grandpa? The only suggestion of his possible residence in Jersey City was a notation in the Jersey City Directory of 1915. It reads:

<blockquote>

Lippsitt Frank Brakeman r (resident) 285 Pavonia Ave

Jno lab (laborer)   r   285 Pavonia Ave

Thos clk (clerk)   r   285 Pavonia Ave

</blockquote>

The abbreviated name *Jno* refers to John or Jonathan. Given the inaccuracies of the census takers, could this *Jno* have been William John? To be listed in a census record or in a city directory just meant that the person had to be present in the house when the census taker came calling. Could William John have been staying with his brothers, Frank and Thomas Michael, even briefly, in 1915? Mom has no recollection of this arrangement, so we will never know for sure.

Below are the addresses where Grandpa lived during his years in the States, according to various federal census records and the Bloomfield and Jersey City Directories:

1904	654 Grand Street (where he stayed with brother Patrick)
1908-1911	2 East Liberty Street, Bloomfield (when married to Winnie) 9 Vine Street, Bloomfield (after Winnie's death; home of Michael and Anna Sexton, Winnie's sister and brother-in-law)
	204 Ninth Street (when Lillie and Thomas Michael came)
1915-16	285 Pavonia Ave (living with Thomas and with "Jno")

1917	294 Pavonia Ave (the address given by both Grandpa and Thomas
	    Michael on June 5, 1917, the day they both applied for and
	    received their World War I Draft Registration cards.)

1920 (census)	334 ½ Seventh Street (a duplex home shared with the Schwartz family;
	    Grandpa, 32 years old and now married, was listed with Loretta C (28),
	    Catherine (7/12), and Thomas Michael. Both Grandpa and Thomas now both
	    worked for the railroad, Grandpa as a "*brakeman*" and Thomas as a
	    "*switchman.*")

1922-1923	262 12th Street (Grandpa ("*conductor*") was listed with Loretta and with Thos M ("*switchman*") but no mention of Mom)
1923 -1965	20 West Hamilton Place (Frank "*Lipsin*" was listed along with Loretta and Thos, now a "*fireman*"; no mention of Mom)
1965-1969	260 Ege Ave.

The 1910 census listing of Grandpa as a "*foreman – railroad terminal*" is the first indication of his railroad career; what jobs he had between his arrival in 1904 and 1910 are unclear. Grandpa always worked; his earlier jobs were in a laundry and as a laborer digging a tunnel (not sure which one). However, it may be safe to assume that his brother Patrick, a railroad man himself, may have been instrumental in getting Grandpa a similar job. He undoubtedly served the Erie Railroad well throughout his 53 years in its employ. Always a vigorous and healthy man, Grandpa worked for the Erie until 1963 when he reached the mandatory retirement age of 75.

The monthly *Erie Railroad Employee Magazine* honored him in several of its issues. A 1913 edition (issue # 3) placed Grandpa on its *ERIE ROLL OF HONOR* for the following:

> *"One night early in February, yard brakeman H.R. Allen and*
> *F.A. Lippsett, discovered fire in coach 1693 lying in Jersey City*
> *Yard, and promptly put out the flames, thereby avoiding*
> *considerable damage to car. For this interest in the Company's*
> *welfare, each of these men have been awarded a credit mark."*

Three years later, a 1916 edition (issue # 12) honored him in the same way with the following description of his service:

> *"F.A. Lipsett, yard brakeman, Jersey City, New York division,*
> *detected brakebeam dragging under N.Y.C. car 13629 in train*
> *extra 1830, while passing Jersey Avenue tower, and took*
> *prompt action to stop train and remove beam."*

Finally, a 1934 edition of the magazine (issue # 10) ran a picture of Grandpa with the caption, *"A Safe Worker."*

Grandpa also won accolades for himself and for the Erie with his athletic prowess, earning several medals in the track and field competitions among the railroad companies. Mom has the gold medal he won in the running high jump in 1916 and a silver medal for the 12-pound shot in the 1917 games. Grandpa gave a second gold medal to his brother, Thomas Michael, but no one has seen that medal since. For some reason (not verifiable), I recall that his second gold medal was for the discus. Grandpa used to exercise regularly with a group of Jersey City policemen who tried to enlist him to join their ranks, but he preferred his railroad connection instead.

John Miller, the Director of Archival Services for the Erie Lackawanna Historical Society (the Lackawanna RR merged with the Erie RR in 1960), was able to send me copies of the magazine pages which honored Grandpa, but he also said that news items regarding athletic competitions among the different railroads had never been indexed, making it close to impossible to find them without going through the editions one-by-one. He also said that the railroads sponsored many different teams and marching bands, among other things.

In addition to his railroad competitions, Grandpa also was an avid bowler for many years until his age and his compromised health put an end to his participation with his team, the *Wanderers*. I found it interesting to note that this team name was the same one as the local Sligo-area *Gaelic Athletic Association's* club back home in the old sod.

A coincidence, perhaps? Or a name chosen purposefully by another Sligo transplant here in the States who also was a teammate of Grandpa's?

It was around 1960 when Grandpa surrendered his bowling ball for good. We were having dinner at 262 Ege that day when he stopped by and handed it over; it actually was a somewhat emotional moment for him, having to concede defeat to his age and to other health issues. It was a two-finger ball, so I took it down the next day to Joe Correale's bowling supply store at the corner of Grant and West Side Aves. to have a third hole drilled in it. I remember being terribly embarrassed, having had only fifty cents with me for the two dollar charge. I promised Joe that I would return with the difference immediately, but Dad told me to tell him that I was the grandson of his old friend, Joe Colford. And so I did, and Joe laughingly let the fifty cent fee suffice for the job.

Grandpa completed his *Second Papers* as the final step in seeking citizenship on January 24, 1913. The Common Pleas Court of Hudson County finally issued *Francis Andrew Lipsett* his *Certificate of Naturalization* two months later on St. Patrick's Day.

What I found interesting was the fact that Grandpa reported that he was *"natural born"* when he completed his World War I Draft Registration Card, although the next line included *"Ireland"* as his place of birth. Brother Thomas Michael, on the other hand, who accompanied Grandpa that same day for the same purpose, reported that he had submitted his *First Papers* for citizenship already.

The Hayes – Crowley – Lipsett Connection

The following section of our story traces four generations of the families of Mom's mother,

Loretta (Crowley) Lipsett:

Peter and Johanna (O'Leary) Hayes and Family
(Our great-great-grandparents)
.
.
.
.
.

Catherine (Katie) Hayes
(Our great-grandmother)

Patrick and Bridget (Crowley) Crowley and Family
(Our great-great-grandparents)
.
.
.
.
.

Denis Crowley
(Our great-grandfather)

Denis and Katie (Hayes) Crowley and Family
(Our great-grandparents)
.
.
.
.

Loretta Crowley
(Our grandmother)

Frank and Loretta (Crowley) Lipsett
(Our grandparents)

Chapter XXVI

Peter and Johanna (O'Leary) Hayes

Our Maternal Great-Great Grandparents

Located in the southwestern part of Cork, the largest of Ireland's 32 counties, lies the townland of Corran (aka: *Corran South*), approximately 509 acres in size. Within its borders is the village of Leap (pronounced *Lep*), considerably smaller at 133 acres only, although it is considered the largest village in all of Cork. Leap is situated at the northernmost end of Glandore Harbor, just a few miles from the Irish Sea. With the populations of Corran and Leap in 1853 at only 38 and 29 inhabitants, respectively, it probably was not too difficult for its residents to meet, to court, and eventually to marry.

In the village of Leap stood a 50-acre farm belonging to the Hayes family. Our maternal great-great-great grandparents, Michael and Mary (Coughlan) Hayes, the owners of this farmhouse, house # 8, Corran, Leap, saw to the birth there of our great-great grandfather, Peter Hayes, who was baptized on October 9, 1826; his sponsors (godparents) were John Coughlan and Mary Hurly. Not far from the Hayes household lived John and Catherine (Murray) Leary, another of our great-great-great grandparents, whose daughter, Johanna, was born and baptized on February 10, 1832; her sponsors were Jeremiah Leary and Judith Walsh. Fr. James Doheny, the pastor of St. Mary's Church, baptized both Peter and Johanna.

Margaret Hayes Sweetnam - Homestead

HOUSE # 8, CORRAN, LEAP

Years later Johanna eventually caught Peter's eye.   They undoubtedly were neighbors, and it was typical for the Irish not to travel too far from their own townlands or villages to find a spouse. I do not know exactly when it all happened, but our great-great-grandparents, Peter Hayes and Johanna O'Leary, eventually met, courted, and wed. Fr. O'Sullivan of St. Mary's Church in Leap, the Diocese of Cork and Ross, Catholic Parish of Dunmanway, reported that they were married in this church sometime before 1856.   However, I have not been able to find their marriage record in the online digitized ones.

Peter and Johanna (O'Leary) Hayes had the following children, most of whom were baptized by Fr. John Donegan in St. Mary's Church:

Mary Ann (baptized Dec. 15, 1856; sponsors: Patrick Hayes and Honora Leary)

Catherine (Katie; our great-grandmother, Feb. 19, 1858 – Oct. 20, 1935; sponsors: Thomas Leary and Catherine Sullivan)

Johanna (baptized Feb. 13, 1860; sponsors: Patrick Donovan and Mary Hayes)

Honora (baptized Feb. 23, 1862; sponsors: John Tobin and Julia Hayes)

JOHANNA (O'LEARY) HAYES

Ellen (aka: *Nellie*; baptized March 8, 1864; sponsors: Lawrence O'Brien and Mary Duggan)

*Julia (born and baptized on the same day, June 30, 1865, an indication that she died in childbirth; sponsors: Michael Leary and Mary Hayes)

John (born Oct. 20, 1866; he died very young; sponsors: Dennis Collins and Hannorah McCarthy)

*Julia (born Feb. 15, 1868; sponsors: Dennis Donovan and Johanna Sheehy)

Margaret (baptized Oct. 21, 1870 – 1945; sponsors: Patrick Whilton and Johanna McCarthy)

This list includes two children by the name of Julia. A common practice in Ireland was for parents to give a child the same name as a brother or sister who predeceased him/her. It would appear that the first Julia died in childbirth. Grandpa Lipsett's parents followed the same practice; Thomas, his oldest sibling, died in 1892 at the age of 18, and his youngest, born just two years later, was named Thomas also.

Peter and Johanna must have come from some very hardy stock. They lived through the potato famine of 1845-49 which cost County Cork 200,000 of its people, a full 25% of its total population, to death (150,000) and to emigration (50,000). Historians consider Cork to be one of the counties most affected by the famine.

Great-great grandpa Peter, however, enjoyed longevity and passed away at the age of 86 on January 20, 1914; I don't know the date when great-great grandma Johanna died, but she was alive and well at 82 years of age when the 1911 census was taken. Peter and Johanna both were still living in the family home at that time along with daughter Margaret (Hayes) Sweetnam and her eight children; Margaret's husband William died of a ruptured appendix just the year before.

A picture of the house which I have seen doesn't do its size justice; in addition to these 11 individuals, a 22-year-old *"domestic servant,"* Jeremiah Sheehy, also was listed in the census as a resident. This census form lists four of Margaret's children as *"scholars"*: Henry Joseph (9; aka: *Harry*), Margareta (8), Willie (7), and Kate Ann (6). The citations for Richard (3) and George (1) were both *"cannot read."*

Although a modernized version of the Hayes family homestead still stands in Leap, it is no longer owned by descendants of the Hayes family. There is an interesting footnote to the story, however. A tradition in Ireland was for the family homestead to be passed down to the oldest son. However, if there was no son or if he decided to pass on this inheritance and seek his fortunes elsewhere, it went to the child who agreed to stay in the home and care for the parents for the rest of their days. Their son, John, did not live long, so Peter and Johanna passed the home onto their youngest daughter, the aforementioned Margaret, and her husband, William Francis Sweetnam, who promised to share the home with them and care for them.

It is the story of Margaret's handing down of the farm which is most interesting. Five of her eight children (she lost two others in childbirth) were sons, three of whom were to predecease her before her own passing in 1945. Sons William and Harry, both of whom left Ireland for the States in 1923, were already dead, and George had emigrated long before then, leaving only Richard behind as the logical inheritor of the farm. However, Richard had married a woman of whom Margaret did not approve, so she cut off all ties with him, never seeing him nor speaking with him again. She left the farm instead to her oldest daughter, Marion. Needless to say, family members considered Margaret to be *"a stern woman."*

What is it they say about "Irish Alzheimer's"? . . . *"You forget everything but the grudges!"*

George had been in the States for several years and settled in Boston before William and Harry arrived. He was known for his great singing voice, recording quite a few Irish ballads for Decca Records, one of which I found by chance being sold on Ebay; the price of *"Hold Your Head up Patsy McCann"* was going for $24.95. He also co-hosted an Irish radio show for WPOW radio every Sunday afternoon and had some of his poems published in *The Irish Echo*. George passed away on September 24, 1981.

When William and Harry left Ireland in 1923, mother Margaret also sent along with them their sister, Kathleen, to take care of them (keep house, wash and iron clothes, cook, etc.). The night before the three of them left for good, Margaret held an *Irish Wake*, a traditional practice among those Irish parents who never expected to see their emigrating children again.

How true and how prophetic that practice was for Margaret; she was not to see either of her sons again.

Older brother Harry was crushed to death in an elevator accident at Macy's on August 5, 1923, only three weeks after his arrival in the States. He apparently had been moving a rack of clothing and happened to look through an open door of a freight elevator which struck him in the head, sending him to the bottom of the shaft. It was his fifth day on the job; he also had completed his *Declaration of Intention* to become a U.S. citizen just 11 days earlier.

At the time of his death, Harry, William, and Kathleen had been staying with their aunt Katie (Hayes) Crowley, their aunt and our great-grandmother, at 242 Eighth Ave. in the Chelsea section of Manhattan. According to Harry's death certificate, his head had been crushed in the accident. Kathleen, his sister, was the one who identified his body at the city morgue; the certificate stated that she knew it was him *"because of his shirt. She had ironed it for him that morning."* His wake was held in Katie's apartment.

A sad note is that Margaret received the first letter from her son Harry about his life in the States several days after his funeral.

The *Southern Star*, the local newspaper in Skibbereen, a town just a few miles from Leap, reported to the locals in County Cork on August 25, 1923, that Harry, *"a most respectable industrious man . . . had been working only four or five days when, unfortunately, he met with an accident to which he succumbed."*

William (aka: *Sonny*), a New York City fireman of Engine Company 147, met a rather untimely death when he was killed in an automobile accident, apparently at the hands of a drunk driver, in the town of Middletown, CT, in 1937. His brother George was in the car at the time and sustained serious injuries but survived. The *Southern Star* reported on September 25, 1937, that Sonny *"was killed in a motor accident at Middletown, Connecticut. There was an attendance of over 1,000 people at the funeral, including Danno O'Mahony, the famous wrestler."*

It was during my Hayes/O'Leary search when I discovered that Mom had a second cousin, Bill Sweetnam, living in Freehold about whom she knew nothing; Bill was the son of the aforementioned William Sweetnam and the grandson of our great-grandma Katie's sister, Margaret. Bill was just two years old when his father was killed.

Bill's wife, Mabel, actually is the family historian who has helped me quite a bit in tracing Mom's family. Jeanne and I took Mom to visit Bill and Mabel in February of 2009. Mabel had the guest book for Bill's father's wedding to Jane (Haggerty) here in the States on October 21, 1931. Grandpa and Grandma (Crowley) Lipsett signed in, as did Katie (Hayes) Crowley, Clara Crowley, and James Crowley and his wife (more on the Crowleys later). Grandpa and Grandma Lipsett are listed among the *"Gifts and Givers"* in the wedding album as having given a *"Comfortable (rose)"* to the couple, and great-grandma Katie gave a *"Cereal Set."*

Sister Kathleen was the only one of the three Sweetnam emigres who ever saw her mother again. She took the first two of her six children, Kathleen and John, back home again in 1932 to visit her. Kathleen married Patrick Tobin, another Irish-born railroad man, on June 2, 1928, and they spent the better part of their 54 years together at 2322 Loring Place in the Bronx. Patrick passed away in 1982, and Kathleen followed on April 30, 2001. She lived until the age of 96 while living with her youngest daughter, Gail, and her family in Virginia.

Mom has very fond memories of Kathleen who visited us at Ege Ave. at one time.

Chapter XXVII

Our Maternal Great-Grandmother

Katie (Hayes) Crowley's Early Years

The details surrounding our great-grandmother, Catherine (aka: *Katie*) Hayes' arrival in the States are not entirely clear. The more plausible of the two stories I have heard is the one that Mom has always told that Katie came through Canada. I have found a number of records that match her approximate age and year of arrival (she has told census-takers that she arrived in 1880, although these years often are incorrectly recalled). A 23-year-old Catherine Hayes arrived at the port of Halifax aboard the *Hibernian* in 1881, and another 23-year-old Catherine came through Quebec on the *Moravian* on October 16, 1880. There also was a Kate Hayes, 20 years of age, who disembarked the *Lake Huron* in Quebec on May 15, 1882.

One of these could indeed have been our Katie.

Another bit of evidence that supports Katie's Canada arrival is Mom's story of her trip to Canada as a sixth or seventh-grader with her Grandma Katie to visit the Guilfoyle family. Unbeknownst to her at the time, Mom actually was paying a visit to the household of the relatives of her great-aunt and great-uncle, Philip and Ellen (aka: *Nellie*) (Hayes) Guilfoyle and their children and grandchildren; Nellie was Katie's younger sister by six years. Mom had always believed that Katie was the only member of her family to have left Ireland for the States, but the Ellen/Nellie Guilfoyle in Canada was indeed Katie's younger sister.

Philip was Canadian-born to Irish-born parents. He and Ellen had seven children, four girls and three boys. The 1910 and 1920 censuses place the family in Baileyville Town, Maine, on Spruce St. and Hemlock St., respectively, but it is clear that they also had resided in both Massachusetts and Canada. Their first two children, Mary and Lauretta, were born in Massachusetts, but the other five entered the world in Canada. Mom always knew of Philip's brother's name as Percy, but his name actually appears as *William P.* Guilfoyle (1930 census) and then as *Percival* (aka: *Percy*) in the 1940 census. Percy, his wife Mary (aka: *Mamie*), and their three children (Emmett, Mona, and Gwendolyn), all were Canadian born. It was around 1920 when Percy and his family left Canada for New York City where this *"welder – steamship company"* could be found over the years at 371 West 117th St., 560 West 149th St., and 110 Morningside Drive. Mom recalls visiting Gwendolyn and Mona often and staying overnight in their Manhattan apartment.

There were two other Guilfoyles whom Mom recalled, a brother Emmett as well as a sister Frances. Frances remained in Canada and would go on to marry Valmore Chartier (*"He was kind of chubby,"* Mom recalled.) Mom, Grandma Crowley, and great-grandma Katie all flew to Canada for the wedding. Years later, one of the Chartier children requested as a grammar school graduation gift a trip to New York's Time Square on New Year's Eve. Mom accompanied him, but her recollection was that the experience was a nightmare, one not to be repeated.

Mom's great-aunt Nellie passed away on January 22, 1929, at the age of 65 after a seven-day battle with pneumonia; contributory to her death, according to the death certificate, was *"diabetes."* Although a resident of Woodland, Maine at the time, she passed away in Chapman Hospital in the town of St. Stephen in New Brunswick, Canada.

I have not found any ship's manifest attesting to Nellie's arrival in Canada, so I am unclear as to whether or not she accompanied Katie or traveled on her own. I almost found the proverbial "smoking gun" on a ship's manifest for the *Arawa* which brought a Catherine Hayes and an Ellen Hayes to Montreal; however, the arrival date was September 22, 1899, a year which is much later than all other indications of Katie's professed 1880 arrival.

The nagging questions raised by the discovery of another Hayes sibling in Canada, of course, include the following:

- Did the Hayes and Guilfoyle families know each other in Ireland, prompting Katie's and/or Nellie's visit to them?
- Did Katie and Nellie travel together to Canada before Katie left Nellie there and made her way to New York?
- Did Nellie arrive in Canada as a lone traveler first, only to be joined later by Katie for a short visit before she left for New York?

Mom always told a great story of her Canada trip with her Grandma Katie which would have taken place in 1930 or 1931, just a couple of years before the repeal of prohibition. Before they left for the trip, Grandpa Lipsett apparently challenged his mother-in-law Katie not to come back from Canada without some whiskey which she would, of course, have to smuggle into the country. As a 12-year-old-or-so young girl, Mom was a complete nervous wreck, knowing that her grandma Katie ran the risk of being apprehended by customs officials as she attempted to bring this illegal hooch across the border. Katie concealed a couple of flasks of whiskey *"in her bosom,"* and covered them with a large scarf. When asked by the border customs officials if she were bringing any whiskey into the country, Katie replied, *"Now what would an old lady like me want with that!"*

And so they let her pass.

Another explanation, far more exciting than Katie's Canada immigration story, is the one that followed her for many years. According to Mom, family members always teased Katie about how she *"chased"* her future husband, Denis Crowley, from Ireland to the States, a claim which she always vehemently denied (*"No such thing!"* she would say.).

Although this may just be teasing family fodder, it is not altogether out of the realm of possibility; in fact, it is likely that she did. The Dunmanway parish register of marriages includes many Hayes and Crowley family members, several of whom married across these families, so I believe that Katie and Denis probably knew each other back home before getting together in the States. Corran, Leap is only a dozen miles from Denis' townland of Ballineen, and fellow genealogists have stated consistently that immigrants to the States typically married someone from their homeland with whom they were familiar. Therefore, despite Katie's assertion that she didn't really *"chase"* her future husband, Denis, it probably is true that she came to the States shortly after his arrival with him in mind. After all, Katie arrived here just a few months after Denis stepped off his ship on May 5, 1880.

Chapter XXVIII

Our Maternal Great-Grandfather

Denis Crowley

O ne of the most common names in the part of Cork where our family is from was *Crowley*, with 116 Crowleys listed in Cork in 1890. This heavy concentration of the Crowley name in the western part of the county helps us to pinpoint this area as the home of our Crowleys. It also would appear that it was not uncommon for one to marry a distant cousin.

Our great-great grandfather, Patrick Crowley, married Bridget Crowley on February 24, 1854; their home townland was Ballineen. They had nine children, as best I can determine:

Nelly (baptized March 27, 1855 - ?)

Denis (baptized January 13, 1857 – August 22, 1911; our great-grandfather)

Catherine (baptized July 20, 1858 – January 25, 1936)

*Mary (baptized June 20, 1860 - ?)

Agnes (born before 1864 - ?)

Annie (born before 1864 – October 21, 1921)

Bridget (born Christmas Day, 1864 - ?)

Julia (born August 25, 1866 – September 25, 1908)

Elizabeth (born October 4, 1869 - ?)

Bridget always said that she had eight children, all of whom survived into adulthood. She declared so in the 1900 census when the census takers were required to ask two questions of the mother, a stark reminder of the high infant and childhood mortality rate at the time (these questions were included in census records until the 1910 census):

Mother of how many children: <u>**8**</u>

Number of these children living: <u>**8**</u>

Census records I have examined tell a sad story for so many families: three children surviving out of eight, four surviving out of six, etc. The nine Crowley children listed above, however, include Mary whose baptismal record I found on the online digitized parish records. It would appear that the Crowleys indeed had nine children, losing one, probably Mary, at an early age. Could Bridget's recall of eight children have been an error?

Probably, but speculation, for sure.

Reverend John Hurley baptized our great-grandfather, Denis Crowley, in the Church of St. Patrick in the town of Dunmanway, County Cork, Ireland, on January 13, 1857; sponsors were Denis Crowley and Mary Crowley. His family's townland of Ballineen was just seven miles east of the more sizable town of Dunmanway.

Matching names and dates from various records with the prevailing cultural practices of the time, I can speculate that our great-great grandfather Patrick died in Ireland and never made it to the States. The ages and dates of the deaths of at least three Patrick Crowleys in Ballineen before 1880 match the Crowley emigration timeline; they suggest that one of them probably was our Patrick. A not uncommon practice among the Irish was for the remaining family members to leave the old sod for America after the patriarch passed away.

Based upon this information along with multiple immigration records and reported dates and ages from other records I have found, it is safe to assume that the two oldest children, our great-grandfather Denis and his sister, Catherine (Kate), left for the States to pave the way for the rest of their family. They arrived at New York aboard the steamship *Abyssinia* on May 5, 1880. The ship's register listed a

Denis Crowley (25) and a Kate Crowley (20) among the passengers it deposited in Castle Garden. Denis was a *"lab"* (laborer) and Kate a *"servt"* (servant).

Where they lived right after they stepped off the boat is open to pure conjecture, but the 1880 census, taken less than a month later, places a Kate Crowley as a *"servant"* along with another servant, Annie Murphy, in the home of Benjamin and Esther Marks and their six children on East 74th St. in Manhattan. A Dennis Crowley, *"car-man,"* appeared in the same census a few blocks away on 95th St. as a *"boarder"* in the home of Richard and Mary Kennedy and their three children. *"Car-man"* is just another version of the occupation *"cartman"* which great-great uncle James Colfer also had. Another boarder, James Hall, lived there as well. Of course, these census entries are no proof that this Kate and Denis are our Crowleys, but it certainly is possible.

Following her children, Denis and Kate, to America a year later on April 11, 1881, was our great-great grandmother, Bridget, 50 years of age, who came on the *City of Montreal* along with the rest of her brood: daughters Anne (15), Brigit (11), Julia (10), and Elizabeth (9). Another sister, Agnes (aka: *Aunt Aggie*) did not accompany her family to the States and apparently traveled alone; she told a census taker that she arrived here in 1879. Staying behind in Ireland, however, was Nelly, the oldest in the family, who had married a Daniel Coghlan on January 17, 1880; Julia, her sister, served as one of her witnesses.

Bridget Crowley took a short-lived trip back to Rosscarbery in September of 1897; this town is within a few miles of where Bridget's family lived. The trip probably indicated that she went back home to visit Nelly and her family.

Great-great-grandma Bridget and her Crowleys settled somewhere in Manhattan when they arrived. There are no remaining 1890 federal census records, so it is unclear where she lived with her children immediately thereafter. The 1900 census, however, placed her in the residence of her daughter, Catherine, and her husband, John Patrick Hutton, along with their six children at 23 Morton Street in Manhattan. Bridget also lived with the Hutton family, all eight of them, at 150 Barrows Street in Manhattan ten years later when the 1910 census taker
came calling.

What is interesting to note in the ages many immigrants reported to the census takers every 10 years is the great disparity between them each time. For example, Bridget reported her age as 84 in the 1910 census but only as 55 just 10 years earlier for the 1900 census. Her stated age in 1910 was the more accurate of the two, however. Such differences in reported ages were quite common. Other genealogists have said that when the immigrant Irish reached their real ages, they reported them accurately, probably because there was some pride in achieving a great age when so many Irish died young. Prior to revealing their true ages, Irish immigrants chose not to admit them to the authorities due to Irish Catholics' skepticism of the government.

Bridget did not appear in any other federal census, an indication that she did not live until 1920; Mom also can't recall her great-grandma Bridget. However, Mom does have memories of her great-aunts Catherine, Agnes, and Julia Crowley; here are those recollections:

Catherine. Mom attended the wedding of her Aunt Catherine (Crowley) Hutton's granddaughter, Hannah, and she tells the story that Elizabeth Hutton (aka: *Libby*), the eldest of the Hutton daughters and first cousin to our grandma Loretta Crowley Lipsett, was an individual of ample size, not unlike Loretta. Libby would stay at 20 West Hamilton Place because, by her own admission, it was *"the only place she got a nightgown to fit her."* The 68-year-old Catherine was a resident of 426 161st St. in Brooklyn when she passed away on January 25, 1936.

Agnes. Mom has vivid recollections of her many visits to William and Aunt Aggie (Crowley) Fitzgerald's spacious corner property home at 27 Newark Ave. in Bloomfield; they had moved there from New York City in order to accommodate their 10 children. Aggie actually had 12 children, two of whom died. I'm sure that the children Mom played with during her visits were the Fitzgerald grandchildren (and Mom's second cousins) who were living there in 1930: Robert, Elizabeth, and Richard. William also was the witness for our great-grandfather, Denis', naturalization ceremony on October 26, 1892; he was an engineer who had a daily commute to his job with Consolidated Edison in New York City.

Family parties typically had Aggie playing the piano as accompaniment to the singing of her husband and sons. Mom also recalls the Easter egg hunts on the grounds of their home. The 1940 census placed William (76) and Aggie (72) at the same address along with their unmarried children, James (45),

Joseph (40), and Agnes (37); each son was employed as a *"pipe caulker – asbestos."* Complications from diabetes eventually cost Aggie a leg, and they were contributory to her death in 1943; Bill outlived her for eight years.

Julia. The second youngest in the Crowley family, Julia had nine children with her first husband, James Mahoney, but only three survived (James, Julia, and Joseph); her second marriage to Otto Kraatz on September 5, 1899, lasted only one year and bore no children. Julia's sons, either James or Joseph, attended our great-grandma Katie's wake. Members of the Mahoney/Kraatz clan were all Brooklyn residents. Julia passed away on September 25, 1908, at the age of 42.

Annie. One of the Crowley great-aunts unknown to Mom was Annie who married a Donovan (first name unknown) and bore him four children: Nora, Joseph, Florence, and Dennis. However, Mom does recall visits with their daughter, Mom's aunt Nora (aka: *Nonnie*), and her husband, Joseph H. King, a New York City policeman, whom she married in 1913. They and their three children, Frances Regina, Dorothy Anne, and Robert, were residents of Manhattan before settling by 1930 at 6th Ave. in Brooklyn. Joseph's brother Benjamin, another policeman, lived with the family for many years as well.

After her first husband's death, Annie married California-born Thomas Kennedy, a New York City fireman, on August 15, 1899; it would appear that she had no children with her second husband. They were on the move to different Manhattan locations as documented by the census takers: 301 Spring St. (1900), 110 Christopher St., (1910), and 784 Greenwich St. (1920). Annie also reported that her year of immigration was 1881, the same year as the ship's manifest that listed her name along with the rest of her family. Her stated age at that time also was consistent with that given to the census taker years later. She passed away on October 21, 1921, at 50 years of age.

Elizabeth. Mom's aunt Elizabeth (aka: *Lizzie*) died on June 18, 1913, at the age of 41. She had been married to Thomas Cruise, a Boston-born New York City fireman, since 1893. The 1900 census had the couple residing at 95 Van Dam St. with their three children: Maria (5), William (1), and Thomas (less than one month old). However, I found no records for the rest of her family in any other census.

Bridget. This sister married another William Fitzgerald, although I am unclear about the date; this Manhattan-based couple had at least one child, Thomas, born on April 5, 1889. Records that might pinpoint other events in their lives are sketchy, however.

What is of interest to me is what Carla McDonald, an Irish genealogist specialist, wrote to me in an email several years ago. The surnames Mahoney, Donovan, Kennedy/McKennedy, and Fitzgerald are all common family names in the western part of Cork where the Crowleys lived. As I have mentioned previously, these names appeared as the names of the men several of Denis' sisters married and of the family which may have taken in Denis as a boarder upon his arrival in the States.

Could it be that our great-aunts married Cork men from home?

Chapter XXIX

Our Maternal Great-Grandparents

Denis and Katie (Hayes) Crowley

Denis and Katie were married on February 4, 1883, at St. Alphonsus Church in New York City. Witnesses to the marriage were Richard Joyce and Anne Crowley, Denis' sister. The newlyweds lived at 46 Laight St. in the Tribeca section of Manhattan, an address that has been granted Landmark status. Now a seven- unit apartment building, it exchanged hands in 2003 for $1.5 million. Other addresses I have found for Denis and Katie before 1900 place them at 439 West 25th St., 25 Bethune St., and then 53 Bethune.

Despite all the Manhattan addresses they occupied for the next few years, it is clear that they also lived in Brooklyn for some time. Our grandmother, Loretta Crowley, was born on November 23, 1891, and was baptized six days later at St. Peter's Church in Brooklyn. Mom has always said that our great-grandmother Katie found Brooklyn to be a bit more boring than she would have preferred, so the Crowley family left this borough before 1900 and took up residence in Manhattan for good.

Denis and Katie lost their first two children to the usual maladies which claimed babies and children in those days. Their first-born, Patrick (named after Denis' father), lived only seven days; he died at home on March 1, 1884, due to *"congestion of lungs – convulsions."* Their second child, daughter (Jo)Hannah, named after Katie's mother, did not fare much better, succumbing to *"acute pneumonia"* at her home at 559 Greenwich St. in the Village on October 12, 1887; her death certificate listed her age as *"two years, seven months, seven days old."*

The 1900 census placed the surviving Crowleys at 437 West 25th St. in Manhattan; the list included:

Denis (40) – Year of Immigration: 1880 - *teamster*
Katie (40) – Year of Immigration: 1880 – *eight children, six living*
Joseph (13)
James (11)
Denis (6)
"Raletta" (Loretta; (7) – our grandmother)
Clara (4)
Irene (2)

The 1910 census placed the family this time at Manhattan's 272 10th Ave:

Dennis (50) - *laborer in brewery*
Katie (52) - *mother of eight, five living*
Loretta (18) - *bookbinder – publishing house*
Dennis (16) - *bookkeeper – milk company*
Clara (14)
Irene (11)
Dennis Delea (25) - *nephew-in-law; conductor – railroad*
Kateleen (aka: Catherine; 4) – *granddaughter*

Missing from the latter census was Joseph, the third-born child and the first to have survived childhood. He had taken up with a young woman, Mary Hogan, of whom neither Denis nor Katie approved. Katie was quite concerned that her son was not ready for marriage, so she went to the local parish priest and asked him to stop their union. *"Was he a good son?"* he asked Katie, to which she replied in the affirmative; *"Then he'll be a good father!"* was his response.

Nevertheless, Joseph, four months before his 19th birthday, married the 15-year-old Mary Hogan on May 14, 1905, at St. Michael's Church in Manhattan; daughter Catherine was born 10 months later. Their daughter was only 18 months old when her 21-year-old father, a *"driver,"* died on September 5, 1907, undoubtedly the result of a work-related accident. The coroner described Joseph's cause of death as *"multiple fractures of fifth cervical vertebra – probably fall upon head."* The young couple had been living at 451 West 16th St.

Another missing Crowley from the 1910 census was son James who had married Catherine (aka: *Kitty*) Ollis on January 30, 1910, just three months before the census taker came calling at his folks' place. *"She was kind of a hard person to take!"* Mom has said; Kitty's father was Irish-born, her mother, a

New York City native. The newlyweds settled for a time at 739 28ᵗʰ St. in Manhattan before moving to Jersey City where they could be found at 1196 Summit Ave. (1920) with their two sons, Thomas (9) and James (six months), and then at 66a Charles St. (1930) where both father James (41) and his son, Thomas (19), were employed as *"stock clerk – electric lighting"* and son James (16) as a *"messenger – bank."* The 1940 census had the family relocating and purchasing a home in Wayne, NJ; James (51) now was working as a *"store room keeper – electrical manufacturer,"* and son James (26) was a *"clerk – Trust Company."*

Mom's folks had little contact with James and Kitty over the years, since there appeared to be no love lost between Kitty and her Crowley in-laws. However, Mom does tell the story of a visit to a place of theirs at Packanack Lake, NJ. She apparently was a guest of son James in a rowboat which he took out to tour the lake. It was when they tried to dock it upon its arrival back in port when Mom extended herself a bit too much to tie it up and took a fall into the brink.

I remember their son Tommy, a Union City resident, visiting us in Jersey City with his wife, Elizabeth, on a number of occasions. He also was the one who drank himself into oblivion at Mom and Dad's 25ᵗʰ anniversary party in the Casino in the Park and who had to be escorted to the taxi stand by Mom's cousin, Fr. Robert McDermott.

I don't understand why the 1910 census included Kateleen (usually a form of *Kaitlyn/Catherine*) as the granddaughter in residence with the Crowleys with no mention of her mother, Joseph's widow, Mary, living there. Perhaps only a census-taker's error? However, four years later on June 1, 1914, Mary was to marry Thomas Gibbons, a *"piano maker – factory,"*, who adopted her daughter and gave her Gibbons as her new surname, much to Katie's chagrin.

Mom always told the story that Mary once said, *"Grandpa Crowley was better to me than my own father."* Kateleen Crowley/Gibbons came to the wake for our great-uncle, Denis, Jr., in 1931, according to Mom.

Dennis Delae, the 25-year-old *"nephew-in-law"* listed in the 1910 census, was the son of Katie's sister, Maryanne, who had married Jeremiah Dullea; Mom recalls him as *"Din"* Dullea. The Dullea family was very close to Mom's family, particularly Ed and his wife, Mary (aka: *Minnie*) Dullea, residents of 97 Dahlgren Place in Brooklyn, where the Dullea descendants remain to this day. Their families exchanged many visits with each other over the years. Ed and Minnie had four children, all Mom's second cousins, the surviving two of whom I have been able to track down and to have communicate with Mom. (Read more about the Dullea family in the *Footnotes* section of our story.)

Within a month of each other in the summer of 1911, Katie was to lose her fourth child, Irene (July 19), as well as her husband, Denis (August 22) both to typhoid fever. Irene was suffering with the fever before she passed away, and father Denis contracted it when he kissed her good night. Irene, just two months before her 12th birthday, died at the end of a two-week stay at St. Mary's Children's Hospital; cause of death was *"typhoid fever – lumbar pneumonia."* Her father, a 52-year-old *"brewer"* for Flanagan Nay Brewery, followed Irene into eternal life a little over a month later; he had been admitted to New York Hospital on July 20 of that year. His death certificate read simply, *"typhoid fever."* Katie and Denis had been married for 28 years at the time of his death. The Crowley family kept undertakers J. Molloy & Sons quite busy; they saw to the funeral and burial arrangements for Patrick, (Jo)Hannah, Joseph, Irene, and Denis.

Great-grandpa Denis Crowley, Mom's maternal grandfather

A widow at the age of 53, Katie was left the mother of only four surviving of her eight children: James (23), Loretta (20), Denis, Jr. (17), and Clara (16). With James off and married, Denis, Jr. was to be the primary breadwinner for his widowed mother Katie and his single sisters, Loretta and Clara.

Katie, someone Mom always described as a fiercely independent woman well ahead of her time, did whatever she could do to keep going and to keep her family together. By the time Mom was born in 1919, 64-year-old Katie had moved to 242 Eighth Ave. in the Chelsea section of Manhattan. She was joined there by her children, Denis (26; *"longshoreman – docks"*) and Clara (24; *"dressmaker – shop"*), and a *"roomer,"* Thomas Simpson, a 50-year-old Swedish-born *"carpenter."*

Katie, Denis, and Clara were residing at 721 Ninth Ave. in Manhattan by 1930, but it was barely a year later on February 3, 1931, when Denis passed away at the age of 36. He dropped dead from *"cardio-vascular disease and cerebral arteriosclerosis"* while sipping morning coffee at the counter of a *"restaurant"* not far from where he worked in the city; he had no sooner passed the morning newspaper to a fellow diner at his request when he keeled over and passed. The death certificate listed him as a *"store keeper."* He was the fifth of Katie's eight children to predecease her. Mom always said that Denis was a red meat-eater to the exclusion of other healthier diets that most folk value these days. His funeral procession passed in front of his place of employment while several of his co-workers stood outside and wept.

Mom's Uncle Denis was always a favorite of hers, thus the middle name of our brother Paul; she has said that she could always get what she wanted from her *Uncle Dinny*, given his tendency to spoil her. Most contemporary records list the name with a double *"n,"* but the original Irish spelling of the name included only a single *"n."* Although Denis *"kept time"* with his long-time girlfriend, Julia Daley, he never married her, choosing instead to support Katie and Clara. Julia eventually was to marry Robert Segrave on July 1, 1933, two years after Denis' death; Mom has described him as a *"very jolly guy."*

Chapter XXX

Grandpa and Grandma (Crowley) Lipsett

Grandpa met Loretta Crowley for the first time in 1917 at the 19th annual Sligo Ladies Ball in New York City. This event, sponsored each year by the *Sligo Ladies Social and Benevolent Association,* was the group's main event, highlighted by the grand march, the promenade of couples around the hall each year. The book, *Sligo in New York,* reported that *"on some occasions the ceremony took 55 minutes to complete because of the sheer number of participants."* I don't know the location of this particular ball, but the 15th annual December 12, 1913, gathering was held at Donovan's Grand Circle Hall on West 59th Street in New York. Tickets for *"admitting Gentleman and Lady, Including Wardrobe,"* were *"50 cents."*

I dare say that Grandpa may have been an active member of the *Sligo Men's Social and Benevolent Association,* a group that also sponsored sports teams and a variety of social events.

Grandpa actually attended the ball in the company of his twin cousins, Anna and Belinda Coleman, the daughters of his mother Kate's sister, Anne (Ryan) and her husband, Thomas Coleman.

Grandpa and Grandma's encounter at the ball must have been quite interesting. Grandma had been getting over a case of erysipelas, a skin infection that manifests itself as red and inflamed blotches. Her case was on her face, so she wore a veil to keep the cold air from irritating it. Grandpa thought this strange, perhaps an indication that she was a widow, but he pursued her, anyway. Their first dance together was to the tune, *"In the Gold Fields of Nevada,"* a waltz written by the song-writing team of Edgar Leslie (lyrics) and Archie Gottler (music).

While they courted, they used to meet at the Flatiron Building in Manhattan. Around the time of their courtship, the building housed *Taverne Louis*, a French restaurant and café which provided dining, music and dancing. The group, *Louis Mitchell and His Southern Symphony Quintette*, provided the music for quite some time.

Could Frank and Loretta have been regulars on the dance floor? Or was the Flatiron little more than a place for them to rendez-vous? Mom has always said, though, that she loved watching Grandpa and Grandma Lipsett dance the waltz. Even Mom's Aunt Clara was known to be an accomplished dancer, winning competitions in various Manhattan dance clubs.

Although Mom has said that Grandma knew of Grandpa's first marriage to Winnie at the time of their own marriage, the state of New York's *Certificate and Record of Marriage* completed by Grandma and Grandpa and witnessed by Thomas and Clara recorded Grandpa as *"Single"* in the space asking whether *"Single, Widowed or Divorced"* and *"1st"* as the *"Number of Groom's Marriage."*

All signed that the information provided was accurate, however.

Reverend Emmett F. Rogers officiated at the wedding of our grandparents, Francis A. Lipsett and Loretta C. Crowley, at St. Columba Church on West 25th St., Manhattan, on Tuesday afternoon, April 30, 1918; best man was Thomas Lipsett, and maid of honor was Clara Crowley. Their wedding reception/dinner took place just around the corner from Grandma's Chelsea apartment at Cavanagh's Irish Steak and Ale House on West 23rd St. The establishment started out as an oyster bar with 12 tables and grew to one of the most popular gathering places in town, attracting Tammany Hall politicos and professional prize fighters as regulars. It closed in 1971; in its place now is a Clearview Cinema.

Grandpa and Grandma Lipsett

Grandma and Grandpa Lipsett lived briefly with her mother (Katie) and the rest of the Crowleys in their 242 8th Ave. Chelsea apartment when first married. The street-level business of their apartment building was a Chinese restaurant whose owner/proprietor Grandpa often met with to play cards. This modest-looking apartment building still contains approximately six apartments, and a bagel shop, Murray's Bagels, now occupies the first floor.

The residence also was the place where Mom was born. Although residents of Pavonia Ave. in Jersey City at the time, Grandma and Grandpa decided to give birth to Mom in the apartment Katie shared with Denis and Clara in order to have Katie serve as a midwife of sorts. The state birth record also included *"242 Eighth Ave."* as Grandpa and Grandma's residence. Grandpa assisted in the delivery with a supply of chloroform, and Dr. Robert Bickley was the physician in charge for Mom's May 25, 1919, birth. According to the Irish naming tradition, Mom was named *Catherine*, after her mother's mother, *Catherine/Katie* Hayes. Six days later, Reverend Rogers baptized Mom at St. Columba's Church, just two blocks from the apartment. Mom's sponsors were her Uncle Dennis and her Aunt Clara.

Grandma and Grandpa's first Jersey City address as a married couple was 334 ½ Seventh St., an attached two-family home they shared with the Schwartz family, a German-born and Polish-speaking family whose address was 334 Seventh St. The head of the household was 59-year-old W. J. Schwartz, MD, according to the 1920 census record; although the names on the record are difficult to read, it appears that he was joined by his wife Georgina and two children, Berthold (19) and Henry (17), both described as *"medical students."* This census also listed Mom (seven months old) and Thomas Michael as residents at 334 ½ Seventh. By 1922, the Lipsetts had moved to 262 12th St., and they were in 20 West Hamilton Place by June 2, 1923.

Grandpa and Grandma purchased 20 West Hamilton on May 31, 1923, from the Coover family who had been in the home since October 19, 1903. Levi and Mary Coover had passed away, and their children, son Edward C., daughter-in-law Lillian H. Coover, and widowed daughter, Effie C. Hutton, sold them the home. They paid $9,500 for it, and Grandpa sold it for the exact same price 42 years later in 1965 when he moved and joined us uptown. I found a copy of the original deed to the house at the Hudson County Register's Office, but there was no purchase price contained in it, just the statement that the sale was *"in consideration of one ($1.00) dollar and other good and valuable consideration of lawful money of the United States of America."*

The deeds I found which did list the selling price, however, indicated that Mary Jane and Martin Moynihan and Caroline White sold it to Philip and Karen Pirecki for $430,000 in 1999; the couple then sold it to Christopher and Schaun Hatcher for $635,000 in 2003. The home changed hands again when David and Karin Piscitelli purchased it from Schaun Ulrikson in 2009 for $910,000.

It currently is on the market one more time for $1,379,714.

Mom remembered starting St. Michael's School as a first grader in 1924 and coming home to eat lunch on an ironing board, a sure indicator that the Lipsetts had moved into 20 West Hamilton only recently and had yet to establish a permanent place for in-home dining.

Grandpa's intention was to rent out the rooms in his home to the local bookmakers, much like the families of his friends and neighbors, the Coynes and the Craigs, did. However, Grandma Lipsett's cooler head prevailed, and she convinced Grandpa that having such an operation right across the street from the wide open Hamilton Park would only invite closer scrutiny by any passers-by. Grandpa relented and chose to take in roomers instead.

(Remember that the bookie of all bookies, Joe *"Newsboy"* Moriarty, lived just next door to them. The 1940 census listed the *"Occupation"* of both Joe and his brother, Albert, as *"peddler"* and their *"Place of Employment"* as *"own place."*)

The home, built in 1862, had no electricity at the time Grandpa and Grandma bought it. Gas was the mode of heating and lighting, but Thomas Michael paid for the installation of an electrical system throughout the house as a gift to his brother and sister-in-law.

I remember 20 West Hamilton very well, particularly the small half-bathroom just outside the kitchen; it had been added at a much later time and was not heated. It was memorable for a young boy like me, because it had a toilet tank mounted high on the wall with a long pull-cord one had to yank in order to flush it. Of course, I always had to use it when I visited, just to be able to flush that toilet tank on the wall; I had never seen one before. Whenever I see them now in those high-end home furnishing magazines, I immediately think of Grandpa's home.

A financial necessity in order to pay the mortgage and to make ends meet, there was always a stream of "*roomers*" living for varying lengths of time in the five rooms allotted to these folk on the second and third floors of this classic brownstone. One can only imagine the myriad responsibilities Grandma had in keeping what was essentially a rooming house afloat: doing laundry for as many as five boarders at a time, cleaning bathrooms, and generally "screening" potential roomers who always heard via word-of-mouth that 20 West Hamilton was the place to stay. She saw to the many housekeeping chores associated with managing such an undertaking. In addition to the roomers, she also tended to Thomas Michael, her brother-in-law, who lived with her from the time she married Grandpa until his own marriage, approximately 17 years later. It also wasn't long after her brother Denis' death in 1931 before her mother Katie and sister Clara moved in as well.

I would imagine that negotiating occasional family disputes also became part of Grandma's responsibilities.

Mom also speaks of the many "*greenhorns,*" those Irish immigrants fresh off the boat, who came to stay for varying amounts of time with the Lipsetts before they were settled. Needless to say, Grandma must have been one tough, hard-working, and flexible individual.

Grandma never accepted roomers without references and the names and addresses of their employers. Mom tells the story of a roomer who left 20 West Hamilton for good one day without having returned the keys to the building or to his room. Grandma apparently went to this guy's place of work to retrieve the keys, but before she could demand them back, he took them from his pocket and handed them over without a word.

A tough cookie, perhaps?

Read more about the 20 West Hamilton roomers in the *Footnotes* section of our story.

When they were both together at 20 West Hamilton, Katie and Clara shared a large third floor bedroom, leading to tensions between the two of them and resulting in Katie leaving and taking up residence in an efficiency apartment in Manhattan for a while; Mom recalls visiting her there. Katie eventually returned to 20 West Hamilton at the urging of Grandma and Grandpa.

Katie lived at 20 West Hamilton for a period of three to four years. She was not one to sit down and take it easy; she was always "*on the go*," trekking on foot from 20 West Hamilton to Journal Square to go shopping or making her way alone through the New York City subway system to visit family and friends, with or without directions. "*You're never lost if you have a tongue!*" she would say.

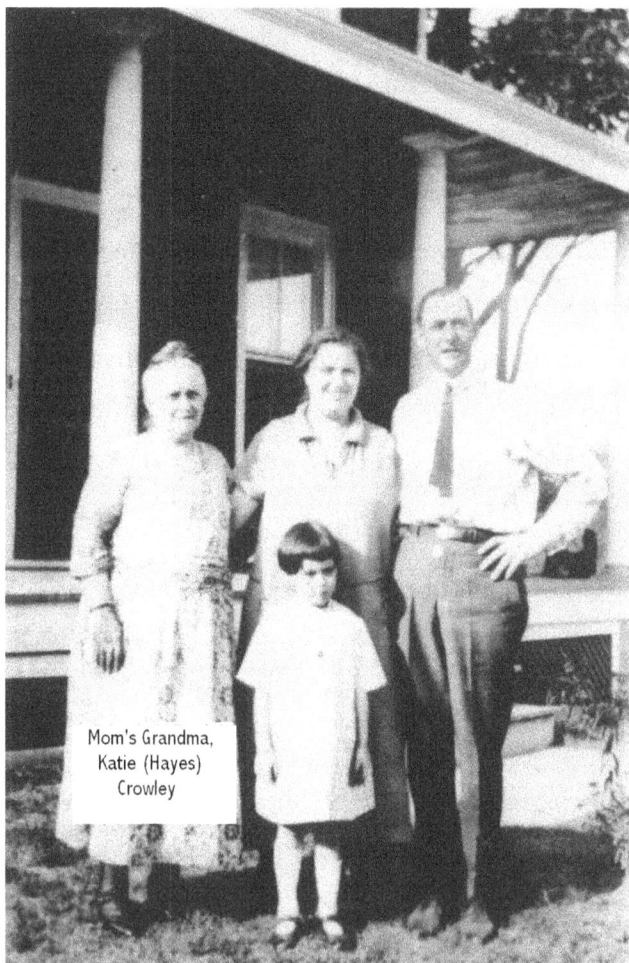

Mom's Grandma, Katie (Hayes) Crowley

The last day trip Katie was to take was on Saturday, October 19, 1935, when she went to see Bill and Ella (O'Donovan) O'Brien at their home at 207th Street in Manhattan; Bill had been ailing for some time. Ella was Katie's niece, the daughter of her sister, Johanna (Hayes) O'Donovan; she worked as a *living out girl* (a maid, nanny, etc.) for an attorney on Park Ave. Mom tells the story that Bill said to Katie as she was leaving, "*I'll bury you, too, before long!*" The comment made in jest turned out to be prophetic; Grandma Lipsett found Katie dead on the floor at 20 West Hamilton the next morning. Bill apparently felt terrible that he had made that comment just the night before her death. Katie was 77 years old when she passed. The paper the next day read thusly:

> *Crowley – On October 20, 1935, Catherine Crowley (nee Hayes), beloved*
> *wife of the late Dennis F. Crowley, devoted mother of James P. Crowley,*
> *Mrs. F.A. Lipsett, Mrs. James McNally, at her late residence, 20 West*

Clara, on the other hand, was a very slim, frail-looking woman, who always had the reputation among the family that she was a bit on the delicate side. In fact, Katie took her and her alone for a trip to Ireland in the summer of 1910 because, according to Mom, *"She was sick and Katie thought it would do her good."* Expecting indoor plumbing during her visit, Clara asked her host where the bathroom was; the reply she received but did not anticipate was *"any place between here and the next field!"* Clara was 14 years old at the time.

Mom's Aunt Clara Crowley

Clara was absent from 20 West Hamilton during her short-lived marriage to James F. McNally. They were wed on June 26, 1932, at the Church of the Sacred Heart at West 51st St. in Manhattan. Their only child, James Dennis, was born almost a year later on May 15, 1933, but he lived only six months. Mom recalls that James left Clara and wasn't even around at the time of his son's death. James also had two daughters from a previous marriage.

Stories of Clara's husband are far from flattering; he apparently misrepresented himself to Clara regarding his background and employment status. Despite his claims to be a *"tenement house inspector,"* there was no proof through the social security administration that he was employed in that capacity at all. Neither Grandpa nor Grandma Lipsett was very fond of him.

Clara remained at 20 West Hamilton for approximately 20 years until the summer of 1954. Clara fell and broke her leg while we were all at Monmouth Beach, so Mom called her cousin, Tommy Crowley, to tend to her. After a trip to the hospital to mend her leg, Clara spent some time at one of the hospitals and treatment centers located at Laurel Hill in Secaucus. The Pollack Hospital in Jersey City then became her home for the last few years of her life until her death on New Year's Eve, 1966. I remember her wake at Marshello's Funeral Home; besides the Colford family, there was barely a handful of mourners who came to pay their respects.

Grandma Lipsett entered Flower Fifth Avenue Hospital in Manhattan for relatively routine gall bladder surgery, an operation she barely survived, succumbing a day later on August 13, 1953, to a *"pulmonary embolism,"* the same diagnosis attributed to Grandma Colford in 1967. Dr. Robert Bickley, the same physician who delivered Mom 34 years earlier, was Grandma's surgeon. I guess that the specialization of medical practices these days didn't apply then; delivering babies and performing surgeries made MDs more like *"jacks of all trades."*

Bickley told Mom after Grandma's death that he also had discovered a large cancerous mass during surgery and suggested that, even if she had survived the surgery, her days would have been numbered. Grandpa and Grandma had been married for 35 years when she died; she was three months shy of her 62nd birthday.

Grandma and Grandpa had always been driven by their strong Catholic faith; they believed in Saint Margaret Mary's promise that anyone who attended nine consecutive First Friday masses would never die without a priest. And it so happened: Grandpa was with Grandma at her hospital bed when she breathed her last, and as he exited her room to seek assistance, he found a priest walking down the halls of the hospital who gave her last rites and helped him in the immediate aftermath of Grandma's death.

Sadly, I have no recollection of Grandma Lipsett who passed away just one month before my third birthday. I know that Mom would have loved to have shared her grandchildren with her. I recall on two separate occasions as a very young child asking Mom to identify a person (her mother) in a particular picture, only to have her break down and identify her as *"Grandma Lipsett."* Nevertheless, Mom has kept her alive with many stories of her larger-than-life personality and of her great wit and charm. *"She never spoke ill of anyone,"* Mom has said.

Always upbeat and positive, Grandma seemed to have been one of those folks who just made others feel good. One of her friends said to Mom, *"Whenever I talk to your mother, I feel like I had a week's vacation."* Her advice to Mom also spoke of her willingness to accept everyone as they were: *"When you know a person's way, you act accordingly."*

In my field we call that *"social intelligence"*; apparently, Grandma Lipsett had plenty of it.

1935

Grandpa originally had planned a return trip to Ireland with Grandma in the summer of 1953. However, Grandma reneged on the trip, citing Mom's pregnancy with Paul and her wish to be around to help. She offered to make the trip the following summer, despite Grandpa's suggestion that Mom would probably be pregnant then, too, but Grandma never made it to 1954.

Grandpa took the Ireland trip himself the next summer, exactly 50 years after he left for good. No steamship travel this time – he took to the air aboard Trans World Airlines (TWA) for Shannon Airport. His trip included visits to several of his siblings, including his brother William John who was quite sick and frail at the time; Mom said that Grandpa was quite shaken at his general condition.

William John passed away at the age of 76, just two months after Grandpa saw him. Grandpa also was able to see Lillie again, his sister Kitty (Kate Ellen; Fr. Robert's mother), and his brother Bob (Maureen's father) during this same trip. His approximate two-week stay ended on June 28, 1954, when he bade farewell one last time to his country of origin and boarded TWA flight 937-28 for his return trip to Idlewild Airport (now Kennedy Airport) in New York.

Mom said that his preparation for the Irish summer weather was far from adequate, despite her urging that he reconsider his travel apparel. Bringing clothes more fitting for a summer at the Jersey shore rather than for one in Ireland, Grandpa shivered his way through his trip. He said to Mom upon his return, *"It was 50 years since the last time I was there, and it'll be 50 more years before I go back!"*

Grandpa remained at 20 West Hamilton for another 11 years. It was around that time that Mom and Dad thought it best that he move closer to us to allow us to keep a closer watch over him. The upkeep at 20 West Hamilton had become a bit much, and his long-standing tenants in the fourth-floor apartment, Tom and Rose Hayes, had passed away, necessitating a search for another tenant. Mom suggested that trying to replace a trusted couple who had become friends with Grandpa through their

20 years at 20 West Hamilton was not a prudent idea, especially considering the downturn in the Hamilton Park area.

I remember visiting the Hayes couple on several occasions when stopping by to drop off Grandpa after a Sunday dinner with us. Tom and Grandpa were big *"rasslin"* (wrestling) fans, and Tom gave me during one visit a couple of them *"rasslin"* magazines which the folks appreciated about as much as me being given a case of typhoid.

Grandpa sold his home in the winter of 1965 to Tom Tansey. The original plan was for him to move in with us, and the folks even looked at other homes in the Ege Ave. area which might accommodate our rather large brood and Grandpa, too. However, they found no such home to satisfy our needs. Another plan developed a few years after the March 12, 1962, death of Helen Costigan, Bill's wife, who lived in the other half of the attached duplex to us at 260 Ege. The Costigans had no children and had lived there since 1948. The folks approached Bill and asked if he might allow Grandpa to live as a roomer with him in one of the upstairs bedrooms. Bill agreed, but after approximately a three-month, $50 per month arrangement in the fall of 1965, the loss of privacy became an issue for Grandpa and this plan less than an optimal one.

However, Bill died on November 13, 1965, and Grandpa purchased the home on February 22, 1966, from Marie Cleary, a Costigan niece to whom he had been bequeathed the property. A conversion of this residence from a one to a two-family soon was underway, and Grandma and Grandpa Colford eventually vacated their 277 Ege Ave. home and moved into the first floor, with Grandpa Lipsett as the upstairs occupant.

Emphysema plagued Grandpa, the result of many years of inhaling cigarette and cigar smoke, and it had gotten the better of him by the time he occupied 260 Ege. He already had surrendered his bowling ball and his long-standing membership with his bowling team, *The Wanderers.* Walking just a few steps soon left him out of breath and gasping for air; several trips to the hospital to stabilize his breathing followed. Watching him trying to pull in air like a longshoreman pulling in freight, particularly on those hot and humid dog days of summer, was just awful.

Grandpa passed away on November 26, 1969, at the age of 81years, five months, 26 days.

216

Chapter XXXI

Some Grandpa Lipsett Recollections

I will always remember Grandpa Lipsett as that iconic figure who stood in sharp contrast to the more reserved, formal Grandpa Colford. Grandpa never failed to get quite a few laughs out of his grandchildren, even if it meant resorting to behaviors considered by some to be a bit on the irreverent side. Blessing himself before grace at the dinner table with *"Knick, knack, nabitty jack, the black pig"* would send us roaring with laughter but only would elicit the exasperated cry, *"Oh, Pop!"* from Mom. (Where that blessing came from I'll never know.) His description of a good meal as *"Dandy eats!"* also resulted in the same pained expression from Mom, and his forced and purposefully overdramatic belching after dinner made all of us, save Mom, laugh at this entertainment.

And we never tired of making him repeat each week a story, the details of which have long since faded from memory, about a German gentleman he knew who was training his dog. The punch line came when Grandpa used his best German accent to imitate this man with the statement, *"Jump, jump Fritz, and I'll give you leefa (liver)."* We would laugh each of the fifty or so times he told that story over the Sunday dinner table.

And, of course, who could forget the question he always asked when listening to some rock singer trying to hit the high notes: *"What is he, singin' or cryin'"*? Or his decrying *"the damndest summer for rain!"* after only a brief daytime spritz. His love for sports never wavered, despite his contention that *"any game today"* was surely rife with cheating and with other less-than-honest shenanigans, except, of course, his beloved wrestling, surely the most staged of all sports, but the one he always insisted was above reproach!

There were times when his playfulness at 262 may have been due to lowered inhibitions after his typical stopover in Cahill's Tavern on West Side Avenue for a good hour or so before he made it to 262 Ege for Sunday dinner. I remember awaiting his 3:00-or-so arrival on the Montgomery West Side bus while seated on the steps of the AME Church on the corner of West Side and Clarke Aves. He would exit the bus and give me a wave, but his whereabouts then were obstructed as he walked behind the passing bus. Of course, I thought that he had gone into Adam's Delicatessen where he always picked up a brick of ice cream and an apple pie, but he obviously had entered Cahill's in its adjoining space to Adam's. When I returned to 262 Ege several minutes later without Grandpa and told Mom of his mysterious disappearance, she knew, of course, what the deal was.

Grandpa spent these pre-dinner visits at Cahill's playing Euchre, a well-known Irish card game, and sipping a pint or two. I met two men over the years who attested to Grandpa's Euchre-playing ability. One was Martin Cahill himself who told me when I met him at the Park Tavern (his own Cahill's had long since closed) that Grandpa *"was the greatest Euchre player I ever saw."* Another testimonial came from one Tom Toolan whom I met during my first Ireland visit in the summer of 1975. I was just outside the Mountain Inn one night when Tom stopped me and told me that he remembered Grandpa from his 1954 Ireland visit and that Grandpa *"was a great Euchre player."*

Great memories indeed.

Besides being an accomplished musician and dancer of sorts, Grandpa also was a lover of music, particularly Irish music. I was in possession of his record collection for many years, trying to donate it to collectors and to record libraries in the New York area. However, there was no interest expressed at all among all those folk. Most of these records dated from 1908 through 1925, long before they were made of vinyl; Grandpa's records were made of a shellac resin, a very hard, but brittle substance. That all 100-or-so of his records lasted all these years with only a minimum of breakage was remarkable. The collection, primarily recordings from Victor and Victrola Records, consisted of both 10-inch and 12-inch-in-diameter sizes, and most, but not all, were one-sided only.

In the spring of 2012, I contacted Carol Buck, the director of the Irish American Cultural Institute (IACI), located at the time in Morristown. She gladly took me up on my offer and accepted 50 of Grandpa's records, many of which still were in their original, yet tattered, covers. This grouping consisted of the Irish recordings of the internationally-known Irish tenor, John McCormack, along with those of a few other singers and comedy sketches. My only stipulation for the IACI was that Grandpa's name be attached to the collection. Carol announced the donation in the IACI's Newsletter Issue No. 912, and she allowed me space to write a brief bio of Grandpa for the issue.

Carol contacted me again (August 21, 2014) to tell me that the IACI had moved its headquarters permanently to the Great Hunger Institute at Quinnipiac University in Hamden, CT. She said that the representatives from the new location were *"thrilled with the collection."*

So Grandpa's name will live on at Quinnipiac.

And should anyone get a chance to visit Ellis Island, please stop by Grandpa's plaque on *"THE AMERICAN IMMIGRANT WALL OF HONOR"* which officially certifies him and others for *"joining those courageous men and women who came to this country in search of personal freedom, economic opportunity and a future hope for their families."*

Chapter XXXII

Footnotes

The "Other" Michael and Margaret Harvey Dunn

T his addendum to our story chronicles a few years in the lives of another Michael and Margaret Harvey Dunn who, I *thought* for several years, were our great-grandparents. Although they are *not*, they might be related to us in some other way. Other explanations might be that our Margaret Harvey Dunn married another Michael Dunn after our Michael died (not very likely) or that this Margaret Harvey, one of many with the same name living in New York City, just coincidentally also married another Michael Dunn (more likely).

Nevertheless, I thought that I would include their story here as another backstory of a hard-working, doomed Irish immigrant couple.

This Michael was a *"truck driver,"* according to his son, Edward's, February 21, 1889, birth certificate; the *"Maiden Name of Mother"* on this same certificate was *"Margaret Harvey."* There was no address included, but there was one (*35 Carmine St.*) two years later when the same Michael and Margaret (Harvey) Dunn welcomed a daughter, Mary, into the world on Christmas Day, 1891. The couple had been in residence at 67 Carmine St. just the year before. The latter birth certificate listed Michael's occupation this time as *"Coachman."* Five months later, I suspect that the Michael in the following newspaper article was the same Michael Dunn of Carmine St. who encountered some difficulty while working the docks.

The July 12, 1889, edition of the New York Times published the following story:

Defied the Police

Michael Dunn, a truckman, while on the Guion wharf at the foot of King-street, was assaulted on Wednesday by one of the hands on the lighter (aka: tugboat) Nameless, lying at the wharf, and was brutally beaten about the head and face. After committing the assault the assailant took refuge on board the lighter, and when Patrolman Gannon of the steamboat squad attempted to arrest the fugitive he was stopped by Capt. Charles McKeegan of the Nameless, who stood at the gangway with a capstan bar in his hands and swore that he would brain the first man who attempted to board the lighter. In this defiance of the officer he was aided by half a dozen hands on the lighter. The assailant of Dunn took advantage of the parleying with the officer to make his escape. Gannon summoned two other officers and boarded the lighter. The fugitive having disappeared he arrested Capt. McKeegan for aiding in his escape. Justice Smith at the Jefferson Market Police Court held McKeegan for trial.

Michael undoubtedly survived this assault, since he was around two years later for the 1891 birth of his daughter, Mary.

The 1894 - 1895 city directory then placed Michael at 46 Clarkson St. where he remained until his death in 1903.

This Michael completed his *Declaration of Intention* (aka: *First Papers*), the first of two steps needed for the granting of citizenship, on December 23, 1890. The clerk at the Court of Common Pleas for the City and County of New York, S. Jones, witnessed his intention which stated the following:

I, Michael Dunn, do declare an oath that it is bona fide my Intention
to become a citizen of the United States and to renounce forever all
allegiance and fidelity to any foreign Prince, Potentate, State or
Sovereignty whatever, and particularly to the QUEEN OF THE
UNITED KINGDOM OF GREAT BRITAIN AND IRELAND of whom
I am a subject.

For some reason, Michael's address at the time, 67 Carmine St., was written on the document right below his name, verifying this address as the same location where this "other" Michael and Margaret lived at the time. However, it is unclear whether or not Michael ever followed through with this process.

Did this Michael ever complete the second step in applying for citizenship? I cannot answer this question, since the many Michael Dunn citizenship papers I have found do not have any identifying information which would verify any one of these Michaels as having done so. It wasn't until the 1906 Naturalization Act when these applications were revised to include much more detailed information for each individual, making a match with one's ancestors much more precise. It also was not unusual for an immigrant to complete the first, but not the second step for citizenship, so perhaps this was true for this Michael as well.

Edward and Mary, the two youngest children of this other Michael/Margaret couple, were born in Charity Hospital on Blackwell's Island; this hospital also was called *Maternity Hospital* or *Maternity and Charity Hospital* or *City Hospital.* Blackwell's Island eventually was renamed Welfare Island, but now it is known as Roosevelt Island.

Giving birth there was a sure sign that family fortunes had reached rock bottom.

Blackwell's Island must have been one miserable place. New York City purchased it for the expressed purpose of putting up charitable and corrective institutions, with top priority given to erecting a state penitentiary. After its construction, the first hospital on Blackwell's, Penitentiary Hospital, was built strictly for the prison's inmates. When it burned down in 1861, it was rebuilt and renamed *City Hospital*, then *Charity Hospital* to signify its purpose to serve both inmates and the poorest of the city's poor population.

An 1890 publication described Charity Hospital for:

"the very poor of the city; some of them are only morally sick and needing a home . . . most of their sickness, as we nurses know, has been brought on by over-work, poverty, drunkenness, laziness, and the like, but some are worthy and deserving persons"

A recent New York Times article on the history of Roosevelt Island claimed that *"as Blackwell's Island, it was a place of quarantine, for the ill, the criminal and the insane."*

Other public institutions eventually were constructed on the island: a workhouse (for drunks and disorderlies), two almshouses for men and women (for the infirm, destitute, and homeless), a smallpox hospital, two Hospitals for Incurables (one for men, one for women), and an Asylum for the Insane, the first of its kind in the country.

This Margaret must have been one of those individuals hospitalized on an island just reeking with the poor, the destitute, the incarcerated, and the infirm. Since she gave birth there to the last two of her four (or five) children, Edward and Mary, her circumstances must have been quite dire at the time and needful of public assistance. I can only assume that her physical condition, her inadequate financial resources, and her poor pre-natal care put both Edward and Mary at high risk for early death. Considering the fact that the infant mortality rate, typically caused by the overcrowded, unsanitary conditions of the tenement-dwelling Irish in the late 1800s was 25%, their demise would be quite understandable. There are probably no baptismal certificates for either Edward or Mary in their parishes, since the priest assigned to Charity Hospital would have been the one to have baptized them there.

I believe that I have found the death certificate for this Michael Dunn, although, at first, I thought that he was our Michael. This 50-year-old Michael Dunn, a *"longshoreman,"* died on February 8, 1903, while a patient in the aforementioned Charity Hospital on Blackwell's Island. His cause of death was *"pneumonia and delirium tremens"* (a severe case of alcohol withdrawal resulting in seizures and often death); alcoholism apparently got the better of him. It is safe to assume that he breathed his last while a lying in a bed in the alcoholism ward of the hospital. His *"last place of residence"* on his death certificate was *"46 Clarkson St."*

The missing information on Michael's death certificate speaks volumes. These certificates include, among other things, spaces for the names of both mother and father, the place where each was born, and the number of years living in the States. It is just those facts which bring to life everyone's forebears. However, each of the spaces allotted to those questions included the notation, *"?,"* nothing but a question mark, an indication that there was no family member alongside Michael when he died who could have provided Dr. M. H. Jackson, the Manhattan Borough Coroner, with that information. Jackson also found Michael's body three days later in the *"morgue,"* according to the certificate, which was located at the time in Bellevue Hospital. This Michael was buried four days later in Calvary Cemetery in a plot purchased by a John Keegan, a name which I cannot connect to our family.

It is quite possible that this Michael may have been a resident of Blackwell's Island's New York Penitentiary on at least three occasions. His first stint was a one-month sentence for *"petit larceny,"* beginning on January 3, 1884. It was standard practice for inmates to be released before serving their full sentence, but Michael was back right away for a four-month stay for the same offense on July 19th of that year. Finally, the charge of *"assault, 2nd degree"* put him back yet again for five months on March 23, 1892.

Another suspicion I have is that the Michael Dunn who was sentenced for six months in the Kings County Penitentiary for *"intoxication"* on May 20, 1902, was this Michael. Longshoreman would have worked the docks in both Manhattan and Brooklyn, so if Michael faced arrest in the latter location, the Kings County facility is where he would have spent his time. However, I am less sure of this incarceration than I am of the others.

The social and economic plights of this Michael and Margaret were hardly atypical for the Irish immigrant population in the States in the mid to late 19th century. In his book, *Finding Your Irish Ancestors in New York City*, genealogist Joseph Buggy wrote:

> *"they started out on the bottom rung of the social and economic ladder . . .*
> *were more likely to be victims of crime, commit crime, have poorer*
> *mental and physical health, and have a greater reliance on charitable,*

city and state institutions . . . the Irish had the highest rates in all

these categories . . . it was a sad and dangerous time to be Irish in New York City."

An 1894 government report also noted that the death rate for the years 1884-1890 among those Manhattan and Brooklyn residents having Irish-born mothers was much higher than the average death rate for the total number of white residents for reasons *"mainly due to consumption, alcoholism and its consequences, and pneumonia."*

Perhaps this Margaret is the subject of the following New York Times article which I found.   The article ran in the January 8, 1899, edition:

MOTHER AND BABE'S SAD PLIGHT

Husband Did Not Return From War,

And Woman Is Homeless

Mrs. Margaret Dunn, a sickly, poorly clad woman twenty-nine years old, with a two weeks' old baby in her arms, asked Magistrate Flammer, in the Yorkville Police Court, yesterday to commit her and her child to prison for the Winter, as she was homeless and friendless. "Where is your husband?" asked the Magistrate.

"He went to the war and never came back," was the woman's reply, as she burst into tears.

In answer to further questions, she said that her husband was dissipated, and that he went to the war in May. She was living out at the time. Her child was born in the Maternity Hospital two weeks ago. "They discharged me from the hospital yesterday'" she added, "and, having no place to go to, I walked about in the rain with my baby in my arms. We were soaked with the rain, and when baby began to cry I entered the hallway at 436 Second Avenue for shelter."

When Mrs. Dunn stepped into the hallway Charles Snyder, a tenant, caught sight of her. He called a policeman and had her arrested for trying to abandon her child. When asked whether she intended to abandon her child she said: "I don't know what I would have done."

On her confession of vagrancy Magistrate Flammer committed her with the baby to the City Prison for three months.

A tragic story, indeed, but who knows how commonplace a story it was among the poor immigrant working class?

Rene Kuhn

With Paul's help I was able to track down Grandma's maid of honor, Rene Kuhn's, granddaughter, Heather Corbally Bryant. We exchanged several emails and a couple of telephone conversations, and she filled me in on her grandmother's fascinating life. Heather holds an undergraduate degree from Harvard and a Ph.D. in Modern English and Irish Literature from the University of Michigan. During the time of our first contact, she was in the English Department at Penn State, but she now is a professor in the Writing Program at Wellesley College. Heather is the author of several books, some of them poetry collections, but she also has written a biography of her grandmother which she has titled, *You Can't Wrap Fire in Paper.* I also have, courtesy of Heather, a hand-signed copy of Rene's 1938 autobiography, *Assigned to Adventure*.

It would appear from Heather's recollections that her grandmother, born Irene Agnes Dolores Corbally, was quite a remarkable person, "*a wild woman*," Heather claimed, at a time when women never ventured far from home. A restless character, Rene only lasted two years at Marymount College in Manhattan before she completed her studies at Columbia. After a brief stint ($18 per week salary) in her first job as a 21-year-old journalist with the Syracuse Herald, she returned to Manhattan for a position with the *New York Daily News* before a downsizing in its staff resulted in her dismissal and to her consideration of a job overseas. She stood up to her family's warnings about foreign travel and conceded that she would be gone for six months only. Thus began her international travels which lasted five years, far more than the six months promised her family, first as a fashion reporter in Paris, but then her career as a foreign correspondent took off for other parts of the globe.

Within six months of her departure, Rene, on impulse, accompanied a friend to Shanghai, China, where she took a position on the editorial staff of the legal *Shanghai Opium Monopoly*. Her first day on the job she met and eventually married Albert Lowenstein Katz, a Chicago newspaperman and a

German Jew whose father fled Germany and changed his last name to *Kuhn* in order to appear less Jewish. Rene simply cabled her family with the news of her spring, 1922, nuptials. The fallout from the marriage from both families was significant; Rene's Irish kin was upset that she married a Jew, and the Katz family was equally as perturbed at his decision to wed an Irish woman. The couple soon took a year's sabbatical from its Shanghai residence to have their only child, Heather's mother, Rene Leilani Kuhn, born in Honolulu, Hawaii. The younger Rene, herself a writing instructor at Harvard and a writer/editor for Life Magazine, also penned two novels, one of which was *34 Charlton*, a novel about growing up in Greenwich Village.

Heather described her grandparents' relationship as *"tempestuous."* After one of their disputes, Rene left Bert in Shanghai and returned to the States where she stayed with the Kuhn family in Chicago, her first encounter with her in-laws. During this separation, however, Bert died. A Dr. Dunn declared the official cause of death as pneumonia, but there also was a strong suspicion that he had been poisoned due to his involvement in undercover work for United States Naval Intelligence. The story is told that an informant let Bert's communist house boy know of his employer's espionage work, and it was he who poisoned Bert. After an unsuccessful first attempt at the poisoning, the second one succeeded. Bert's ashes were sent to Rene back home in Chicago; Rene was left a widow at the age of 28.

Rene eventually remarried, this time to Eugene Monahan, *"but it didn't work out,"* Heather said. There also was a rift that developed between her and her only brother, Clarence. Her marriage to a Jew didn't help, but Heather reported that Clarence, a hefty baby at birth at 12 pounds, was born with a withered right arm, *"so he got all the attention."* Rene lived until the age of 97, passing away the night before New Year's Eve, 1995.

It would appear that she outlived her single brother Clarence. He was listed as a *"public school teacher"* and as a *"chemist – educational"* on the 1930 and 1940 censuses, respectively, still living with his mother and his two maiden aunts, Margaret and Mary, in Manhattan. However, there was a Clarence Corbally who passed away at the age of 80 in February, 1984 (a match with his DOB of 1904), while a resident of Little Silver, NJ. Given his uncommon name, I am betting that he was the one and only brother to Rene, but I cannot confirm that without scouring more obituaries of the local Monmouth County newspapers of 1984. I was unable to find his obituary in my microfilm search of the Asbury Park Press for that time period, but perhaps a return trip to the Monmouth County Library might yield some fruit the next time.

Radermacher – Dunn Connection

The information in this section concerns the relationship, although not quite understood, between our Dunns and the Radermacher clan which housed our Grandma in 1905 and another family of Dunns soon after she left for Jersey City (or perhaps even before she left). Remember that Grandma was gone from the Radermacher household by 1908-09.

Anna, the eldest of the Dunn siblings who was in the Radermacher household by 1910, must have caught John Radermacher's eye, since the two eventually were to wed sometime between 1910 and 1915, the latter year that the New York State census listed him as married. However, I have not been able to locate their marriage certificate. The newlyweds were at 769 Ridgewood Heights, Queens, NY, by 1915, sharing their residence for the first time with Anna's widowed father, Andrew Dunn (67; "*retired*"), while the rest of Andrew's children were with Livinia at 107 123rd St. in Manhattan. Yet one more Dunn, a younger brother, Joseph (18; "*office clerk*"), joined his siblings there also.

By 1920, John and Anna had relocated to Bellmore Ave. in Queens, NY; their household this time included the regulars, Livinia (57) and the single Mary Leonard/Linnard (59). Andrew was still with the family in 1925 when the group moved once again to 266 123rd St. in Manhattan. Joining the regulars there (John, Anna, Andrew, Mary, Joseph, now a "*Pennsylvania railroad watchman*," and Livinia) was William Bradley, a 13-year-old nephew, the son of Anna's widowed sister, Irene. However, Andrew passed away from "*angina pectoris*" on December 26, 1925, soon after the city census was taken.

It would appear, however, that things did not go well for John Radermacher. Although he had been employed as a "*bookkeeper*" and "*stenographer*" over the years, he apparently was unable to work by the time of the 1925 city census. There was simply an "*X*" in the space allotted for "*occupation*" in that record, and more interestingly, his wife Anna ("*telephone operator*") was listed as the "*head*," a highly unusual title for a woman whose husband was alive and well and living in the home.

The 1930 census sheds some light on John's inability to work. It places him as an *"inmate"* in the Manhattan State Hospital for the Insane on Ward's Island in NY, formerly known as the New York City Asylum for the Insane. How long his mental health was in decline is not known, but his assignment to that hospital meant that he had serious psychiatric problems. He and Anna had no children.

While her husband was hospitalized in 1930, Anna, still a telephone operator, was living with Livinia, Mary, and Joseph Dunn (now a *"salesman – grocer"*) at 69 106th St. In addition to the nephew William Bradley, his mother Irene (39), also was in the household. Irene was a nurse in a local hospital.

The last record I have for Anna is the 1940 census which has her at 111-32 209th St. in Queens as a 53-year-old *"widow."* This time she was the *"sister-in-law"* living with 53-year-old NYC police lieutenant, Hector Rose, and his children: Marie (23), Edward (21), and Robert (20). Hector had married Anna's sister, Teresa, on November 17, 1915. However, Teresa never made it to the 1940 census, passing away on December 17, 1938, at the age of 49.

Ege Avenue

Grandpa and Grandma Colford purchased 277 Ege Ave. from the Pettit family who themselves had bought it from a Massachusetts-born couple, Aubrey and Mary (Hardy) Armstrong, who had been in the home for approximately 18 years. A cabinet maker by trade, Aubrey and his wife spent no fewer than 15 years wandering throughout various residences in Jersey City's eighth ward before settling into 277 in 1900 with their three children: Henry (11); Elida (6); Aubrey Irving, Jr. (5). They had lived in at least seven other area locations for no longer than three years at each one before landing at 277 Ege; prior to their purchase, they spent one year (1899) at 261 Ege. The Armstrongs relocated to Bloomfield after the sale.

Neighbors of the Armstrongs in 1900 were the residents of the attached duplex at 260 – 262 Ege just across the street. Ellsworth (37; *"carpenter"*) and Mary (35) Schultz were at 260, and Henry (33; *"clerk"*) and Ella (34) Smith and their five-year-old daughter, Elsie, occupied 262. Ownership of 260 would change over the years; William (44; *"superintendent – mercantile house"*) and Mary Hickerson

(45) and their three children were there by 1910. There they remained until sometime just before the 1930 census which then listed the widow Olive Marshall (58) and her son, James (22), there along with four lodgers and one boarder.

Two of those lodgers, as you may recall from earlier in this story, were William Colford, Grandpa's youngest sibling, and his son, George. The Marshalls were at 260 again in the 1940 census, this time with only one lodger, 51-year-old Henry Rolffs ("*salesman – haberdashery*"). Helen and Bill Costigan purchased 260 in 1948.

Ownership at 262 changed also; the Field family, William (46; "*printer – own shop*"), his wife, Mary (58), and their six children, the oldest of whom was Augusta (aka: *Gussy;* 21), were there in time for the 1910 census. The Fields were there again for the 1920 and 1930 censuses, the latter which included only the unmarried Gussy and her parents. Gussy, listed in the census counts throughout the years as "*stenographer,*" "*secretary – social agency,*" and "*secretary – welfare work,*" occupied 262 Ege in 1940 along with her married sister Marion, her husband Donald Nutting, and their three children. With the help of Grandma and Grandpa Lipsett's largesse, Dad and Mom would purchase 262 from Gussy in 1950 for $6,200; she was its sole resident at the time. The value of the property had increased somewhat, since the census ten years earlier had placed it at $4,700, although its worth in 1930 was $7,500.

There is an interesting footnote to the Field - Colford real estate deal, however. After all the parties had agreed on the sale, Gussy begged the indulgence of the folks to let her continue to live in the home until she found a suitable apartment for herself somewhere in Jersey City. Our kindly folks accommodated her request and charged her a nominal fee to remain in 262 until she relocated. After several months of this arrangement, however, it became clear to the folks that she was not particularly motivated to change her residence. Dad then took the initiative to look for an apartment for her; he found one and took her to view it. Gussy apparently approved of it and then made her move, freeing up 262 for the Colfords.

Harry Crook and Sons

A little over a year after our great-aunt, Anna (Harvey) Crook's death, allegedly by her own hand, husband Harry relocated to Asbury Park and purchased a home there at 1016 Fourth Ave. Other residents in his home included the following: his three sons, John (18), Harry, Jr. (16), and Edward (14); his sister, Helen, her husband Edward Stahl, and their two-year old daughter Gloria; and Harry's brother, Frederick (19), a *"private investigator,"* according to the 1930 census. This same census record has Harry as the *"chief investigator – Monmouth County."*

While the chief of detectives, he opened his own business, the *Crook Armored Car Service*, at the intersection of Main St. and Sylvania Ave. in Avon, a business made possible by the federal government which sold off all the surplus armored cars left over from World War I. His purchases apparently were a stroke of genius for someone intent on using them for his own nefarious pursuits. Although he had no experience in law enforcement, save for a brief stint as a security guard in an apartment store somewhere in Asbury Park, Harry had befriended Jonas Tumen, the county prosecutor, who gave him the unlikely appointment as Chief of the Monmouth County Detectives. In his book, Linderoth wrote: *"The two men turned the office into an extortion racket . . . Tumen and Crook were by far the most glaring examples of corruption the state dealt with."* The bulk of Crook's cash came from extorting money from owners of speakeasies, and he also consorted with area mobsters in helping them protect their own rackets.

Harry must have had friends in high places who accepted his claim that he was totally unaware as to how all those slot machines and their proceeds wound up in his home!

However, his reign only lasted from 1930-1935. It was just after New Year's Day, 1935, when Edward Currie, a special prosecutor assigned to the Crook/Tumen fiasco, replaced Crook with William Mustoe as acting Chief of Detectives. Tumen, Harry's co-conspirator, had been ousted just a week earlier, replaced by Currie himself, at the time an assistant district attorney. Mustoe ordered Harry to resign or have charges brought against him; an investigation into Harry's activities was underway. The Red Bank Register reported on January 10, 1935, that Harry had only 48 hours to turn in, among other things, *"his county owned car, his service revolver, machine gun, and five clips of ammunition."* This he did, but he refused to hand over his badge, claiming that he was innocent and that he planned to fight any charges in court.

In the middle of his reign, January 9, 1932, Helen Manion of Long Branch became Harry's second wife. However, the couple made a hasty retreat to Florida right after Harry's ouster to avoid being taken in by the authorities; the destination was another property Harry owned at 1216 Southeast Sixth St. in Fort Lauderdale. His occupation there in 1940 was a familiar one: *"operator of armored cars – public service."* Records showed him eventually living with another woman, a Marion J. Crook, although there is no certificate anywhere to document their marriage. His marriage to Helen, however, ended on February 7, 1949, when the circuit court judge granted her a divorce on the grounds of *"extreme cruelty."* The divorce decree ordered Harry to *"pay to the plaintiff $25.00 per week as alimony until she may remarry."*

After the "heat" died down, Harry returned to NJ right after his divorce and married yet again, this third time to Annie Sullivan. The couple was in residence in Avon when he died on September 9, 1973, at the age of 82. Perhaps he had turned his life around, since his obituary in the Red Bank Register spoke of his involvement in the Holy Name Society in St. Elizabeth Church and of the nine grandchildren and 13 great-grandchildren he left behind. He is buried in St. Catherine's Cemetery in Sea Girt, NJ, never having been arrested nor prosecuted for his misdeeds. Apparently, not enough evidence was gathered to make a case.

John, Harry's oldest son, eloped with a nursing student, Marjorie Scheupp, and married on May 23, 1932, at St. Paul the Apostle Church in Manhattan. The couple eventually relocated to Syracuse, NY, where they had four children and where John ran a restaurant and hotel, the Chateau, before moving onto the management of other food and entertainment-based businesses. His name appeared in the local newspapers on several occasions for things like a shooting in his bar, a fire of unknown origin, and for withholding pay from one of his employees. The last newspaper article which featured him in the fall of 1992 reported his arrest at the age of 80 for scalping hundreds of tickets to local sporting events and concerts; he and his wife were residents of a senior citizen complex at the time. John and his wife passed away the following year, Marjorie on May 26, 1993, and John seven months later on December 23rd.

Harry's namesake and second son, Harry, Jr., served in the army during the Second World War before joining his father in his armored car business. He eventually followed Harry, Sr. to Florida for a time, but he returned to Avon where he became involved in the local Republican Party and would go on to serve as the mayor of Avon in the 1970s. He was in this capacity at the time of his father's death. He and his wife Patricia (Frank) relocated one last time back to Florida, self-employed once again in his Crook Armored Car business. The 84-year-old Harry passed away on May 6, 1999.

Edward, the youngest, was 83 years old when he took his own life on July 9, 1999, by lying down on the railroad tracks in front of an oncoming commuter train bound for Newark, NJ. North Jersey Coast Line train # 5308, carrying 400 passengers on its six cars, was unable to stop before it struck Edward in Middletown, NJ, at 8:08 a.m., just a few minutes after it pulled out of the Red Bank train station. Monmouth County's Chief Medical Examiner, Dr. Stanley Becker, ruled the death of this "*salesman – liquor distributor*" a "*suicide.*" His death came just two months after that of his older brother, Harry.

Dullea Family

One of Mom's second cousins was Catherine Dullea who became a nun and joined the Dominican Sisters as *Sister Fabian*; she earned a doctorate in English and served as chair of the English Department at Molloy College after working as a missionary for several years in Puerto Rico. She eventually changed her name to *Sister Catherine Dullea.* I remember looking her up at a Saint Peter's College Glee Club road trip to Molloy College back in 1970 or 1971. Catherine now is a resident of the Dominican's retirement community in Amityville, Long Island; as of this writing, the 93-year-old Catherine was celebrating 75 years as a Dominican. She spent the week before she entered the convent at 20 West Hamilton Place where Mom entertained her; "*She treated me to a nice Chinese dinner,*" Catherine recalled for me when I spoke with her.

Catherine's younger sister, Mary/Marie (Dullea) Molony (88), also was alive and well and back into her home on Breezy Point after its restoration due to the Superstorm Sandy devastation. She was quite a lively, engaging individual who had a great recall of family history. Mom said that Marie "*practically danced my feet off*" at the 50th anniversary celebration of Sr. Catherine's entry into the convent.

Marie's recollection and that of her sister's was that the aforementioned Denis Dullea showed up on the steps of 97 Dahlgren Place one day to visit and remained for several years! They both told the story that Denis wasn't employed much, so he did Marie's arithmetic homework for her each day, despite her parents' preference that he not do so. Marie and Catherine both called Mom and exchanged this and other stories with her.

As a matter of pure happenstance, Marie Molony's daughter, Kathleen McGowan, our third cousin, is a good friend to a neighbor of ours, Bert Byrnes. I met Kathleen recently at the surprise 60th birthday party for Bert. She was quite friendly, and she wanted me to bring Mom to see Marie at her home in Breezy Point. Although that will not happen, Jeanne and I plan to visit even more cousins there one of these days.

Another small world story.

20 West Hamilton Place

Mom has lots of humorous stories about the many roomers Grandpa and Grandma took in over the years at 20 West Hamilton Place. The 1930 federal census listed four of them living there along with Francis, Loretta, Catherine C, and Thomas Michael:

> Harry Dunlap, a 20-year-old *electrician*
> George Meyers, a 31-year-old *railroad worker*
> William Bertrand, a 28-year-old *clerk*
> John King, Jr., a 26-year-old (occupation unclear on record)

Mom also recalls other names:

> Mr. Callahan
> George Campbell and his son
> Mr. Smith
> Nancy and Eddie Bonaski (the first tenants in the new apartment
> created on the third floor)
> Mr. Gant
> Tom and Rose Hayes (the second and last tenants to occupy the
> third-floor apartment for more than 20 years)

The 1940 census listed the Hayes couple in the third-floor apartment; *"roomers"* Peter Missitt (29), a Jersey City fireman, and his older sister Elizabeth (33), a switchboard operator in the Jersey City Medical Center, occupied the second-floor rooms. Mom (20) was listed as a *"clerk – bank"* whose salary the previous year was $1,240. Grandpa listed the value of his home at $6,000.

Roomer Elizabeth Missitt was celebrating a birthday one day while also enjoying a movie date with a gentleman caller. Mom made a cake for her, expecting to surprise her with it upon her return that night. However, when Elizabeth arrived home from the movies, she broke down in tears and explained to Mom that her date had died alongside her moments earlier while seated in the theater!

Another story has one of the roomers, Mr. Callahan, the paymaster for the railroad, counting out piles of money in his room one night. Meanwhile, another roomer on the next floor, Mr. Smith (aka: *Smitty*), was three sheets to the wind, as he was wont to be, according to Mom, and he took a tumble down the stairs, knocked Mr. Callahan's bedroom door off its hinges, and fell at his feet amid the money piles!

Can't make this stuff up.

Chapter XXXIII

Summary, At Last

Filling in some of the gaps in our story requires a full-time commitment, but even a 40-hour week devoted to this research does not guarantee the discovery of all the details missing here. So I have put together this story with the information I have come across through all the many sources I have found. The information contained in our story is that which I have uncovered, stumbled upon, was given, or was told by Mom and by other relatives of ours.

Some of the missing information could indeed be "hiding in plain sight," hidden by the simplest of misspellings or by erroneous first names in any or all municipal or parish or immigration records. For example, it took me quite a while to locate our great-grandfather, Michael Colfer's, name on the register of the ship *Atmosphere* on which he sailed to the States along with his future wife and her siblings, because the person who recorded the name for the Mormon Church's Family History Center misread it as *"Colper."* And James Colfer was listed as *"Celper"* on the 1870 census record and as *"Colfax"* on his marriage record.

With nary a picture of any of our forebears, we will have to conjure up our own images of them in our minds' eyes. And without any firm recall of the more humanizing details of their lives from other descendants, particularly of the Dunn and Harvey lines, we are left with just the blueprints of their lives which I hope this story has put together.

I am reminded of a comment a volunteer at the Mormon Church's Family History Center made to me during the last of my six visits there. It had been approximately one year between this visit and the previous one, so she looked up at me as I signed in and said, *"I haven't seen you for a while!"* I replied that I thought that I would have been finished with our story some time ago, but that new information kept coming across my desk. At this point, another volunteer, a gentleman working away at one of the microfilm readers, smiled and said, *"Don't you know it's never over!"*

How true, how true.

For now, this is our story, but I will continue to investigate the whereabouts of great-grandma Margaret and of our other missing details in order to revise our story as these new facts reveal themselves. Stay tuned.

I just hope that you have read this story and that you have held onto it for your children who also might want to read it one day.

So there you have it. And thanks for listening.

Brother Joe signing off . . . for now . . .

www.ingramcontent.com/pod-product-compliance
Lightning Source LLC
Chambersburg PA
CBHW081407270326
41931CB00016B/3404